BEACHWAY PRESS

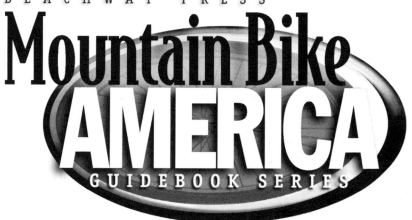

Mountain Bike AMERICA

GUIDEBOOK SERIES

WASHINGTON

Beachway Press Publishing, Inc.

Publisher Scott Adams

Series Editor Scott Adams
Senior Editor Tyler Beck
Ast Editors Shelley Girdner
Dillon Holly

Art Director/Series Designer Chuck Samuels

Production Ast Amy Phillips
Phoebe Lawless
Jeff Brooks
Mason Carpenter

Cartographers Dan Dunham
Porter Bosco
Gus Phillips

Photographers
Mark Poffenbarger, Amy Poffenbarger, Matt VanEnkevort,
John Flinn, Robert Jimenez, Jackie Livingston, Brian Dumais,
Jon Eacrett, Kevin Dentler, Santo Criscuolo, Washington
Tourism

Advertising Sales (804) 360-7581
Regional Book Sales (West Coast)
Frank McCormick
Distribution 1-888-BEACHWAY (232-2492)

Maps designed and produced by Beachway Press

Beachway Custom Maps (804) 360-7581

Printed in the United States of America by
Automated Graphic Systems, Inc., White Plains, MD

Published by
Beachway Press Publishing, Inc.
9201 Beachway Lane
Springfield, VA 22153-1441

10 9 8 7 6 5 4 3 2

Cover: Juniper Ridge Loop "Honorable Mention Ride O" with
Mount Adams in the distance. Photo by Matt VanEnkevort

ISBN 1-882997-09-3

Library of Congress Cataloguing-in-Publication Data
Poffenbarger, Amy & Mark
Mountain Bike America: Washington
An Atlas of Washington State's
Greatest Off-Road Bicycle Rides/by Amy & Mark Poffenbarger
1st ed. Springfield, VA: Beachway Press, ©1998
256 pages: Illustrations, Photographs, Maps, Graphics
1. All-terrain cycling–Washington–Guidebooks
Washington–Guidebooks
98-071367
CIP

From the Publisher...

We at Beachway Press look at guidebook publishing a little differently. There's just no reason that a guidebook has to look like it was published out of your Uncle Ernie's woodshed. Granted, we may go a little too far with our 3-D maps, sidebars, shaded relief maps, and adventure directories. We just feel that guidebooks need to be both easy to use and nice to look at. And that takes an innovative approach to design. See, we want you to spend less time fumbling through your guidebook and more time enjoying the adventure at hand.

Then there's the written content. There are only so many times one can say a ride is "awesome" or that a view is, well, "awesome." You'd expect as much. We want you to know why the view looks like it does and what occurred on that spot where you're standing. In many cases, where the views may fail you, the history alone can make the ride unforgettable. When there's so much out there to appreciate, it would be a shame to let one element govern whether a ride is good or bad. Our objective is to introduce you to the greatest off-road bicycle rides in each region of the state. We're not interested in saturating one popular region, outling every possible trail combination. We want you to see the entire state. In a way, then, you could almost call **Mountain Bike Washington** *a guide to Washington* **by mountain bike**. *Whatever you decide to call it, we hope you enjoy it, and we'd like to thank you for taking an adventure with us.*

Happy Trails!

BEACHWAY PRESS

Mountain Bike
AMERICA
GUIDEBOOK SERIES

WASHINGTON

An Atlas of Washington State's
Greatest Off-Road Bicycle Rides

By Amy & Mark Poffenbarger

Introduction by Scott Adams, Series Editor

BEACHWAY PRESS

An addition to the
Mountain Bike America Guidebook Series

Table Of Contents

Dear Readers:

Every effort was made to make this the most accurate, informative, and easy-to-use guidebook on the planet. Any comments, suggestions, and/or corrections regarding this guide are welcome and should be sent to:

Beachway Press
c/o Editorial Dept.
9201 Beachway Lane
Springfield, VA 22153

We'd love to hear from you so we can make future editions and future guides even better.

Thanks and happy trails!

Table of Contents

Table of Contents

Preface

ashington is a living, breathing wonderland for mountain biking exploration. The shades of history, the colors of the mountains and valleys, and the hues of the western sky paint a delicious picture of what Washington is and who Northwesterners are. As folks continue to relocate here for the benefits of western living, we mountain bikers are going to rely even more heavily on our trusty steeds and trails to help us "get back to nature." As you experience these rides, we'll show you old-growth forests, teach you Native American folklore, and bring you to elevations with views unimaginable. You'll learn why Washington's landscape is so different from west to east, and also a little bit of Western American history. And, if we've done our job right, you'll also have some wonderful adventures.

Getting my education in the art of singletrack from my husband, Mark, was a fine way to be introduced to this dirt-grinding sport. My strong will and fear of disappointing him directed me forward, and I worked hard at getting as muddy as I could.

My initiation into Northwest mountain biking occurred on a very rainy day in January 1990, at Wallace Falls. My cycling days in Texas required technical skill but not always that special muscle for climbing. The highest peaks usually equaled that of a highway overpass, so, needless to say, I got a good first workout on the climb up to Wallace Lake. It was raining and cold—rare weather conditions for Texas. I bit my lip, keeping quiet the entire way up. Mark was impressed.

Then we arrived at the river crossing. The water from Wallace Lake was racing toward the pinnacle of its decent faster than a filling bathtub and was running about as high as hip-waders. It was so coooold! Mark, the gentleman that he is, carried my mountain bike across the river, while I scurried my overheated body through the glacial melt like I was born with ice water for blood. After the ride, Mark told a friend: "I knew from that moment on that she was my woman!" Good ol' Mark; he's still proud of my performance that day, and we've been adventuring together ever since.

Mountain biking opened up many doors for me—a new cardiovascular sport for one, not to mention the enlarging vastus medialis muscles above my knees. This unique sport has also given me an enlightened sense of respect for the power Mother Nature wields over her mountains. Overall, my respect and interest in global environmental conditions result from our experiences mountain biking and the places we've seen along the way.

We were very lucky. We were given the opportunity to do the two things we love —mountain biking and being together. As a writer, it's always been my goal to have my writing published in a book. Mark and I love to ride our mountain bikes; it was pure luck, combined determination, dedication, a pinch of will to succeed, and a ton of hard work that our dream has come to fruition. It is our sincere hope that you have as much fun riding these rides as we did researching and charting them for you. We believe the best guidebooks don't leave you at an intersection scratching your head, and hopefully you'll find ours to be one of the best.

There are many outstanding rides in this state, but we had to draw the line somewhere. But the research hasn't stopped. As you read this, we're out discovering new rides to include in future editions, and we welcome your comments and suggestions. We know you have a choice of mountain biking guidebooks and we thank you for choosing ours from the *Mountain Bike America* series. But most of all, we wish you lots of fun and good adventures.

Amy Poffenbarger

Acknowledgment

True believers in the buddy system, we have a tremendous support network to thank. But none of this would have been possible without Scott Adams and his team at Beachway Press. Thank you very much for the opportunity. It has been quite the adventure.

Special thanks to our great friends Matt and Lisa VanEnkevort, for the adventures and the pictures! John Flinn, thank you for your incredible contributions. Mimi Day, Jeff Day—and of course Helen and the hounds—It's always so much fun with you guys. To Betsy and Brian, my special cousins, thanks for discovering new rides and sharing your favorites. Robert! Dude! Came all the way from Texas just to ride! Robin Laughlin, Dave Hull, and Simon Roland: Thanks for sharing the first official book ride with me. Jon Eacrett, we owe the birds-eye view of the Straight to you. Thanks to Ryan Dean for traveling with me. Cindy Hazzard, you are a true sport. Santo Criscuolo and Kevin Dentler, a special thanks for your contributions of two awesome areas to ride. Brad and Kathy Schmidt, the food, hospitality, and warm beds at the Mountain Home Lodge are divine. Melt-in-your-mouth scones are found only at Dan and Sally Kuperberg's Chewuch Inn. Thanks for everything. Clif Bars and Clif Shot saved us on more than one occasion. Great work on the energy food. And to Tammy White, thanks for your "secret" recipe and caring support. Many thanks to Marvin Moline for the contacts, the Department of Natural Resources, the National Forest Service, and everyone at the bike shops who led us to great ride destinations. To my talented friend Amy Gulick: Triple thank you's for your tireless effort—who needs an editor? Our little buddy, Pancho, who runs like the wind, never runs out of steam, and travels with us everywhere, but when he has to stay home, Tim O'Neill's always there to toss the ball and feed him— Thank you. To our supportive families we owe many thanks: Betty, Toner, and Saba, you make our daily lives a happy place; Muazzez, our friends will never know how good börek really are on rides because we eat them all ourselves! Jim, Mary, Staesha, Sarah, Roman, and Sam: I get all choked up when I remember how much incredible support and love you put forth to us during this whole project—I love you guys! For my grandmother, Phyllis McKendry, I dedicate this book, and all the fun we had putting it together, to you and Pappa. You guys enjoyed over 60 years of fun together. I hope we do, too.

Introduction

Introduction

Welcome to the new generation of bicycling! Indeed, the sport has evolved dramatically from the thin-tired, featherweight-frame days of old. The sleek geometry and lightweight frames of racing bicycles, still the heart and soul of bicycling worldwide, have lost much ground in recent years, unpaving the way for the mountain bike, which now accounts for the majority of all bicycle sales in the U.S. And with this change comes a new breed of cyclist, less concerned with smooth roads and long rides, who thrives in places once inaccessible to the mortal road bike.

The mountain bike, with its knobby tread and reinforced frame, takes cyclists to places once unheard of—down rugged mountain trails, through streams of rushing water and thick mud, across the frozen Alaskan tundra, and even to work in the city. There seem to be few limits on what this fat-tired beast can do and where it can take us. Few obstacles stand in its way, few boundaries slow its progress. Except for one—its own success. If trail closure means little to you now, read on and discover how a trail can be here today and gone tomorrow. With so many new off-road cyclists taking to the trails each year, it's no wonder trail access hinges precariously between universal acceptance and complete termination. But a little work on your part can go a long way to preserving trail access for future use. Nothing is more crucial to the survival of mountain biking itself than to read the examples set forth in the following pages and practice their message. Then turn to the maps, pick out your favorite ride, and hit the dirt!

WHAT THIS BOOK IS ABOUT

Within these pages you will find everything you need to know about off-road bicycling in Washington. This guidebook begins by exploring the fascinating history of the mountain bike itself, then goes on to discuss everything from the health benefits of off-road cycling to tips and techniques for bicycling over logs and up hills. Also included are the types of clothing to keep you comfortable and in style, essential equipment ideas to keep your rides smooth and trouble-free, and descriptions of off-road terrain to prepare you for the kinds of bumps and bounces you can expect to encounter. The major provisions of this book, though, are its unique perspectives on each ride, it detailed maps, and its relentless dedication to trail preservation.

Without open trails, the maps in this book are virtually useless. Cyclists must learn to be responsible for the trails they use and to share these trails with others. This guidebook addresses such issues as why trail use has become so controversial, what can be done to improve the image of mountain biking, how to have fun and ride responsibly, on-the-spot trail repair techniques, trail maintenance hotlines for each trail, and the worldwide-standard Rules of the Trail.

Each of the 40 rides is complete with maps, photos, trail descriptions and directions, local history, and a quick-reference ride information guide including such items as trail-maintenance hotlines, park schedules, costs, local bike stores, dining, lodging, entertainment, and alternative maps. Also included at the end of each regional section is an "Honorable Mentions" list of alternative off-road rides (41 rides total).

It's important to note that mountain bike rides tend to take longer than road rides because the average speed is often much slower. Average speeds can vary from a climbing pace of three to four miles per hour to 12 to 13 miles per hour on flatter roads and trails. Keep this in mind when planning your trip.

MOUNTAIN BIKE BEGINNINGS

It seems the mountain bike, originally designed for lunatic adventurists bored with straight lines, clean clothes, and smooth tires, has become globally popular in as short a time as it would take to race down a mountain trail.

Like many things of a revolutionary nature, the mountain bike was born on the west coast. But unlike Rollerblades, purple hair, and the peace sign, the concept of the off-road bike cannot be credited solely to the imaginative Californians—they were just the first to make waves.

The design of the first off-road specific bike was based on the geometry of the old Schwinn Excelsior, a one-speed, camel-back cruiser with balloon tires. Joe Breeze was the creator behind it, and in 1977 he built 10 of these "Breezers" for himself and his Marin County, California, friends at $750 apiece—a bargain.

Breeze was a serious competitor in bicycle racing, placing 13th in the 1977 U.S. Road Racing National Championships. After races, he and friends would scour local bike shops hoping to find old bikes they could then restore.

It was the 1941 Schwinn Excelsior, for which Breeze paid just five dollars, that began to shape and change bicycling history forever. After taking the bike home, removing the fenders, oiling the chain, and pumping up the tires, Breeze hit the dirt. He loved it.

His inspiration, while forerunning, was not altogether unique. On the opposite end of the country, near-

ly 2,500 miles from Marin County, east coast bike bums were also growing restless. More and more old, beat-up clunkers were being restored and modified. These behemoths often weighed as much as 80 pounds and were so reinforced they seemed virtually indestructible. But rides that take just 40 minutes on today's 25-pound feather-weights took the steel-toed-boot- and-blue-jean-clad bikers of the late 1970s and early 1980s near-ly four hours to complete.

Not until 1981 was it possible to purchase a production mountain bike, but local retailers found these ungainly bicycles difficult to sell and rarely kept them in stock. By 1983, however, mountain bikes were no longer such a fringe item, and large bike manufacturers quickly jumped into the action, producing their own versions of the off-road bike. By the 1990s, the mountain bike had firmly established its place with bicyclists of nearly all ages and abilities, and now command nearly 90 percent of the U.S. bike market.

There are many reasons for the mountain bike's success in becoming the hottest two-wheeled vehicle in the nation. They are much friendlier to the cyclist than traditional road bikes because of their comfort-able upright position and shock-absorbing fat tires. And because of the health-conscious, environmental-ist movement of the late 1980s and 1990s, people are more activity minded and seek nature on a closer front than paved roads can allow. The mountain bike gives you these things and takes you far away from the daily grind—even if you're only minutes from the city.

MOUNTAIN BIKING INTO SHAPE

If your objective is to get in shape and lose weight, then you're on the right track, because mountain biking is one of the best ways to get started.

One way many of us have lost weight in this sport is the crash-and-burn-it-off method. Picture this: you're speeding uncontrollably down a vertical drop that you realize you shouldn't be on—only after it is too late. Your front wheel lodges into a rut and launches you through endless weeds, trees, and pointy rocks before coming to an abrupt halt in a puddle of thick mud. Surveying the damage, you discover, with the layers of skin, body parts, and lost confidence littering the trail above, that those unwanted pounds have been shed-permanently. Instant weight loss.

There is, of course, a more conventional (and quite a bit less painful) approach to losing weight and gaining fitness on a mountain bike. It's called the workout, and bicycles provide an ideal way to get physical. Take a look at some of the benefits associated with cycling.

Cycling helps you shed pounds without gimmicky diet fads or weight-loss programs. You can explore the countryside and burn nearly 10 to 16 calories per minute or close to 600 to 1,000 calories per hour. Moreover, it's a great way to spend an afternoon.

No less significant than the external and cosmetic changes of your body from riding are the internal changes taking place. Over time, cycling regularly will strengthen your heart as your body grows vast networks of new capillaries to carry blood to all those working muscles. This will, in turn, give your skin a healthier glow. The capacity of your lungs may increase up to 20 percent, and your resting heart rate will drop significantly. The Stanford University School of Medicine reports to the American Heart Association that people can reduce their risk of heart attack by nearly 64 percent if they can burn up to 2,000 calories per week. This is only two to three hours of bike riding!

Recommended for insomnia, hypertension, indigestion, anxiety, and even for recuperation from major heart attacks, bicycling can be an excellent cure-all as well as a great preventive. Cycling just a few hours per week can improve your figure and sleeping habits, give you greater resistance to illness, increase your energy levels, and provide feelings of accomplishment and heightened self-esteem.

BE SAFE—KNOW THE LAW

Occasionally, even the hard-core off-road cyclists will find they have no choice but to ride the pavement. When you are forced to hit the road, it's important for you to know and understand the rules.

Outlined below are a few of the common laws found in Washington's Vehicle Code book.

- *Bicycles are legally classified as vehicles in Washington.* This means that as a bicyclist, you are responsible for obeying the same rules of the road as a driver of a motor vehicle.
- *Bicyclists must ride with the traffic—NOT AGAINST IT!* Because bicycles are considered vehicles, you must ride your bicycle just as you would drive a car—with traffic. Only pedestrians should travel against the flow of traffic.
- *You must obey all traffic signs.* This includes stop signs and stoplights.
- *Always signal your turns.* Most drivers aren't expecting bicyclists to be on the roads, and many drivers would prefer that cyclists stay off the roads altogether. It's important, therefore, to clearly signal your intentions to motorists both in front and behind you.
- *Bicyclists are entitled to the same roads as cars (except controlled-access highways).* Unfortunately, cyclists are rarely given this consideration.
- *Be a responsible cyclist.* Do not abuse your rights to ride on open roads. Follow the rules and set a good example for all of us as you roll along.

THE MOUNTAIN BIKE CONTROVERSY

Are Mountain Bicyclists Environmental Outlaws?
Do We have the Right to Use Public Trails?

Mountain bikers have long endured the animosity of folks in the backcountry who complain about the consequences of off-road bicycling. Many people believe that the fat tires and knobby tread do unacceptable environmental damage and that our uncontrollable riding habits are a danger to animals and to other trail users. To the contrary, mountain bikes have no more environmental impact than hiking boots or horseshoes. This does not mean, however, that mountain bikes leave no imprint at all. Wherever man treads, there is an impact. By riding responsibly, though, it is possible to leave only a minimum impact—something we all must take care to achieve.

Unfortunately, it is often people of great influence who view the mountain bike as the environment's worst enemy. Consequently, we as mountain bike riders and environmentally concerned citizens must be educators, impressing upon others that we also deserve the right to use these trails. Our responsibilities as bicyclists are no more and no less than any other trail user. We must all take the soft-cycling approach and show that mountain bicyclists are not environmental outlaws.

ETIQUETTE OF MOUNTAIN BIKING

Moving softly across the land means leaving no more than an echo.

Hank Barlow

When discussing mountain biking etiquette, we are in essence discussing the soft-cycling approach. This term, as mentioned previously, describes the art of minimum-impact bicycling and should apply to both the physical and social dimensions of the sport. But make no mistake—it is possible to ride fast and furiously while maintaining the balance of soft-cycling. Here first are a few ways to minimize the physical impact of mountain bike riding.

- *Stay on the trail.* Don't ride around fallen trees or mud holes that block your path. Stop and cross over them. When you come to a vista overlooking a deep valley, don't ride off the trail for a better vantage point. Instead, leave the bike and walk to see the view. Riding off the trail may seem inconsequential when done only once, but soon someone else will follow, then others, and the cumulative results can be catastrophic. Each time you wander from the trail you begin creating a new path, adding one more scar to the earth's surface.

- *Do not disturb the soil.* Follow a line within the trail that will not disturb or damage the soil.

- *Do not ride over soft or wet trails.* After a rain shower or during the thawing season, trails will often resemble muddy, oozing swampland. The best thing to do is stay off the trails altogether. Realistically,

however, we're all going to come across some muddy trails we cannot anticipate. Instead of blasting through each section of mud, which may seem both easier and more fun, lift the bike and walk past. Each time a cyclist rides through a soft or muddy section of trail, that part of the trail is permanently damaged. Regardless of the trail's conditions, though, remember always to go over the obstacles across the path, not around them. Stay on the trail.

- *Avoid trails that, for all but God, are considered impassable and impossible.* Don't take a leap of faith down a kamikaze descent on which you will be forced to lock your brakes and skid to the bottom, ripping the ground apart as you go.

Soft-cycling should apply to the social dimensions of the sport as well, since mountain bikers are not the only folks who use the trails. Hikers, equestrians, cross-country skiers, and other outdoors people use many of the same trails and can be easily spooked by a marauding mountain biker tearing through the trees. Be friendly in the forest and give ample warning of your approach.

- *Take out what you bring in.* Don't leave broken bike pieces and banana peels scattered along the trail.

- *Be aware of your surroundings.* Don't use popular hiking trails for race training.

- *Slow down!* Rocketing around blind corners is a sure way to ruin an unsuspecting hiker's day. Consider this—If you fly down a quick singletrack descent at 20 mph, then hit the brakes and slow down to only six mph to pass someone, you're still moving twice as fast as they are!

Like the trails we ride on, the social dimension of mountain biking is very fragile and must be cared for responsibly. We should not want to destroy another person's enjoyment of the outdoors. By riding in the backcountry with caution, control, and responsibility, our presence should be felt positively by other trail users. By adhering to these rules, trail riding—a privilege that can quickly be taken away—will continue to be ours to share.

TRAIL MAINTENANCE

Unfortunately, despite all of the preventive measures taken to avoid trail damage, we're still going to run into many trails requiring attention. Simply put, a lot of hikers, equestrians, and cyclists alike use the same trails—some wear and tear is unavoidable. But like your bike, if you want to use these trails for a long time to come, you must also maintain them.

Trail maintenance and restoration can be accomplished in a variety of ways. One way is for mountain bike clubs to combine efforts with other trail users (i.e. hikers and equestrians) and work closely with land managers to cut new trails or repair existing ones. This not only reinforces to others the commitment cyclists have in caring for and maintaining the land, but also breaks the ice that often separates cyclists from their fellow trailmates. Another good way to help out is to show up on a Saturday morning with a few riding buddies at your favorite off-road domain ready to work. With a good attitude, thick gloves, and the local land manager's supervision, trail repair is fun and very rewarding. It's important, of course, that you arrange a trail-repair outing with the local land manager before you start pounding shovels into the dirt. They can lead you to the most needy sections of trail and instruct you on what repairs should be done and how best to accomplish the task. Perhaps the most effective means of trail maintenance, though, can be done by yourself and while you're riding. Read on.

ON-THE-SPOT QUICK FIX

Most of us, when we're riding, have at one time or another come upon muddy trails or fallen trees blocking our path. We notice that over time the mud gets deeper and the trail gets wider as people go through or around the obstacles. We worry that the problem will become so severe and repairs too difficult that the trail's access may be threatened. We also know that our ambition to do anything about it is greatest at that moment, not after a hot shower and a plate of spaghetti. Here are a few on-the-spot quick fixes you can do that will hopefully correct a problem before it gets out of hand and get you back on your bike within minutes.

- **MUDDY TRAILS.** What do you do when trails develop huge mud holes destined for the EPA's Superfund status? The technique is called corduroying, and it works much like building a pontoon over the mud to support bikes, horses, or hikers as they cross. Corduroy (not the pants) is the term for roads made of logs laid down crosswise. Use small-and medium-sized sticks and lay them side by side across the trail until they cover the length of the muddy section (break the sticks to fit the width of the trail). Press them into the mud with your feet, then lay more on top if needed. Keep adding sticks until the trail is firm. Not only will you stay clean as you cross, but the sticks may soak up some of the water and help the puddle dry. This quick fix may last as long as one month before needing to be redone. And as time goes on, with new layers added to the trail, the soil will grow stronger, thicker, and more resistant to erosion. This whole process may take fewer than five minutes, and you can be on your way, knowing the trail behind you is in good repair.
- **LEAVING THE TRAIL.** What do you do to keep cyclists from cutting corners and leaving the designated trail? The solution is much simpler than you may think. (No, don't hire an off-road police force.) Notice where people are leaving the trail and throw a pile of thick branches or brush along the path, or place logs across the opening to block the way through. There are probably dozens of subtle tricks like these that will manipulate people into staying on the designated trail. If executed well, no one will even notice that the thick branches scattered along the ground in the woods weren't always there. And most folks would probably rather take a moment to hop a log in the trail than get tangled in a web of branches.
- **OBSTACLES IN THE WAY.** If there are large obstacles blocking the trail, try and remove them or push them aside. If you cannot do this by yourself, call the trail maintenance hotline to speak with the land manager of that particular trail and see what can be done.

We must be willing to *sweat for* our trails in order to *sweat on* them. Police yourself and point out to others the significance of trail maintenance. "Sweat Equity," the rewards of continued land use won with a fair share of sweat, pays off when the trail is "up for review" by the land manager and he or she remembers the efforts made by trail-conscious mountain bikers.

RULES OF THE TRAIL

The International Mountain Bicycling Association (IMBA) has developed these guidelines to trail riding. These "Rules of the Trail" are accepted worldwide and will go a long way in keeping trails open. Please respect and follow these rules for everyone's sake.

1. *Ride only on open trails.* Respect trail and road closures (if you're not sure, ask a park or state official first), do not trespass on private property, and obtain permits or authorization if required. Federal and state wilderness areas are off-limits to cycling. Parks and state forests may also have certain trails closed to cycling.

2. *Leave no trace.* Be sensitive to the dirt beneath you. Even on open trails, you should not ride under conditions by which you will leave evidence of your passing, such as on certain soils or shortly after a rainfall. Be sure to observe the different types of soils and trails you're riding on, practicing minimum-impact cycling. Never ride off the trail, don't skid your tires, and be sure to bring out at least as much as you bring in.

3. *Control your bicycle!* Inattention for even one second can cause disaster for yourself or for others. Excessive speed frightens and can injure people, gives mountain biking a bad name, and can result in trail closures.

4. *Always yield.* Let others know you're coming well in advance (a friendly greeting is always good and often appreciated). Show your respect when passing others by slowing to walking speed or stopping altogether, especially in the presence of horses. Horses can be unpredictable, so be very careful. Anticipate that other trail users may be around corners or in blind spots.

5. *Never spook animals.* All animals are spooked by sudden movements, unannounced approaches, or loud noises. Give the animals extra room and time so they can adjust to you. Move slowly or dismount around animals. Running cattle and disturbing wild animals are serious offenses. Leave gates as you find them, or as marked.

6. *Plan ahead.* Know your equipment, your ability, and the area in which you are riding, and plan your trip accordingly. Be self-sufficient at all times, keep your bike in good repair, and carry necessary supplies for changes in weather or other conditions. You can help keep trails open by setting an example of responsible, courteous, and controlled mountain bike riding.

7. *Always wear a helmet when you ride.* For your own safety and protection, a helmet should be worn whenever you are riding your bike. You never know when a tree root or small rock will throw you the wrong way and send you tumbling.

Thousands of miles of dirt trails have been closed to mountain bicycling because of the irresponsible riding habits of just a few riders. Don't follow the example of these offending riders. Don't take away trail privileges from thousands of others who work hard each year to keep the backcountry avenues open to us all.

THE NECESSITIES OF CYCLING

When discussing the most important items to have on a bike ride, cyclists generally agree on the following four items.

- **HELMET.** The reasons to wear a helmet should be obvious. Helmets are discussed in more detail in the Be Safe—Wear Your Armor section.
- **WATER.** Without it, cyclists may face dehydration, which may result in dizziness and fatigue. On a warm day, cyclists should drink at least one full bottle during every hour of riding. Remember, it's always good to drink before you feel thirsty—otherwise, it may be too late.
- **CYCLING SHORTS.** These are necessary if you plan to ride your bike more than 20 to 30 minutes. Padded cycling shorts may be the only thing preventing your derriere from serious saddle soreness by ride's end. There are two types of cycling shorts you can buy. Touring shorts are good for people who don't want to look like they're wearing anatomically correct cellophane. These look like regular athletic shorts with pockets, but have built-in padding in the crotch area for protection from chafing and saddle sores. The more popular, traditional cycling shorts are made of skin-tight material, also with a padded crotch. Whichever style you find most comfortable, cycling shorts are a necessity for long rides.
- **FOOD.** This essential item will keep you rolling. Cycling burns up a lot of calories and is among the

few sports in which no one is safe from the "Bonk." Bonking feels like it sounds. Without food in your system, your blood sugar level collapses, and there is no longer any energy in your body. This instantly results in total fatigue and light-headedness. So when you're filling your water bottle, remember to bring along some food. Fruit, energy bars, or some other forms of high-energy food are highly recommended. Candy bars are not, however, because they will deliver a sudden burst of high energy, then let you down soon after, causing you to feel worse than before. Energy bars are available at most bike stores and are similar to candy bars, but provide complex carbohydrate energy and high nutrition rather than fast-burning simple sugars.

BE PREPARED OR DIE

Essential equipment that will keep you from dying alone in the woods:

- **SPARE TUBE**
- **TIRE IRONS**—See the Appendix for instructions on fixing flat tires.
- **PATCH KIT**
- **PUMP**
- **MONEY**—Spare change for emergency calls.
- **SPOKE WRENCH**
- **SPARE SPOKES**—To fit your wheel. Tape these to the chain stay.
- **CHAIN TOOL**
- **ALLEN KEYS**—Bring appropriate sizes to fit your bike.
- **COMPASS**
- **FIRST-AID KIT**
- **MATCHES**
- **GUIDEBOOK**—In case all else fails and you must start a fire to survive, this guidebook will serve as excellent fire starter!

To carry these items, you may need a bike bag. A bag mounted in front of the handlebars provides quick access to your belongings, whereas a saddle bag fitted underneath the saddle keeps things out of your way. If you're carrying lots of equipment, you may want to consider a set of panniers. These are much larger and mount on either side of each wheel on a rack. Many cyclists, though, prefer not to use a bag at all. They just slip all they need into their jersey pockets, and off they go.

BE SAFE—WEAR YOUR ARMOR

While on the subject of jerseys, it's crucial to discuss the clothing you must wear to be safe, practical, and—if you prefer—stylish. The following is a list of items that will save you from disaster, outfit you comfortably, and most important, keep you looking cool.

- **HELMET.** A helmet is an absolute necessity because it protects your head from complete annihilation. It is the only thing that will not disintegrate into a million pieces after a wicked crash on a descent you shouldn't have been on in the first place. A helmet with a solid exterior shell will also

protect your head from sharp or protruding objects. Of course, with a hard-shelled helmet, you can paste several stickers of your favorite bicycle manufacturers all over the outer shell, giving companies even more free advertising for your dollar.

- **SHORTS.** Let's just say Lycra cycling shorts are considered a major safety item if you plan to ride for more than 20 or 30 minutes at a time. As mentioned in The Necessities of Cycling section, cycling shorts are well regarded as the leading cure-all for chafing and saddle sores. The most preventive cycling shorts have padded "chamois" (most chamois is synthetic nowadays) in the crotch area. Of course, if you choose to wear these traditional cycling shorts, it's imperative that they look as if someone spray painted them onto your body.

- **GLOVES.** You may find well-padded cycling gloves invaluable when traveling over rocky trails and gravelly roads for hours on end. Long-fingered gloves may also be useful, as branches, trees, assorted hard objects, and, occasionally, small animals will reach out and whack your knuckles.

- **GLASSES.** Not only do sunglasses give you an imposing presence and make you look cool (both are extremely important), they also protect your eyes from harmful ultraviolet rays, invisible branches, creepy bugs, dirt, and may prevent you from being caught sneaking glances at riders of the opposite sex also wearing skintight, revealing Lycra.

- **SHOES.** Mountain bike shoes should have stiff soles to help make pedaling easier and provide better traction when walking your bike up a trail becomes necessary. Virtually any kind of good outdoor hiking footwear will work, but specific mountain bike shoes (especially those with inset cleats) are best. It is vital that these shoes look as ugly as humanly possible. Those closest in style to bowling shoes are, of course, the most popular.

- **JERSEY or SHIRT.** Bicycling jerseys are popular because of their snug fit and back pockets. When purchasing a jersey, look for ones that are loaded with bright, blinding, neon logos and manufacturers' names. These loudly decorated billboards are also good for drawing unnecessary attention to yourself just before taking a mean spill while trying to hop a curb. A cotton T-shirt is a good alternative in warm weather, but when the weather turns cold, cotton becomes a chilling substitute for the jersey. Cotton retains moisture and sweat against your body, which may cause you to get the chills and ills on those cold-weather rides.

OH, THOSE COLD, WET WASHINGTON DAYS

If the weather chooses not to cooperate on the day you've set aside for a bike ride, it's helpful to be prepared.

- *Tights or leg warmers.* These are best in temperatures below 55 degrees. Knees are sensitive and can develop all kinds of problems if they get cold. Common problems include tendinitis, bursitis, and arthritis.
- *Plenty of layers on your upper body.* When the air has a nip in it, layers of clothing will keep the chill away from your chest and help prevent the development of bronchitis. If the air is cool, a polypropylene long-sleeved shirt is best to wear against the skin beneath other layers of clothing. Polypropylene, like wool, wicks away moisture from your skin to keep your body dry. Try to avoid wearing cotton or baggy clothing when the temperature falls. Cotton, as mentioned before, holds moisture like a sponge, and baggy clothing catches cold air and swirls it around your body. Good cold-weather clothing should fit snugly against your body, but not be restrictive.
- **Wool socks.** Don't pack too many layers under those shoes, though. You may stand the chance of restricting circulation, and your feet will get real cold, real fast.
- *Thinsulate or Gortex gloves.* We may all agree that there is nothing worse than frozen feet—unless your hands are frozen. A good pair of Thinsulate or Gortex gloves should keep your hands toasty and warm.

- *Hat or helmet on cold days?* Sometimes, when the weather gets really cold and you still want to hit the trails, it's tough to stay warm. We all know that 130 percent of the body's heat escapes through the head (overactive brains, I imagine), so it's important to keep the cranium warm. Ventilated helmets are designed to keep heads cool in the summer heat, but they do little to help keep heads warm during rides in sub-zero temperatures. Cyclists should consider wearing a hat on extremely cold days. Polypropylene Skullcaps are great head and ear warmers that snugly fit over your head beneath the helmet. Head protection is not lost. Another option is a helmet cover that covers those ventilating gaps and helps keep the body heat in. These do not, however, keep your ears warm. Some cyclists will opt for a simple knit cycling cap sans the helmet, but these have never been shown to be very good cranium protectors.

All of this clothing can be found at your local bike store, where the staff should be happy to help fit you into the seasons of the year.

TO HAVE OR NOT TO HAVE...

(Other Very Useful Items)

Though mountain biking is relatively new to the cycling scene, there is no shortage of items for you and your bike to make riding better, safer, and easier. We have rummaged through the unending lists and separated the gadgets from the good stuff, coming up with what we believe are items certain to make mountain bike riding easier and more enjoyable.

- **TIRES.** Buying yourself a good pair of knobby tires is the quickest way to enhance the off-road handling capabilities of your bike. There are many types of mountain bike tires on the market. Some are made exclusively for very rugged off-road terrain. These big-knobbed, soft rubber tires virtually stick to the ground with unforgiving traction, but tend to deteriorate quickly on pavement. There are other tires made exclusively for the road. These are called "slicks" and have no tread at all. For the average cyclist, though, a good tire somewhere in the middle of these two extremes should do the trick.

- **TOE CLIPS or CLIPLESS PEDALS.** With these, you will ride with more power. Toe clips attach to your pedals and strap your feet firmly in place, allowing you to exert pressure on the pedals on both the downstroke and the upstroke. They will increase your pedaling efficiency by 30 percent to 50 percent. Clipless pedals, which liberate your feet from the traditional straps and clips, have made toe clips virtually obsolete. Like ski bindings, they attach your shoe directly to the pedal. They are, however, much more expensive than toe clips.
- **BAR ENDS.** These great clamp-on additions to your original straight bar will provide more leverage, an excellent grip for climbing, and a more natural position for your hands. Be aware, however, of the bar end's propensity for hooking trees on fast descents, sending you, the cyclist, airborne.
- **FANNY PACK.** These bags are ideal for carrying keys, extra food, guidebooks, tools, spare tubes, and a cellular phone, in case you need to call for help.
- **SUSPENSION FORKS.** For the more serious off-roaders who want nothing to impede their speed on the trails, investing in a pair of suspension forks is a good idea. Like tires, there are plenty of brands to choose from, and they all do the same thing—absorb the brutal beatings of a rough trail. The cost of these forks, however, is sometimes more brutal than the trail itself.
- **BIKE COMPUTERS.** These are fun gadgets to own and are much less expensive than in years past. They have such features as trip distance, speedometer, odometer, time of day, altitude, alarm,

average speed, maximum speed, heart rate, global satellite positioning, etc. Bike computers will come in handy when following these maps or to know just how far you've ridden in the wrong direction.

TYPES OF OFF-ROAD TERRAIN

Before roughing it off road, we may first have to ride the pavement to get to our destination. Please, don't be dismayed. Some of the country's best rides are on the road. Once we get past these smooth-surfaced pathways, though, adventures in dirt await us.

- **RAILS-TO-TRAILS.** Abandoned rail lines are converted into usable public resources for exercising, commuting, or just enjoying nature. Old rails and ties are torn up and a trail, paved or unpaved, is laid along the existing corridor. This completes the cycle from ancient Indian trading routes to railroad corridors and back again to hiking and cycling trails.
- **UNPAVED ROADS.** These are typically found in rural areas and are most often public roads. Be careful when exploring, though, not to ride on someone's unpaved private drive.
- **FOREST ROADS.** These dirt and gravel roads are used primarily as access to forest land and are kept in good condition. They are almost always open to public use.
- **SINGLETRACK.** Singletrack can be the most fun on a mountain bike. These trails, with only one track to follow, are often narrow, challenging pathways through the woods. Remember to make sure these trails are open before zipping into the woods. (At the time of this printing, all trails and roads in this guidebook were open to mountain bikes.)
- **OPEN LAND.** Unless there is a marked trail through a field or open space, you should not plan to ride here. Once one person cuts his or her wheels through a field or meadow, many more are sure to follow, causing irreparable damage to the landscape.

TECHNIQUES TO SHARPEN YOUR SKILLS

Many of us see ourselves as pure athletes—blessed with power, strength, and endless endurance. However, it may be those with finesse, balance, agility, and grace that get around most quickly on a mountain bike. Although power, strength, and endurance do have their places in mountain biking, these elements don't necessarily form the framework for a champion mountain biker.

The bike should become an extension of your body. Slight shifts in your hips or knees can have remarkable results. Experienced bike handlers seem to flash down technical descents, dashing over obstacles in a smooth and graceful effort as if pirouetting in Swan Lake. Here are some tips and techniques to help you connect with your bike and float gracefully over the dirt.

Braking

Using your brakes requires using your head, especially when descending. This doesn't mean using your head as a stopping block, but rather to think intelligently. Use your best judgment in terms of how much or how little to squeeze those brake levers.

The more weight a tire is carrying, the more braking power it has. When you're going downhill, your front wheel carries more weight than the rear. Braking with the front brake will help keep you in control without going into a skid. Be careful, though, not to overdo it with the front brakes and accidentally toss yourself over the handlebars. And don't neglect your rear brake! When descending, shift your weight back over the rear wheel, thus increasing your rear braking power as well. This will balance the power of both brakes and give you maximum control.

Good riders learn just how much of their weight to shift over each wheel and how to apply just enough braking power to each brake, so not to "endo" over the handlebars or skid down a trail.

GOING UPHILL—Climbing Those Treacherous Hills

- *Shift into a low gear* (push the thumb shifter away from you). Before shifting, be sure to ease up on your pedaling so there is not too much pressure on the chain. Find the gear best for you that matches the terrain and steepness of each climb.
- *Stay seated.* Standing out of the saddle is often helpful when climbing steep hills with a road bike, but you may find that on dirt, standing may cause your rear tire to lose its grip and spin out. Climbing requires traction. Stay seated as long as you can, and keep the rear tire digging into the ground. Ascending skyward may prove to be much easier in the saddle.
- *Lean forward.* On very steep hills, the front end may feel unweighted and suddenly pop up. Slide forward on the saddle and lean over the handlebars. This will add more weight to the front wheel and should keep you grounded.
- *Keep pedaling.* On rocky climbs, be sure to keep the pressure on, and don't let up on those pedals! The slower you go through rough trail sections, the harder you will work.

GOING DOWNHILL—
The Real Reason We Get Up in the Morning

- *Shift into the big chainring.* Shifting into the big ring before a bumpy descent will help keep the chain from bouncing off. And should you crash or disengage your leg from the pedal, the chain will cover the teeth of the big ring so they don't bite into your leg.
- *Relax.* Stay loose on the bike, and don't lock your elbows or clench your grip. Your elbows need to bend with the bumps and absorb the shock, while your hands should have a firm but controlled grip on the bars to keep things steady. Steer with your body, allowing your shoulders to guide you through each turn and around each obstacle.
- *Don't oversteer or lose control.* Mountain biking is much like downhill skiing, since you must shift your weight from side to side down narrow, bumpy descents. Your bike will have the tendency to track in the direction you look and follow the slight shifts and leans of your body. You should not think so much about steering, but rather in what direction you wish to go.
- *Rise above the saddle.* When racing down bumpy, technical descents, you should not be sitting on the saddle, but standing on the pedals, allowing your legs and knees to absorb the rocky trail instead of your rear.

- *Drop your saddle.* For steep, technical descents, you may want to drop your saddle three or four inches. This lowers your center of gravity, giving you much more room to bounce around.
- *Keep your pedals parallel to the ground.* The front pedal should be slightly higher so that it doesn't catch on small rocks or logs.
- *Stay focused.* Many descents require your utmost concentration and focus just to reach the bottom. You must notice every groove, every root, every rock, every hole, every bump. You, the bike, and the trail should all become one as you seek singletrack nirvana on your way down the mountain. But if your thoughts wander, however, then so may your bike, and you may instead become one with the trees!

WATCH OUT!
Back-road Obstacles

- **LOGS.** When you want to hop a log, throw your body back, yank up on the handlebars, and pedal forward in one swift motion. This clears the front end of the bike. Then quickly scoot forward and

pedal the rear wheel up and over. Keep the forward momentum until you've cleared the log, and by all means, don't hit the brakes, or you may do some interesting acrobatic maneuvers!

- **ROCKS.** Worse than highway potholes! Stay relaxed, let your elbows and knees absorb the shock, and always continue applying power to your pedals. Staying seated will keep the rear wheel weighted to prevent slipping, and a light front end will help you to respond quickly to each new obstacle. The slower you go, the more time your tires will have to get caught between the grooves.

- **WATER.** Before crossing a stream or puddle, be sure to first check the depth and bottom surface. There may be an unseen hole or large rock hidden under the water that could wash you up if you're not careful. After you're sure all is safe, hit the water at a good speed, pedal steadily, and allow the bike to steer you through. Once you're across, tap the breaks to squeegee the water off the rims.

- **LEAVES.** Be careful of wet leaves. These may look pretty, but a trail covered with leaves may cause your wheels to slip out from under you. Leaves are not nearly as unpredictable and dangerous as ice, but they do warrant your attention on a rainy day.

- **MUD.** If you must ride through mud, hit it head on and keep pedaling. You want to part the ooze with your front wheel and get across before it swallows you up. Above all, don't leave the trail to go around the mud. This just widens the path even more and leads to increased trail erosion.

Urban Obstacles

- **CURBS** are fun to jump, but like with logs, be careful.
- **CURBSIDE DRAINS** are typically not a problem for bikes. Just be careful not to get a wheel caught in the grate.
- **DOGS** make great pets, but seem to have it in for bicyclists. If you think you can't outrun a dog that's chasing you, stop and walk your bike out of its territory. A loud yell to Get! or Go home! often works, as does a sharp squirt from your water bottle right between the eyes.
- **CARS** are tremendously convenient when we're in them, but dodging irate motorists in big automobiles becomes a real hazard when riding a bike. As a cyclist, you must realize most drivers aren't expecting you to be there and often wish you weren't. Stay alert and ride carefully, clearly signaling all of your intentions.

- **POTHOLES,** like grates and back-road canyons, should be avoided. Just because you're on an all-terrain bicycle doesn't mean you're indestructible. Potholes regularly damage rims, pop tires, and sometimes lift unsuspecting cyclists into a spectacular swan dive over the handlebars.

LAST-MINUTE CHECKOVER

Before a ride, it's a good idea to give your bike a once-over to make sure everything is in working order. Begin by checking the air pressure in your tires before each ride to make sure they are properly inflated. Mountain bikes require about 45 to 55 pounds per square inch of air pressure. If your tires are underinflated, there is greater likelihood that the tubes may get pinched on a bump or rock, causing the tire to flat.

Looking over your bike to make sure everything is secure and in its place is the next step. Go through the following checklist before each ride.

- *Pinch the tires to feel for proper inflation.* They should give just a little on the sides, but feel very hard on the treads. If you have a pressure gauge, use that.

- *Check your brakes.* Squeeze the rear brake and roll your bike forward. The rear tire should skid. Next, squeeze the front brake and roll your bike forward. The rear wheel should lift into the air. If this doesn't happen, then your brakes are too loose. Make sure the brake levers don't touch the handlebars when squeezed with full force.

- *Check all quick releases on your bike.* Make sure they are all securely tightened.

- *Lube up.* If your chain squeaks, apply some lubricant.

- *Check your nuts and bolts.* Check the handlebars, saddle, cranks, and pedals to make sure that each is tight and securely fastened to your bike.

- *Check your wheels.* Spin each wheel to see that they spin through the frame and between brake pads freely.

- *Have you got everything?* Make sure you have your spare tube, tire irons patch kit, frame pump, tools, food, water, and guidebook.

Liability Disclaimer

Beachway Press assumes no liability for cyclists traveling along any of the suggested routes in this book. At the time of publication, all routes shown on the following maps were open to bicycles. They were chosen for their safety, aesthetics, and pleasure, and are deemed acceptable and accommodating to bicyclists. Safety upon these routes, however, cannot be guaranteed. Cyclists must assume their own responsibility when riding these routes and understand that with an activity such as mountain bike riding, there may be unforeseen risks and dangers.

THE MAPS   Map Legend

We don't want anyone, by any means, to feel restricted to just the roads and trails that are mapped here. We hope you will have an adventurous spirit and use this guide as a platform to dive into Washington's backcountry and discover new routes for yourself. One of the simplest ways to begin this is to just turn the map upside down and ride the course in reverse. The change in perspective is fantastic and the ride should feel quite different. With this in mind, it will be like getting two distinctly different rides on each map.

For your own purposes, you may wish to copy the directions for the course onto a small sheet to help you while riding, or photocopy the map and cue sheet to take with you. These pages can be folded into a bike bag, stuffed into a jersey pocket, or better still, used with the **BarMap** or **BarMapOTG** (see page 225 for more info). Just remember to slow or even stop when you want to read the map.

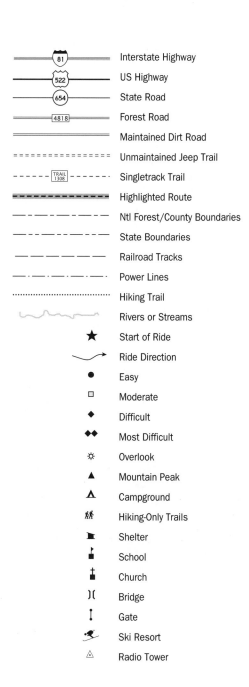

81	Interstate Highway
522	US Highway
654	State Road
4818	Forest Road
	Maintained Dirt Road
	Unmaintained Jeep Trail
TRAIL 1308	Singletrack Trail
	Highlighted Route
	Ntl Forest/County Boundaries
	State Boundaries
	Railroad Tracks
	Power Lines
	Hiking Trail
	Rivers or Streams
★	Start of Ride
	Ride Direction
●	Easy
□	Moderate
◆	Difficult
◆◆	Most Difficult
☼	Overlook
▲	Mountain Peak
⋀	Campground
炏	Hiking-Only Trails
▰	Shelter
▮	School
▯	Church
)(	Bridge
I	Gate
⚞	Ski Resort
△	Radio Tower

WA

OR

MOUNTAIN BIKE WASHINGTON

The Rides

1. Mount Pickett Loop
2. Lily/Lizard Lakes Loop
3. Spruce Railroad Trail
4. Foothills Trail
5. Gold Creek
6. Wildcat Trail
7. Cedar Creek
8. Walker Valley/Cavanaugh Loop
9. Wallace Falls Loop
10. Silver Creek
11. Nason Ridge
12. Mountain Home Loops
13. Jolly Mountain
14. Kachess Ridge
15. West Fork of the Teanaway
16. Capitol Forest—Lost Valley Loop
17. Capitol Forest—Larch Mountain
18. Tiger Mountain
19. Ranger Creek
20. Skookum Flats
21. Crystal Mountain Loop
22. Fifes Ridge
23. Osborne Mountain
24. Tongue Mountain
25. Chain of Lakes
26. Mount St. Helens—Mc Bride/Kalama Loop
27. Mount St. Helens—Blue Lake Loop
28. Mount St. Helens—Plains of Abraham
29. Service Trail/Surprise Lakes
30. Gotchen Creek
31. Siouxon Creek
32. Falls Creek Shuttle
33. Yacolt's Larch Mountain
34. Sun Mountain Trails
35. Lightning Creek
36. Foggy Dew/Merchants Basin
37. Pot Peak
38. Mission Ridge
39. Devils Gulch
40. Riverside State Park—Centennial Trail

Honorable Mentions

A. Lake Padden Park
B. Bellingham Interurban Trail
C. Cranberry Lake in Anacortes
D. Sadie Creek
E. Tahuya River Ride
F. Tolt Pipeline Trail
G. Mad Lake
H. Summit at Snoqualmie
I. Money Creek Trail
J. Mill Creek Valley
K. Iron Horse Trail
L. Taneum Creek Loop
M. Oak Creek Trail
N. Cowiche Canyons Conservancy Trail
O. Juniper Ridge Loop
P. Lewis River
Q. Siouxon Peak and Huffman Peak Loop
R. Buck Creek Trail System
S. Sawtooth Backcountry
T. Echo Valley
U. Steamboat Rock State Park
W. 13-Mile ORV Area
X. TaylorRidge Trail
Y. Narcisse Block of the Oreille
Z. Batey/Bould Trails
AA. 49-Degrees North Alpine Ski Area
BB. Mt. Spokane State Park
CC. Liberty Lake Regional Park
EE. Snake River Bikeway
FF. Asotin Creek Trail
GG. North Fork Trail/Table State Park
HH. South Fork Trail
II. Elbow Creek

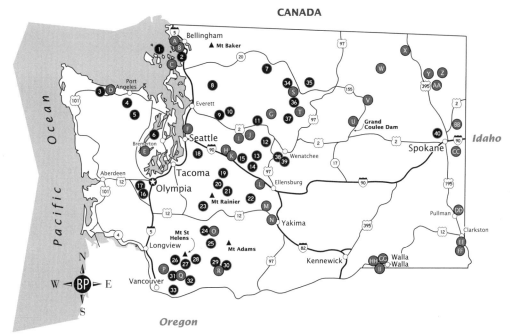

COURSES AT A GLANCE Ride Profiles

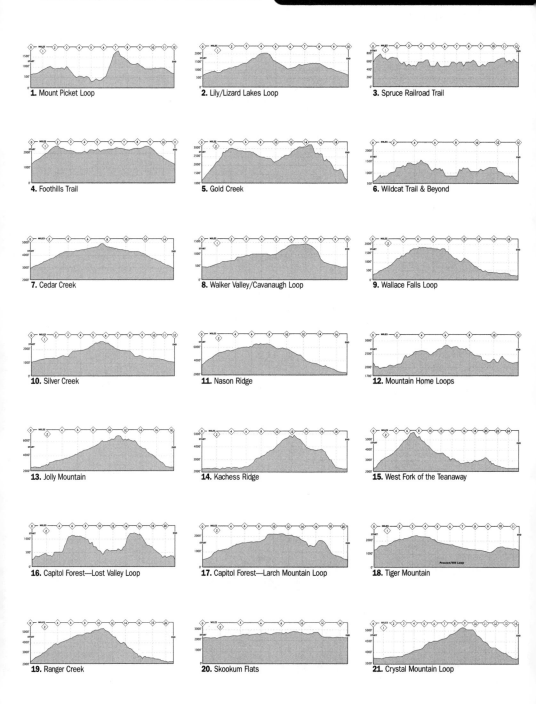

1. Mount Picket Loop

2. Lily/Lizard Lakes Loop

3. Spruce Railroad Trail

4. Foothills Trail

5. Gold Creek

6. Wildcat Trail & Beyond

7. Cedar Creek

8. Walker Valley/Cavanaugh Loop

9. Wallace Falls Loop

10. Silver Creek

11. Nason Ridge

12. Mountain Home Loops

13. Jolly Mountain

14. Kachess Ridge

15. West Fork of the Teanaway

16. Capitol Forest—Lost Valley Loop

17. Capitol Forest—Larch Mountain Loop

18. Tiger Mountain

19. Ranger Creek

20. Skookum Flats

21. Crystal Mountain Loop

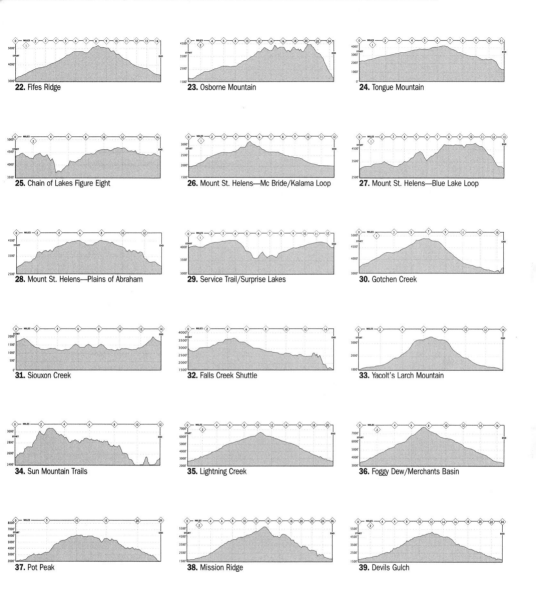

22. Fifes Ridge

23. Osborne Mountain

24. Tongue Mountain

25. Chain of Lakes Figure Eight

26. Mount St. Helens—Mc Bride/Kalama Loop

27. Mount St. Helens—Blue Lake Loop

28. Mount St. Helens—Plains of Abraham

29. Service Trail/Surprise Lakes

30. Gotchen Creek

31. Siouxon Creek

32. Falls Creek Shuttle

33. Yacolt's Larch Mountain

34. Sun Mountain Trails

35. Lightning Creek

36. Foggy Dew/Merchants Basin

37. Pot Peak

38. Mission Ridge

39. Devils Gulch

No Profile Available

40. Riverside State Park—Centennial Trail

HOW TO USE THE MAPS Map Descriptions

Area Locator Map

This thumbnail relief map at the beginning of each ride shows you where the ride is within the state. The ride area is indicated with a star.

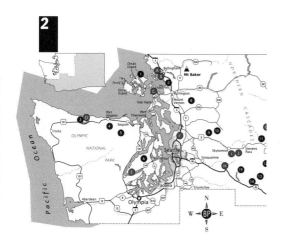

Regional Location Map

This map helps you find your way to the start of each ride from the nearest sizeable town or city. Coupled with the detailed directions at the beginning of the cue, this map should visually lead you to where you need to be for each ride.

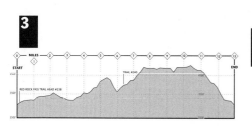

Profile Map

This helpful profile gives you a cross-sectional look at the ride's ups and downs. Elevation is labeled on the left, mileage is indicated on the top. Road and trail names are shown along the route with towns and points of interest labeled in bold.

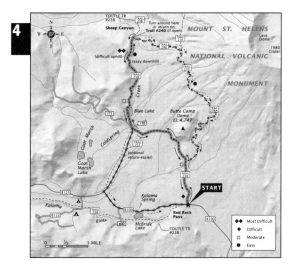

Route Map

This is your primary guide to each ride. It shows all of the accessible roads and trails, points of interest, water, towns, landmarks, and geographical features. It also distinguishes trails from roads, and paved roads from unpaved roads. The selected route is highlighted, and directional arrows point the way. Shaded topographic relief in the background gives you an accurate representation of the terrain and landscape in the ride area.

Ride Information Board *(Included in each ride section)*

This is a small bulletin board with important information concerning each ride.

- The **Trail Maintenance Hotline** is the direct number for the local land managers in charge of all the trails within the selected ride. Use this hotline to call ahead for trail access information, or after your visit if you see problems with trail erosion, damage, or misuse.
- **Cost.** What money, if any, you may need to carry with you for park entrance fees or tolls.
- **Schedule.** This tells you at what times trails open and close, if on private or park land.
- **Maps.** This is a list of other maps to supplement the maps in this book. They are listed in order from most detailed to most general.
- Any other important or useful information will also be listed here such as local attractions, bike shops, nearby accomodations, etc.

Northwest Washington

"Here is the fringey edge where elements meet and realms mingle, where time and eternity spatter each other with foam. The salt sea and the islands, molding and molding, row upon rolling row, don't quit, nor do winds end nor skies cease from spreading in curves."

Anne Dillard, *Holy the Firm*

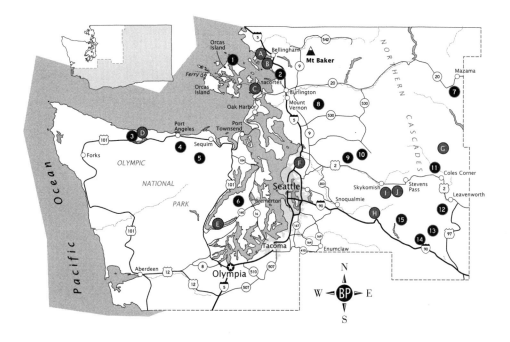

From the foothills of the Cascade range, in the direction of the setting sun, lies the Puget Sound and the ancient, evergreen arm of the Olympic Peninsula. Home to big trees, big fish, and only a few venomous spiders (but no poisonous snakes), the Puget Sound region is primed for the adventurer. Speckled with alpine peaks and gallons of both salt and fresh water, Northwest Washington enjoys fairly mild temperatures year-round, allowing for especially long mountain bike seasons. The rides here may get muddy from time to time—the blustering force of the Pacific winds accounts for that—but that's precisely what makes Washington the Evergreen State. From the San Juans to Tacoma to the Olympics, the elevation gains can range from gentle to intense, but the beauty of this region is its diversity. There are more than enough trails to choose from for a sensational singletrack experience.

Orcas Island

From the top of Orcas Island's Mount Constitution (the highest point in the San Juans), you get a bird's-eye view of the 172 named islands that form the archipelago—including the countless incidental islands that tend to appear, and then disappear, with the tides. What is truly amazing to imagine is that you are looking down at the peaks of a sunken mountain range that stretches from the American mainland to Vancouver Island—a range that actually pre-dates the mainland. Just twelve thousand years ago this same vantage would have revealed fully land-bound mountains. Blanketing the base of the mountains and the better part of the region was the enormous Vashon Glacier, which is responsible for much of the

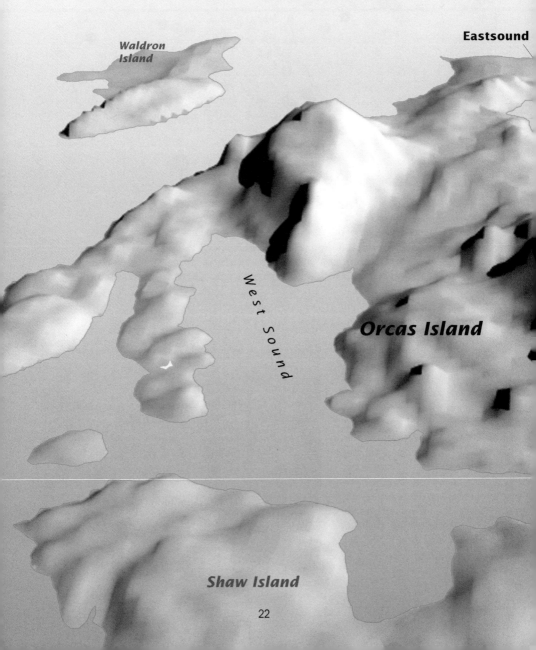

Eastsound

Waldron Island

West Sound

Orcas Island

Shaw Island

San Juans' physical presence. The glacier stripped patches of land down to bare rock and carved out the deep valleys. As the ice age came to an end and the glaciers began to melt, the ocean level rose, submerging much of the coastal region in water (clear into the Puget Sound) and isolating the San Juan peaks forever in a sea of water.

Mt Constitution
El. 2,407

East Sound

Mount Pickett Loop

Ride Summary

This loop is one of the most popular on Orcas Island and one of the few rides within Moran State Park open year-round. The trails within the park are well tended and in excellent condition. This loop begins in an area with four waterfalls then climbs singletrack passing scenic lakes for stunning views of the salty Rosario Straight. Although the backside of the loop gets a little tough to ride because of a few steep sections, it's really a superb route for both intermediate and beginner cyclists. However, after September 1998 watch for changes in trail access for bikes. Check with the information station for more details.

Ride Specs

Start: Cascade Falls Trailhead (1.6 miles from Moran State Park entrance)
Other Starting Locations: Parking lot at Cascade Lake
Length: 11.5 miles
Approximate Riding Time: 2-3 hours
Nearest Town: Eastsound
Rating: Easy to Moderate with some steep climbing
Terrain: Doubletrack and singletrack; paved road from some starting locations
Other Trail Users: Hikers

Getting There

From Anacortes: Take the ferry to Orcas Island. Land on Orcas and follow the main road into the interior. Turn left at the "Y" intersection—the large outdoor map of Orcas is your landmark. At the "T" intersection, turn right. Follow the signs for Eastsound. Keep left at Eastsound heading directly to Moran State Park. Pass a small airfield and proceed directly to the entrance of Moran State Park.

Orcas Island, with its 3,500 residents, is the largest of the San Juan Islands (San Juan is the second largest), and is deservedly hailed as "The Gem of the San Juans." The horse-shoe-shaped island is divided into two lobes bridged by the town of Eastsound. Once a profitable supplier of produce (particularly in the Crow Valley along the island's western leg), Orcas Island spent the later part of the nineteenth century blanketed in fruit orchards and hop fields. The island even tried its hand at growing bulbs. But when railroads began supplanting steamships as the dominant means for transporting goods, the island lost favor with mainland buyers and in time found itself commercially isolated. The fertile fields were abandoned. Today the island functions primarily as a recreational destination, with a number of B&Bs and miles of winding trails to explore.

Located on the island's eastern leg is the Moran State Park. The 5,175 acres of parkland were donated to Washington and Orcas Island in 1921 by Robert Moran—formerly the mayor of Seattle and credited with the city's recovery after the great fire of 1889. After mak-

ing a fortune selling steamships to anxious Klondike gold-rushers, Moran retired to Orcas Island in 1906, buying over 5,000 acres (the better part of Orcas' eastern leg) and designing a 19-bedroom "getaway" overlooking the East Sound (now the Rosario Island Resort). Further contributing to his island-playground atmosphere, Moran constructed a network of trails, roads, and bridges. In the 1930s the Civilian Conservation Corps extended the trail system and built campsites, stone gazebos, and a stone lookout tower.

The Mount Pickett Ride winds through the park's eastern side, which is home to some of the most cared for trail in the state. If you do nothing else on Orcas, ride the steep paved road to the top of Mount Constitution (2,407 feet)—the highest point in the San Juans—for spectacular, panoramic views, from Vancouver Island clear to Mount Baker. Lt. Charles Wilkes, head of the 1841 U.S. Exploring Expedition, named the mountain after the famous naval ship the Constitution ("Old Ironsides"). At the mountain's summit you'll find the Civilian Conservation Corps' 52-foot stone observation tower, built in 1935.

Before beginning your ride, be sure to acquaint yourself with any new trail openings or closings at the information center across from Cascade Lake. The trails along Mountain Lake are some of the best around, fast and virtually flawless—though they're only seasonally open to bikes. Picturesque snapshots of the lake peak through the trees, making this ride simply sublime on sunny days. All the trails of Moran State Park are near perfect for the beginning/intermediate mountain biker, with the exception of the South Boundary Trail which has some tight, steep singletrack.

While visiting Orcas Island, try to check out one or more of the other islands if you have time, like Lopez, Shaw, or San Juan—all of which are served by the Anacortes and Inter-Island ferries. The smaller islands are a little harder to reach. You'll have to rent a private boat or plane to get to them. The San Juans provide a great escape, but as is apparent in the crowded ferry lines come Sundays, they're no secret.

MilesDirections

0.0 START from the parking area and ride through the gate to Mount Pickett Road. Follow Mount Pickett Road, passing the trail for Cascade, Rustic, Hidden, and Cavern Falls.

0.3 Pass another trail intersection on the right for the falls. Continue straight along the river.

0.5 Pass a trail on the left to Twin Lakes and Mountain Lake Landing. This trail is open to bikes between Sept. 15 and May 15 and is another option for reaching Mountain Lake and connecting with the trail to Mount Pickett. Stay right on Mount Pickett Road (which is open year-round to mountain bikes).

1.7 Come to a "Y" intersection and turn left.

2.0 Turn right at the "Y" and head up Twin lakes Trail. The left takes you 50 yards to a great view of Mountain Lake.

4.1 Reach the northern end of the lake.

4.2 Continuing toward Twin Lakes: At the "T" intersection, turn right on the trail for bikes only. The left is hikers only.

5.0 Arrive at Twin Lakes. Turn right at the "T" intersection. The left trail takes you to Cold Springs via the North Trail (3.85 miles); 1.5 miles to the summit straight up. Mount Pickett lies to the right.

5.1 Follow the trail around Little Twin to the right (elevation is 1,100 feet).

5.2 Follow the trail on the right to Mount Pickett.

5.6 Pass a marsh area and a trail to the left.

5.7 Pass an unmarked trail.

6.7 Reach the summit of Mount Pickett (1,750 feet), a 650-foot climb from Twin Lakes.

6.75 At the trail intersection, the sign reads: "4.2 miles on South Arch or continue on the main trail to Mountain Lakes at 4.1 miles." Follow the South Arch trail to the South Boundary Trail.

6.8 At the "Y" intersection, turn left down the South Arch Trail.

8.0 Reach the intersection of the Mount Pickett Trail and South Boundary Trail. Stay straight on South Boundary Trail (open year-round to cyclists).

9.3 Pass a large lean-to opposite the park boundary. **Do Not Trespass.** The lean-to is on private property. Cross a couple of streams and head up.

9.5 Pass permanent houses across the park boundary.

9.6 Turn left at the "Y" intersection for Cascade Lake. The other trail leads to Pickett Road.

10.3 Pass a water pipeline cut on the left. Follow the singletrack up to the right.

11.0 Arrive back at the intersection to Hidden Falls and the wooden bridge to Mountain Lake. Turn left down the forest service road.

11.5 Reach the end of the ride.

READER ALERT! Immediately prior to publication of this edition we learned that there are plans to close sections of these trails to mountain bikes as of September 1998. The trail between Mountain Lake and Twin Lakes, South Arch Trail, and a section of Mount Pickett Road will become hiker only. Please check with the information station and be aware of all current trail closings prior to setting out on the trails.

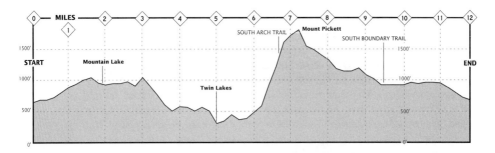

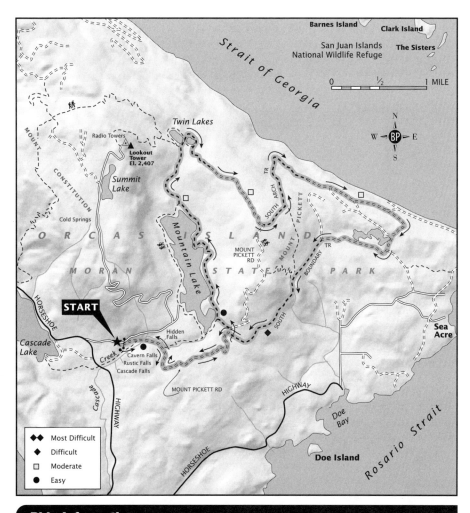

Ride Information

Trail Maintenance Hotlines:
  Moran State Park
  (360) 376-2326

Costs:
  • For ferry rates:
    1-800-84-FERRY (WA only) or
    www.wsdot.wa.gov/ferries
  • Camping fees are $11/night

Local Information:
  Orcas Island Chamber of Commerce
    (360) 376-2273
  www.sanjuan.com/orcasislandchamber

Local Events/Attractions:
  • Rosario Island Resort & Spa,

  Eastsound, WA; (360) 376-2222
  or 1-800-562-8820
  • Orcas Island Farmers Market
    Saturdays, April to October
    Eastsound, WA

Local Bike Shops:
  • Dolphin Bay Bicycles, Orcas, WA
    (360) 376-4157
  • Wildlife Cycles, Eastsound, WA
    (360) 376-4708

Maps:
  • Maptech CD-ROM:
    Mount Constitution, WA
  • DeLorme's Washington Atlas & Gazetteer
    Page 108 C2

27

In Addition:**The Pig Wars**

The Oregon Treaty of 1846 was supposed to settle America and Britain's petty territory wrangling. It stated that the dividing line between the U.S. and Canada would run to the north along the 49th parallel and to the west along the strait between Vancouver Island and the mainland. Simple enough...the 49th parallel and the strait. Except, there are two straits. Britain, rather conveniently, interpreted the treaty to mean the Rosario Strait, which separates the San Juans from the mainland—meaning they'd own the island chain. The U.S., equally self-serving, understood the language to mean the Haro Strait, which runs between the San Juan Islands and Vancouver Island—which would give them the islands. And so, each country went about its business assuming it owned the islands.

In those days there weren't too many people living on any of the islands, so land rights were rarely at issue; that is, until 1855 when the U.S. attempted to collect import duties from the Hudson's Bay Company's sheep farm on San Juan (the chain's principle island). The British-owned company refused to pay the duty, so the county sheriff seized the valuable livestock and sold it at auction. The governor of Vancouver, B.C., James Douglas, protested the action but was, for the most part, ignored. Douglas was no doubt angry, but this just wasn't enough to spark a war.

Four years later, an American, Lyman Cutler, fed-up with the Hudson's Bay Company's roaming livestock, shot an errant pig for rooting in his potato patch. Once again tensions were flared. Demands for compensation were made, but Cutler refused to pay. The British threatened arrest. The American army responded to the rising tensions by sending Captain George E. Pickett [of future Gettysburg fame] with 66 men to establish Camp Pickett (now called American Camp). Their purpose was to protect the American settlers in their "present exposed and defenseless position" against the Hudson's Bay Company. The British countered by building a fort on the opposite end of the island and by amassing 2,140 men, five warships, and 167 canons—sorely outnumbering the Americans.

The two countries were poised at the brink of war. Before shots were fired, both sides agreed to meet at the table. President Buchanan called on the head of his army, Gen. Winfield Scott, to negotiate the terms. After long discussion, both sides agreed that war was not the answer—but that's about all they could decide upon. And so once again the territorial debate was tabled. Both countries agreed that in the meantime they would maintain a joint military presence on the island. For 12 years the island-bound soldiers held their posts until finally Britain and the U.S. sought the German Kaiser Wilhelm I to arbitrate a settlement. His decision?

We, William, by the grace of God, German Emperor...
find...the claim of the Government of the United States...
is most in accordance with the true interpretation of the Treaty.

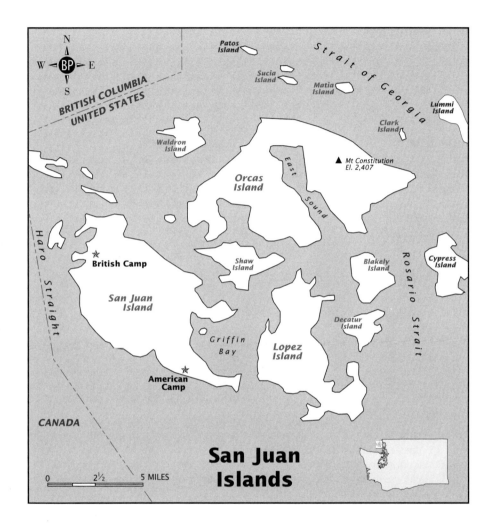

San Juan Islands

With the San Juans fairly in U.S. possession, both military camps disbanded quietly, leaving behind only one casualty: *the pig*.

To learn more about the Pig Wars, visit the quaint Pig War Museum in Friday Harbor on San Juan Island: (360) 378-6495; or visit the American and British Camps themselves—sorry, no mountain bikes are allowed on the trails at either camp. For more information, call (360) 378-2240.

Lily/Lizard Lakes Loop

Ride Summary

Located on Chuckanut Mountain, one of the most popular recreational areas in Bellingham, the trails in and around Lily Lake and Lizard Lake are fun and semi-technical (the loop we've chosen has a descent that even Hans Rey might have trouble negotiating). But the views of the water, the San Juan Islands, the hang gliders, and the trail itself, make that one small, annoyingly steep section not so bad after all. This loop can be completed in just a couple of hours, leaving plenty of time to explore the mountain's other trails.

Ride Specs

Start: B-1000 parking lot
Other Starting Locations: The second gravel parking lot on the B-1000 Road around the bend.
Length: 10 miles
Approximate Riding Time: 2 hours
Nearest Town: Bellingham
Rating: Moderate, with one short difficult section
Terrain: Singletrack
Other Trail Users: Hikers and horseback riders

Getting There

From Bellingham: Take I-5 South to Exit 240, Alger Road. Head left/west over the freeway. Take the first left on Barrel Springs Road toward the Blanchard Hill Trail System. Pass Shaw Road. Turn right in 0.75 miles on B-1000 Road. Park at the Blanchard Hill Trails parking area.

Hang glider off the Samish Overlook.

The scenic Chuckanut Drive—the state's first designated scenic highway—travels north and south along an 11-mile stretch of State Route 11, passing the Samish, Chuckanut, and Bellingham Bays. To the south, the by-way stretches across the bulb-growing flatlands of the Skagit Valley and then travels north along the bay side of the Chuckanut Mountain Range. Hugging to the foothills of the mountains, the drive brushes the 2,500-acre Larrabee State Park—Washington's first— and then skirts along the Chuckanut Bay until the mountains give way to the city of Bellingham—the last major town before the Canadian border.

Bellingham is just 18 miles south of the Canadian border and is home to Western Washington University. The city has an interesting history in that it has *four* histories. Present-day Bellingham began as the four independent and clearly distinct communities of Fairhaven, Sehome, Whatcom, and Bellingham. Bellingham was the smallest of these communities, but when it came time to choose a name for the consolidated city, the other towns fought so hard that the only acceptable compromise was the less significant "Bellingham." If you have time, you'll want to visit some of the area's points of interest such as Fairhaven, where you can take a self-guided tour of some of the more interesting historic sites (just follow the granite plaques). One such site is where an entire freight wagon was engulfed in quicksand.

This ride takes place a few miles south of Bellingham in the Blanchard Hill area, sandwiched between I-5 and the Samish Bay in the southern portion of the Chuckanut Mountain range. You'll likely share the mountain with hang gliders launching from the Samish Overlook, llama-trekkers out for a stroll, equestrians, hikers, and of course, mountain bikers.

Some local riders recommended the Lily Lake/Lizard Lake Trail to us. We like it because you can go at your own pace, for as long or as far as you want, without ever being too far from your car. There's even a popular spot along the trail if you're interested in learning a little bit about the geologic make-up of the Chuckanut Mountains. The attraction is an enormous boulder—which happens to tell the story itself. A sign on the rock reads:

Grooved striations atop this particular matrix of Chuckanut sandstone were made by regolith slowly rumbling along about 18,000 years ago under the pressure of glaciers one mile high. Ice extended westward over Vancouver Island and worldwide freezing lowered the sea level 100 meters.

A "regolith" is just a fancy name for the layer of loose rock that rests on the earth's mantle. It's not an easy climb up the boulder, but the view on top is worth it.

The ride starts from the B-1000 parking lot and begins ascending rather quickly—a great climb that will leave you gasping for air within half a mile. The trail switches back and forth through a clearcut area into a gravel parking lot on the B-1000 Road (which could easily substitute as a starting point). Once across B-1000, the well-groomed trail makes for an enjoyable ride. The trail wanders by a couple of "window" openings in the trees offering spectacular views of the salty waters of Samish Bay speckled with islands: Samish, Vendovi, Guemes, Sinclair, and Cypress. The turtle-like hump of Orcas Island's Mount Constitution can be seen along the horizon.

Continuing toward the lakes, the climb intensifies. Tree roots pose the most difficulty for non-technical climbers. After passing the lakes, there is an intersection for Max's Shortcut. Horses use this shortcut frequently, so depending on the weather, the conditions may be challenging. On wet days, it'll likely be slippery and bumpy, on dry days, just bumpy. Max's Shortcut empties on to the Larry Reed Trail and heads back on the Lily Lake Trail for some fun descents.

Our directions take a slightly longer route that involves some hiking. Passing Max's Shortcut, the descending trail gets pretty difficult at times. You can ride some of it, but after

passing the Talus Trail to the Bat Caves, forget it. There is an incredible hike down which covers some amazingly beautiful (though absolutely non-rideable) trail. But it is worth the effort. The forest here is textured with boulders and rocks of all kinds, deep green plant life, huge fallen trees, and colored mushrooms. The Rosario Strait catches your eye from time to time as the nastiness of the trail gives way to incredible singletrack riding again. The trail then leads to the hang gliding overlook, which is definitely worth a stopover before riding back to the B-1000 Road on fabulous singletrack.

MilesDirections

0.0 START at the B-1000 parking area and take B-1000 to where it meets the Lower Link Trail.

0.1 Take the Lower Link Trail (marked Lily Lake/Lizard Lake Trails).

0.7 Reach a small opening for a view. You've just covered 740 feet of elevation.

0.9 Reach the B-1000 road again. Turn left to pick up trail on the right.

1.0 Begin the ascent up the Lily Lake Trail.

1.3 Notice the spectacular view of the San Juan Islands, Samish Bay, and Rosario Strait. The long island to the right is Lummi Island. The large mass out in front is the east side of Orcas Island.

2.3 Reach an intersection with the Department of Natural Resources' Samish Overlook/Larry Reed trails. Continue straight. Watch for the waterfall.

2.9 Run into a swamp area and follow the trail to the right.

3.0 Cross a log bridge and follow the trail left.

3.3 Cross another wooden bridge and start climbing again.

3.6 Reach the intersection of the Lily Lake and Lizard Lake trails. Turn left toward Lily Lake.

3.7 Cross a wooden bridge.

3.9 Arrive at the intersection of Max's Shortcut. Stay straight.

4.0 Cross a creek and pass the Lily Lake Trail. Continue straight ahead for the Samish Bay Connection.

4.1 Cross the river again.

4.4 Reach the intersection of Rock Trail and a view of Oyster Dome. Follow the trail left toward the Bat Caves. Prepare to descend some incredibly steep trail.

4.5 Arrive at the intersection of the Talus Trail and the Bat Caves. Continue down.

4.6 Riding once again! Arrive at the great boulder. Stop and climb over for a look. The trail continuing on is somewhat rideable.

4.8 Cross the river.

5.0 Arrive at the intersection of Oyster Bay and the Samish Bay Connection. This trail is open to bikes but you wouldn't think so. Stay on the Samish Bay Connection.

5.4 Descend man-made steps in the trail.

5.5 Arrive at a "Y" intersection in the trail. Follow the Larry Reed Trail left and up. The right continues down to the Samish Bay.

5.9 Arrive at a parking lot for the Samish Overlook where hang gliders launch. Hang out and drink in the views.

6.2 Reach the B-2000 Road and follow the Pacific Northwest /Larry Reed Trails to the east.

6.9 Reach the intersection with Max's Shortcut. Continue straight.

7.5 Arrive at an intersection, a "Y" in reverse, with the Lily Lake Trail. Follow the trail sharply to the right.

8.9 Arrive at the B-1000 Road. Turn left and then right for the last mile of singletrack, or turn right down the road and arrive at the parking lot in a little over the same distance.

9.0 Arrive at the small parking area and catch the trail on the right.

9.9 Arrive at the base of the singletrack. Turn left.

10.0 Back at the parking lot.

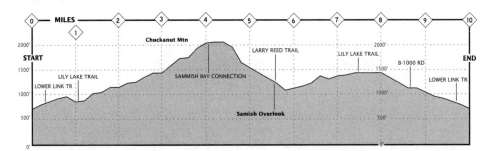

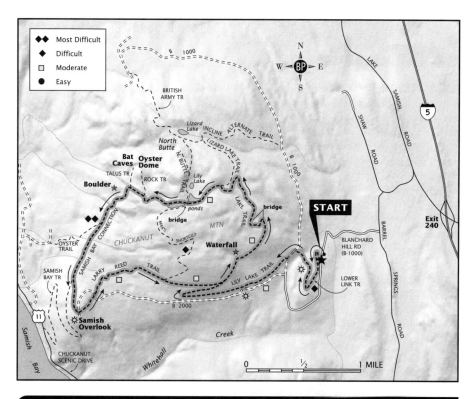

Ride Information

Trail Maintenance Hotlines:
- Pacific Northwest Trails Association:
  (360) 424-0407 or
  pnt@sos.net (**www.pnt.org**)
- Department of Natural Resources:
  (360) 856-3500 or 1-800-527-3305

Schedule:
Open year-round

Local Information:
Bellingham and Whatcom County
Convention and Visitors Bureau:
(360) 671-3990 or 1-800-487-2032

Local Events/Attractions:
- Ski to Sea Race/Festival in late May,
  Bellingham, WA; (360) 734-1330
- Chalk Art Festival in late August,
  Bellingham, WA; (360) 676-8548

Local Bike Shops:
- Fairhaven Bicycle & Ski, Bellingham, WA
  (360) 733-4433
- Kulshan Cycles, Bellingham, WA
  (360) 733-6440 or 1-888-733-6440
- Old Town Cycles, Bellingham, WA
  (360) 734-9749
- Baker Bike & Board, Bellingham, WA
  (360) 738-3728

Maps:
- Maptech CD-ROM:
  Bellingham South, WA; Bow, WA
- DeLorme's Washington Atlas & Gazetteer
  Page 109 C5

Spruce Railroad Trail

Ride Summary

A perfect trail for the whole family, this old railroad grade runs right next to Lake Crescent and is wide enough for even a bike trailer! Everyone can enjoy riding on the dirt road, then advancing to its mountain trail. If there are two cars to shuttle you, you may choose to continue all the way to the beach along a paved road, or you can turn around and enjoy the trail in the other direction. This is a very pretty ride along the water as the trail goes in and out of the trees. It's also very popular, especially in the summer.

Ride Specs

Start: North Shore Road
Length: 12.2 miles one way
Approximate Riding Time: 2-3 hours
Nearest Town: Port Angeles
Rating: Easy—Good family ride
Terrain: Flat singletrack, dirt and paved road
Other Trail Users: Hikers. No dogs allowed

Getting There

From Port Angeles: Take U.S. Route 101 west to Lake Crescent. Just past the west end of the lake, turn right on Camp David Junior Road (also North Shore Road), just past the Fairholm Store and Campground. Park here or at the boat launch area. Parking is also available at the trailhead (4.6 miles ahead) for a shorter ride.

Lake Crescent

The Olympic Mountains are relatively young as mountains go, and contain some of the largest and "healthiest" glaciers in the lower 48 states, even though the mountains are all less than 8,000 feet tall (not to mention that they're right next to the ocean). Olympic National Park is considered an International Biosphere Reserve because within its boundaries there exists everything from glaciated peaks to sea level shores. The forest was first set aside as a reserve in 1897 and was later enlarged and dedicated as Mount Olympus National Monument in 1906. In 1938, at the urging of President Franklin D. Roosevelt and Congressman Monrad Wallgren, Congress gave the area its National Park status—creating what is today the largest coniferous forest in the lower 48. Congress enlarged the park in 1953 to include a 57-mile coastal strip. All in all, of the remaining fifteen percent of old-growth in the Pacific Northwest, nearly half lies within the Olympic and Mount Rainier National Parks.

Nestled in the foothills of the Olympic Mountains is the ten-mile long Lake Crescent, sitting at 620 feet above sea level—and interestingly enough, with a depth of 620 feet. Wrapped along its northern edge is the scenic Spruce Railroad Trail. The actual railroad (which lent the trail both its path and its name) hasn't been in operation since 1918. Built to transport spruce from the Olympic forest to Port Angeles, the railroad never saw completion—nor did the Port Angeles sawmill (which, even shy of completion, ranked among the world's largest). The U.S. military was responsible for the great and sudden demand for timber. With the birth of aerial warfare in W.W.I, the military needed spruce for airplane production. But in November of 1918 the war ended and so, too, did the need for spruce. The logging was discontinued and the sawmill closed.

The Spruce Railroad Grade was converted specifically for bicycle use as an alternative to riding on U.S. Route 101. The trail's wide paths (trailer-width in some parts) make it ideal for beginners or families. Generally smooth, the trail has a few rough sections that are easily negotiated on foot. Because this trail is flat, the natural tendency is to pedal fast. But, out of common courtesy, avoid the impulse. After all, this is a family trail. The ride begins on the northwestern edge of the lake by the boathouse on Camp David Jr. Road.

Camp David Jr. is a county youth camp where once a naturopathic doctor named Louis Dechmann built and operated a lakeside resort called Qui Si Sana (Latin for "Here Get Well"). Hot baths, vinegar wraps, open-air cabins, and the promise of good health through diet and exercise were his techniques. He lost his spa in a battle over water rights in the early 1900s. Many groups tried to reopen the business, but none could make it a profitable venture. In the 1970s, due to vandalism and deterioration, the buildings were torn down and rebuilt to replicate the resort. Camp David Jr. moved in soon after the new buildings were dedicated in 1981. Today, the camp is open for retreats and reunions whenever the youth camp is not in session.

Two and a half miles west along Lake Crescent is the Olympic National Park Information Station. This station is housed in an historic cabin, built in 1905 by Chris Morgenroth, an early forest ranger. Morgenroth is best known for advocating the preservation of old-growth forests and for planting trees after the 1907 Soleduck fire. His reseeding efforts are considered to be the Forest Service's first motion toward official reforestation.

The Spruce Railroad Trail is one of only two trails open to bicycles inside the national park. The other trail is the relatively easy route to Olympic Hot Springs. To get there, take U.S. Route 101 west from Port Angeles. Turn left on Olympic Hot Springs Road. Drive to the Elwa Ranger Station to park your car. From there, ride your bike up the road by Lake

Mills for about six miles to the trail (actually an old beat-up paved road). This ride can be fun, but it's a popular area because of the free hot springs, and most of the ride is on a paved road shared with vehicles. The mere 2.2-mile stretch that's closed to traffic is frequently bustling with a traffic of its own—other cyclists and hikers. There is a trailhead for the final hike up to the hot springs. No bicycle access is permitted beyond this point (you may walk your bike), and dogs aren't allowed beyond the trailhead, either—even on a leash.

Ride Information

Trail Maintenance Hotlines:
- Storm King Ranger Station: (360) 928-3380 (during summer)
- Olympic National Park Headquarters: (360) 452-4501

Schedule:
The trail is open year-round but is best April through November

Local Information:
- Port Angeles Chamber of Commerce Visitors Center: (360) 452-2363
- Olympic National Park Visitor Center, Port Angeles, WA (360) 452-0330

Local Events/Attractions:
Juan De Fuca Festival of the Arts in May, Port Angeles, WA; (360) 457-5411 or 1-800-942-4042

Local Bike Shops:
Pedal 'N' Paddle, Port Angeles, WA (360) 457-1240

Maps:
- Maptech CD-ROM: Mount Muller, WA; Lake Crescent, WA; Lake Sutherland, WA
- DeLorme's Washington Atlas & Gazetteer Page 92 D1&2

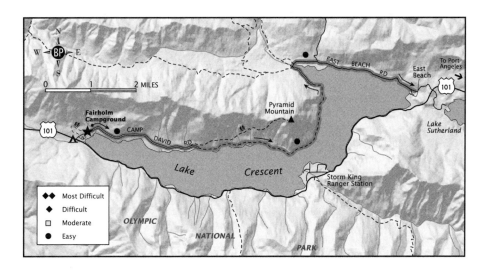

MilesDirections

0.0 START riding east on Camp David Junior Road.

1.5 Pass Eagle View Lane heading down to the lake. Stay on the road.

2.5 Come to a wooden car bridge. Cross with care.

3.0 Pass the Pyramid Creek Trail to the left (open to hikers only).

4.6 Reach the Spruce Railroad Grade trailhead. Optional parking is available here, too.

Trail mileage:

4.7 Super nice singletrack, wide and mellow. There is a restroom at the trailhead (in the woods, away from the lake).

5.7 Cross a small rocky section.

6.0 Cross another rockslide area.

7.4 Cross the bridge and a great swimming hole. Hike up a little here.

7.9 Cross a footbridge.

8.0 Cross a substantial ascent.

8.5 Pass an abandoned trail on the left, head downhill and then cross a wooden bridge. Look for deer that like to hang out here.

8.6 Arrive at the end of the singletrack. The trailhead from the east end of Lake Crescent is below.

8.7 Turn left onto the improved gravel road.

8.8 Cross the bridge of the lake drainage. Now on paved road.

8.9 Head downhill.

9.5 Turn right at the intersection. Watch for oncoming traffic.

9.6 Pass the Log Cabin Resort on the right.

12.2 Hit the East Beach Picnic Area on the right. You can quit here if you have a shuttle, or turn around anywhere and head back.

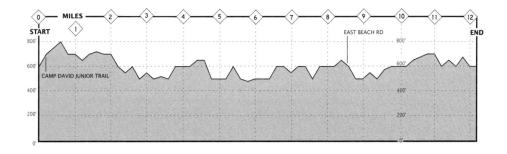

Foothills Trail

Ride Summary

Rising above the Straight of Juan de Fuca, these moderate trails are popular among the locals. Within the Foothills there are several loop combinations that can keep you riding all day. You can complete the main course in a couple of hours, enjoying keen views of the Straight before the trail heads into the forest. Most of the intersections are very well marked, so if you choose to create your own loops, you'll have a tough time getting lost. The singletrack is in good condition, and most of the climbs are only moderately tough.

Ride Specs

Start: Mount Angeles Road
Length: 11.1 miles
Approximate Riding Time: 2 hours
Nearest Town: Port Angeles
Rating: Moderate
Terrain: Double wide, singletrack, and little pavement
Other Trail Users: Hikers, horseback riders, and motorcyclists

View of Port Angeles.

Getting There

From Port Angeles: The "locals way": Take U.S. Route 101, following the signs for the Heart of the Hills Parkway and Hurricane Ridge. Just before entering the park boundary, turn left onto Mount Angeles Road. Follow two-and-a-half miles to Road 6804. It's easy to miss this little turn-off, so look for the almost 90-degree turn to the left, and Road 6804 is right there on the right. This is where you'll park to start the ride.

Alternate entry directions: The "official" trailhead: From 8th and Pine streets in Port Angeles, head south on Pine (Old Black Diamond Road) for almost five miles. Turn left on Little River Road. Travel 1.1 miles, turn left. Travel 0.2 miles on Foothills Trailhead Road. The trailhead is on the right.

Mountain biking on the northern tip of the Olympic Peninsula can be a challenge. It's not that the terrain is especially difficult—there's a fair sampling of both easy and difficult rides. It's that the Olympic National Park covers so many acres! And of course, mountain biking is prohibited in the national park, with the exception of the Spruce Railroad Trail and the Olympic Hot Springs Trail, both farther west. So the locals look to The Foothills to stretch their mountain biking legs. The Foothills are barely five miles from Port Angeles and convenient to some spectacular natural landmarks that should not be overlooked. Among these landmarks are Hurricane Ridge, the Dungeness Spit, and Ediz Hook.

Hurricane Ridge is one mile above sea level and a mere 18 miles from Port Angeles. From the top of Hurricane Ridge, at 6,000 feet, visitors can see the interior of the Olympic Range, its peaks and valleys created by glacial change. Some of the lowest glaciers in the lower 48 can be seen here, too, while wispy clouds waft up and out of the valley making the lush hillsides appear and disappear like phantoms. A Visitor Center at the top offers an outstanding observation deck, with indoor and outdoor viewing, an information center, snack bar, gift shop, and rest rooms. To ride your bike up the road to the top of Hurricane Ridge is to expe-

rience the cleansing power of fresh air and unadulterated sweat. The ride down is pedal-free, just make sure you apply alternating brake pressure so you don't heat your rims up too much—which makes for nasty blowouts.

Located about 14 miles east of Port Angeles is the Dungeness Spit, a five-and-a-half-mile long protrusion that frames in the Dungeness Bay. Said to be the longest natural spit in the world, the Dungeness Spit was designated a National Wildlife Refuge in 1915 and makes for a relaxing place to stroll during warm, summer days. A "spit" is simply a narrow point of land (or reef) that extends into a body of water. The Dungeness Spit's sandy soil, littered with driftwood and eelgrass, is home to a variety of wild birds like loons, Canadian geese, and the black brant, as well as seals.

The Ediz Hook is a three and a half-mile long spit reaching into the Strait of Juan de Fuca to guard the Port Angeles harbor. It has provided many a sailor safe haven, including Francisco de Eliza who named the harbor Puerto de Nuestra Senora de Los Angeles—Port of Our Lady of the Angels. It was under President Abraham Lincoln's administration that the spit was officially reserved for military purposes. A lighthouse and U.S. Coast Guard station sit at its tip and a Navy and Military Reservation at its base.

This area of Washington is said to be in a "rain shadow"—sheltered from the Pacific Ocean by the Olympic Mountains. Storms rising from the ocean hit the Olympics first and are rung, like a sponge, of the majority of their rain. The Hoh Rainforest, for instance, snags an average 150 inches of rain a year, leaving only 24 inches for Port Angeles and merely 12 inches for Sequim. So enjoy this pocket of heavenly weather while you're there. The trail in the Foothills is a great place to start.

"Steep," "lush," and "fun" are just a few of the things that can be said about the Foothills Trails. Incredibly convenient to Port Angeles, and incredibly popular, these trails are extremely well maintained—considering the amount of use they get. There are all sorts of loops you can make. This particular loop was designed for shorter climbs and lots of descending.

The climb starts out on an old paved road no longer open to cars. It crosses over the Heart of the Hills Road to Hurricane Ridge and then turns into a dirt road with deep ruts that can be annoying to some and out-of-control fun for others. The road climbs a fair distance and in some places is pretty steep. As the view opens up to the Straight of Juan de Fuca, the switchbacks become more intense. Once you reach the trails you head deeper into the woods. With the exception of one short chewed-up section, these trails are heaven. There are great map markers at almost every intersection. Some new logging has begun in the area, so trails in our directions may unexpectedly reroute briefly.

MilesDirections

0.0 START at the locals parking area. Ride around the gate and up the semi-dirt, semi-paved Road 6804.

0.1 Cross the overpass of the Heart of the Hills Parkway.

0.3 Pass an overgrown spur on the right. The trail has deep erosion ruts—careful not to fall in.

0.4 Pass another overgrown spur.

0.6 Big ol' switchback left... up, up, up. Wide doubletrack now.

1.0 At the "Y" intersection, turn left. The trail is overgrown to the right.

1.6 Take a half turn and head straight up the mountain without a switchback.

1.7 The trail levels out a little here. Pass a spur trail on the right. 100 yards ahead is the single-track trail for the loop of this ride. It's marked with a sign and a map. Turn right on the trail, or take a side trip 0.2 mile down the road to see a huge billboard-sized radio wave reflector that faces the water. Turn around and head back up.

2.2 Back at the trail intersection, turn left and continue up.

2.3 Pass the top of the trail spur you passed on the road just a bit ago.

2.6 Cross over a loosely boarded bridge.

2.8 At the intersection, turn left heading down.

3.7 Turn left at the "Y" intersection. The right is a short cut back.

4.4 Come upon a new logging road, turn right and hook up with the trail in 0.5 mile.

4.5 Hit the trail on the right next to a huge berm. Climb up a quick, steep section.

4.8 At the "Y" intersection, turn right.

6.0 Reach a parking area. Follow along the right to meet the trailhead again.

6.5 Pass an overgrown trail on the right. Follow the bend left.

7.9 At the intersection, turn left.

8.9 Back at the original intersection where you started the loop. Head straight.

9.3 Take the spur to the left.

9.4 Hit the road. Turn left and head down.

11.1 Arrive at the parking area.

Ride Information

Trail Maintenance Hotlines:
  Department of Natural Resources:
    (360) 374-6131 or
    1-800-527-3305

Schedule:
  Open year-round

Local Information:
  • Port Angeles Chamber of Commerce Visitors Center: (360) 452-2363
  • Sequim-Dungeness Valley Chamber of Commerce Visitor Information: (360) 683-6197 or 1-800-737-8462
  • Port Townsend Chamber of Commerce Tourist Information Center: (360) 385-2722

Local Events/Attractions:
  • Hurricane Ridge Visitor Center: (360) 452-0330
  • Dungeness National Wildlife Refuge: (360) 457-8451 or (360) 683-5847

  • Juan De Fuca Festival of the Arts in May, Port Angeles, WA (360) 457-5411 or 1-800-942-4042 **www.northolympic.com/jffa**
  • Classic Mariners Regatta in June, Port Townsend, WA (360) 385-3628
  • Premiere Jazz Festival in July, Port Townsend, WA; 1-800-733-3608
  • All That Jazz Festival in June, Sequim, WA; 1-800-737-8462
  • Salmon Bake in August, Sequim, WA (360) 683-7988

Local Bike Shops:
  Pedal 'N' Paddle, Port Angeles, WA (360) 457-1240

Maps:
  • Maptech CD-ROM: Port Angeles, WA
  • Custom Correct Map: Hurricane Ridge, WA
  • DeLorme's Washington Atlas & Gazetteer—Page 93 D5

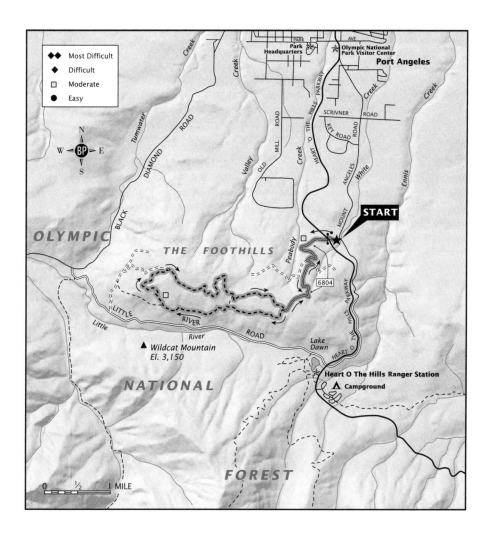

Legend:
- ◆◆ Most Difficult
- ◆ Difficult
- □ Moderate
- ● Easy

N
W —BP— E
S

OLYMPIC

Tumwater Creek

Creek

Creek

PARK
Park Headquarters

AVE
Olympic National Park Visitor Center

Port Angeles

SCRIVNER ROAD
KEY ROAD
ROAD

BLACK DIAMOND ROAD

VALLEY

OLD MILL ROAD

HEART 'O THE HILLS PARKWAY

Peabody Creek

ANGELES

MOUNT

White

Ennis Creek

Creek

THE FOOTHILLS

START

6804

LITTLE RIVER ROAD

Little River

Wildcat Mountain
El. 3,150

Lake Dawn

HEART O THE HILLS PARKWAY

Heart O The Hills Ranger Station
▲ Campground

NATIONAL

FOREST

0   ½   1 MILE

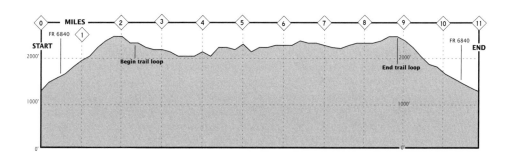

0 MILES 1 2 3 4 5 6 7 8 9 10 11

FR 6840

START

FR 6840

END

2000'

2000'

Begin trail loop

End trail loop

1000'

1000'

0'

0'

Gold Creek

Ride Summary

This sensational ride weaves around the base of Dirty Face Ridge within the Olympic Range, just outside the boundaries of the national forest and the Buckhorn Wilderness Area. Wide switchbacks in the forest road take you up the west side of the Dungeness River to some adventuresome singletrack on the eastern side of the river below Dirty Face Ridge. The trail is steep and narrow and has several drop-offs. It's a ripping good ride that will take you by surprise.

Ride Specs

Start: Gold Creek Trailhead
Other Starting Locations: Anywhere along the logging road
Length: 19.6 miles
Approximate Riding Time: 3 hours
Nearest Town: Sequim (pronounced "skwim")
Rating: Moderate
Terrain: Singletrack and Forest Service Roads
Other Trail Users: Hikers

Getting There

From U.S. Route 101: Head west toward Port Angeles. Just before Sequim turn left onto Louella Road toward the Dungeness Trail. (The left turn to Louella Road is approximately 55 miles from the Bainbridge Ferry landing.) In about one mile, turn left at the "T" intersection on Palo Alto Road, again toward the Dungeness and Tubal Cain Trails. Follow the paved road. After 6.2 miles the road forks. Turn left toward the Dungeness Trail where the pavement ends. Don't confuse this with Dungeness Forks. After 7.1 miles, turn right at the fork. While on Road 28, a sign says "11 miles to Dungeness Fork Trail." At 9.2 miles, see the campground on the right. At 11 miles, you're at the trailhead. Park on either side of the bridge. You'll begin the ride up the road, across the bridge from the trailhead.

The Olympic foothills.

Have you ever imagined yourself as a link in the food chain? Well, it's unlikely you'll have to consider it, but this is cougar country. It's more of an academic issue than a real concern, but should you come across a cougar (which again, is unlikely), don't stop to chat (he won't want to talk anyway). We have run across cubs on trails before, and yes, they are cute to look at, but you definitely do not want to meet the parents. In the interest of excessive preparedness, since forewarned is forearmed, you should know what to do in case you're cornered or jumped.

Chances are the noise you'll be making will keep the wildlife away, but should you have an encounter, don't run. Maintain eye contact and back off slowly. Don't cower or look scared. The more imposing you look, the less inviting you look—you could try raising your arms or spreading your jacket to appear larger than you actually are (a common defense tactic among animals). Like most cats (as the saying goes), cougars are simply curious. They're less likely to have dinner on their mind than play—and humans aren't exactly a delicacy (how unfortunate). Their idea of play, however, doesn't necessarily jibe with ours. So in the worst case scenario, if you are jumped, try to protect your head and stomach area, but by all

means fight back. The majority of experts say that a forceful defense sends the message that you don't want to play. Otherwise, to the cougar, you're just a big ball of yarn.

White-tailed deer and Roosevelt elk populations in the Olympic range have been a topic of debate lately. At the center of this discussion is *over*population. With a lack of natural predators (like the cougar), there's an increase in the number of wildlife crossing paths with people. This has urged some to consider allowing limited hunting in the national park. As of yet, no decision has been made. Along this ride you'll most likely see footprints and scat (animal excrement)—and maybe, if you're lucky, you'll catch a glimpse of a deer along the riverbank.

In the early part of summer you may run across a far safer encounter: *berries*. Just some of the varieties you may see are saskatoon, wild blueberry, huckleberry, raspberry, blackberry, gooseberry, currants, and even a bunchberry or two. In late fall, the salal berry arrives along with the blue elderberry and cranberry or rosehip. Though typically smaller than our cultivated varieties, wild berries have an intensely sweet flavor.

Err on the side of caution when berry picking. You don't want to eat a berry that you cannot identify. With over 200 varieties in Washington, identification however can be difficult. Aside from making a proper identification, there's no sure-fire sign that a berry is safe to eat, so get a good field guide or travel with someone who knows his or her berries.

In short, this ride is fun, though maybe a little short. It's probably not the best ride for beginners or intermediates since there are drop-offs and some rather steep sections. Be sure to concentrate on the trail ahead. Consider taking the Three O'clock Ridge Trail to add a little more singletrack to the ride's downhill. The real challenge comes with the descent. Roots and rocks won't present too much of a problem. The downhill is sweet, steep, and narrow. Although water is scarce along this trail, the Dungeness Creek is always down in the valley to the left. Watch out for blind corners, and enjoy the few short, grunting climbs.

If you find yourself with some time before or after your ride, and you happen to be in the area during July, head out to Port Townsend. July is jumpin' in Port Townsend starting with the Festival of American Fiddle Tunes and ending with the Port Townsend Jazz Festival. If you're into jazz, don't miss this last event—it always draws great performers from across the nation.

MilesDirections

0.0 START at the Gold Creek trailhead, climbing up the fire road away from the river and the trailhead.

0.4 Pass a parking lot pullout on left for the Lower Dungeness Trail #833.

1.9 Follow the main road left. The sign says the Dungeness Trail is in seven miles and the Tubal Cane is in 11—Gold Creek Trail is just across the road from the Tubal Cane Trail, so 11 miles to go!

2.9 Continue up. Pass a spur road on the right.

3.8 Pass a nice view of the valley.

4.1 The climb levels out a little.

4.4 Start the descent.

7.0 Turn left on Forest Road 2860. The sign reads: "Dungeness Trail: 2 miles; Tubal Cane Trail: 6 miles."

8.6 Cross a bridge over Mueller Creek and Lower Dungeness Trail (which enters Buckhorn Wilderness Area—so it's closed to bikes).

8.8 Cross the creek and the climb begins again.

11.3 Cross a small paved section and a bridge. Continue the climb.

11.8 Pass two short spurs on the left. Keep right, riding around the pyramid-shaped mountain and continue climbing.

12.8 Turn left onto the Gold Creek Trailhead #830 at the parking lot. The sign reads: "Shelter 6.1 miles; Forest Road 2860 6.3 miles." There is 20% maximum grade on the downhill from here, losing 2,050 feet. Head into the Quilcene District of Olympic National Forest.

16.6 Stay left at the fork, heading downhill.

19.5 Pass the remains of an old shelter. Go over the one-log bridge.

19.6 Come to the end of the trail and Forest Road 2860.

Ride Information

Trail Maintenance Hotlines:
   Ranger District: (360) 765-2200 (also for
      cougar sightings)

Costs:
   For ferry rates:
      1-800-84-FERRY (WA only) or
      www.wsdot.wa.gov/ferries

Local Information:
   • Sequim-Dungeness Valley Chamber of
      Commerce Visitor Information Center:
      (360) 683-6197
   • Port Townsend Chamber of Commerce
      Tourist Information Center:
      (360) 385-2722
   • Port Angeles Chamber of Commerce
      Visitor Center: (360) 452-2363

Local Events/Attractions:
   • All That Jazz Festival in June,
      Sequim, WA; 1-800-737-8462
   • Sequim Salmon Bake in August,
      Sequim, WA; (360) 683-7988
   • Port Townsend Classic Mariners Regatta
      in June, Port Townsend, WA
      (360) 385-3628

   • Port Townsend Premiere Jazz Festival in
      July, Port Townsend, WA
      1-800-733-3608
   • Juan De Fuca Festival of the Arts in May,
      Port Angeles, WA (360) 457-5411 or
      1-800-942-4042
      www.northolympic.com/jffa
   • Kingston Bluegrass Festival in
      September, Kingston, WA
      (360) 297-7866

Local Bike Shops:
   Pedal 'N' Paddle, Port Angeles, WA
      (360) 457-1240

Maps:
   • Maptech CD-ROM: Tyler Peak, WA
      Mount Zion, WA
   • DeLorme's Washington Atlas &
      Gazetteer—Page 77 A8

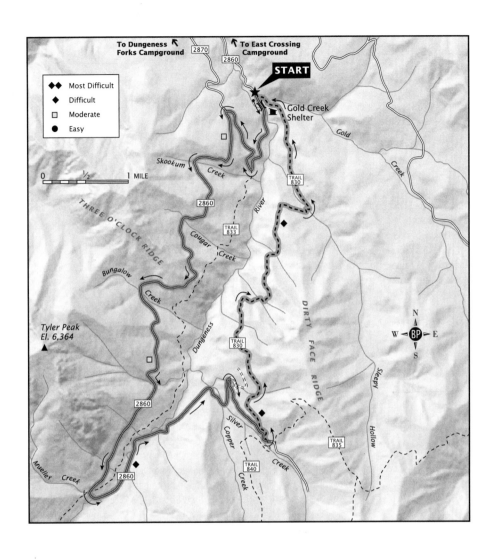

Most Difficult ◆◆
Difficult ◆
Moderate □
Easy ●

To Dungeness Forks Campground ↖ 2870

To East Crossing Campground ↑ 2860

START

Gold Creek Shelter

TRAIL 830

Gold Creek

Skookum Creek

River

TRAIL 833

THREE O'CLOCK RIDGE

Cougar Creek

Bungalow Creek

Dungeness

DIRTY FACE RIDGE

Tyler Peak El. 6,364 ▲

TRAIL 830

Silver Creek

Copper Creek

TRAIL 835

Sleepy Hollow

2860

Mueller Creek

TRAIL 840

0 ½ 1 MILE

N W BP E S

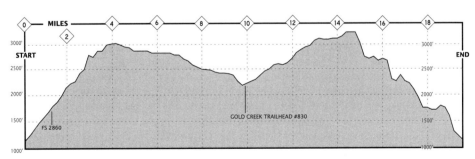

MILES 0 2 4 6 8 10 12 14 16 18

3000' — 3000'

START END

2500' — 2500'

2000' — 2000'

1500' — 1500'

FS 2860

GOLD CREEK TRAILHEAD #830

1000' — 1000'

6

Wildcat Trail & Beyond

Ride Summary

A mere ferry ride away for mountain bikers in the Seattle/Tacoma area, the Wildcat Trail makes a great afternoon get-away. Entirely on singletrack, except for a few road crossings here and there, the trails on Green Mountain are a blast, only occasionally technical, and offer a great workout. Local groups keep these trails in excellent condition. Beginners may struggle with some of the climbs, but more experienced riders will definitely enjoy the ride.

Ride Specs

Start: Wildcat Trailhead
Other Starting Locations: Green Mountain Camp and Picnic Area
Length: 13.5 miles out and back, with a 10-mile out and back option
Approximate Riding Time: 2-4 hours
Nearest City: Bremerton
Rating: Beginner/Moderate
Terrain: Singletrack
Other Trail Users: Motorcyclists, hikers, and horseback riders

Getting There

From Seattle: Take the Bremerton Ferry from Seattle. *Special note: Sunday nights during the summer months are heavy traffic times for ferries. This ride will be less crowded during the week and very early on weekends.* After disembarking the ferry, follow 11th Street through town. After two miles, turn right onto Kitsap Way (State Route 310). Follow the Bike Route signs toward Silverdale. Take State Route 3 north toward the Hood Canal Bridge and Silverdale. After five or six miles, exit onto Chico Way. Follow the exit left under the bridge heading toward Seabeck. Turn right on Northlake Way NW. Turn right at the first intersection onto Seabeck Highway, toward Luther Haven Park. At the stop sign, keep right, continuing up the hill. Turn left onto NW Holly Road (flashing yellow light). Turn left into the Wildcat Lake Trailhead parking lot. This trailhead has outdoor facilities.

From Tacoma: Take I-5 to State Route 16 north. Follow SR 16 to Bremerton. Take State Route 3 north toward Silverdale and follow the directions above.

T he Wildcat Trail sits within a few miles of Bremerton. Like many northwestern towns, Bremerton began as a logging community. In 1891 U.S. Navy Lieutenant A.B. Wycoff purchased 190 acres of waterfront property—now home to the oldest naval installation on Puget Sound. In that same year, William Bremer laid out the town of Bremerton, and in no time the local industry shifted to shipping.

Bremerton (now home to some 37,000 people) has experienced a few hard times since its ship-building heyday, particularly with recent military downsizing. But the city is currently experiencing a period of revitalization—the Sinclair Landing Waterfront Redevelopment Project is just one sign of that. *Money Magazine* recognized as much by citing Bremerton as the most livable city in America in 1990. Narrated boat tours are available of the Navy shipyard and the mothballed fleet of battleships. The USS *Turner Joy*, a Forest Sherman-Class destroyer, has been turned over to a private group and is open to the public as a floating museum on the Bremerton boardwalk. The Bremerton Naval Museum

has an interesting collection of naval artifacts as well—and it's free. The Naval Undersea Museum, located a few miles north of Bremerton in Keyport, contains the largest collection of naval undersea artifact exhibits in the U.S.— and it's free too!

Aside from shipyards, the Bremerton area is able to tout both seaside and mountain recreation: from swimming at Miami Beach near Seabeck to mountain-lake fishing at Kitsap and Wildcat Lakes. And of course there's always mountain biking. The Wildcat Trail itself is located within the sprawling hillsides of Green Mountain, a 6,000-acre Department of Natural Resources state forest. Since 1970, the harvest of timber, rock, and brush in this area has brought Washington State over $4 billion. These monies go to building new schools, as well as to stocking the Kitsap County general fund which insures the protection of fish and wildlife habitats, as well as recreational sites used by hikers and mountain bikers.

In 1993, the Department of Natural Resources had to close down Green Mountain area and the Wildcat Trailhead because of vandalism. The concerted efforts of supportive citizens allowed the area to reopen. Today, with the help of volunteers who take care of the trails, host campgrounds, open and close the gates, as well as make sure visitors don't get locked inside, the Wildcat Trail is again a clean place to play. Local groups keep the trail well marked and in excellent condition. They have work parties on alternate Saturdays. Feel free to join in.

Don't be surprised if the parking lot at Green Mountain has a few cars in it on the weekend. Because of its accessibility to some major urban centers and because it's simply a great ride, this park gets a lot of attention. From the parking lot, the singletrack heads directly into the woods. The dense forest canopy serves as the perfect bumbershoot—shading the trail on warm days and keeping it dry on rainy days. The surface of the trail is smooth, with the occasional forest rock or root. The climbs are gradual; the descents are fast. This trail offers simple pleasures and good views.

Traversing the hillsides, the Wildcat Trail meanders through groves of rhododendrons and crosses a couple of logging roads. Logged hillsides are soft in places and negotiating your way down them may seem more like skiing or skidding than actually riding—but these sections are brief. From there, the trail leads up to a scenic vista—a panoramic picnic spot. From the vantage of 1,690 feet, the Puget Sound weaves its way around its evergreen banks like a silky blue ribbon. Heading down from the vista, the singletrack is narrow and steep. Because this is an out and back, when the trail ends on the opposite side of Green Mountain, it's time to turn around and ride back up and over. The entire ride is less than 15 miles, making this an ideal afternoon get-away, with many trails left to explore.

Ride Information

Trail Maintenance Hotlines:

Department of Natural Resources South Puget Sound Region (360) 825-1631 or 1-800-527-3305

Schedule:

The trail is open seven days a week year-round. Vehicle access is limited—the road to the Vista and the Green Mountain Campground is open from 9 a.m. to 6 p.m. on Saturday and Sunday, June through September.

Costs:

For ferry rates:
1-800-84-FERRY (WA only) or
www.wsdot.wa.gov/ferries

Local Information:

Bremerton/Kitsap Peninsula Visitor and Convention Bureau: (360) 297-8200

Local Events/Attractions:

• Bremerton Naval Museum, Bremerton, WA; (360) 479-7447
• Kitsap Harbor Tours, Bremerton, WA (360) 377-8924
• USS Turner Joy Tours, Bremerton, WA (360) 792-1008
• Blackberry Festival in August, Bremerton, WA; (360) 377-3041
• Armed Forces Festival and Parade in May, Bremerton, WA (360) 479-3579
• The Naval Undersea Museum, Keyport, WA; (360) 396-2894

Local Bike Shops:

• Northwest Bike & Lock, Bremerton, WA (360) 479-4833
• Kitsap Key & Bike, Bremerton, WA (360) 373-6133 or 1-888-373-6133

Maps:

• Maptech CD-ROM: Wildcat Lake, WA
• DeLorme's Washington Atlas & Gazetteer Page 78 D2

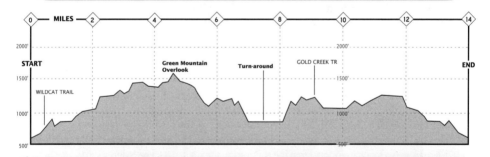

MilesDirections

0.0 START at the Wildcat Trailhead.

1.0 Cross GM 41, following the trail straight-ahead.

1.3 Climb a steep section, the worst of the ride.

1.5 Come to a fabulous viewpoint of Seattle. The trail continues down.

1.7 Turn left onto GM 41, catching the trail immediately on the right that's marked "Wildcat Trail."

2.0 Cross GM 41 switchback following the trail straight-ahead.

2.7 Cross GM 3 at a three-way intersection. Turn right up the steep trail to the Trail Vista. To the left is the Green Mountain Camp and Picnic Area. The trail to Beaver Pond is on the right.

2.8 Pass a river wash on the right, stay to the trail on the left. Cross the forest road again, turn right and continue on the Wildcat Trail on the left.

3.5 Come to Forest Road GM1. At the "Y" intersection follow the trail left by the gate and the road. It's marked so you can't miss it.

4.0 Cross GM 41 and head back into woods.

4.3 Reach the junction of Gold Creek/Beaver Pond and Vista trails.

To the vista: Take a hard left up the Vista Trail. Reach the Green Mountain Vista parking lot. There's a picnic area and an outdoor toilet here. Follow the trail around the gate continuing up to the

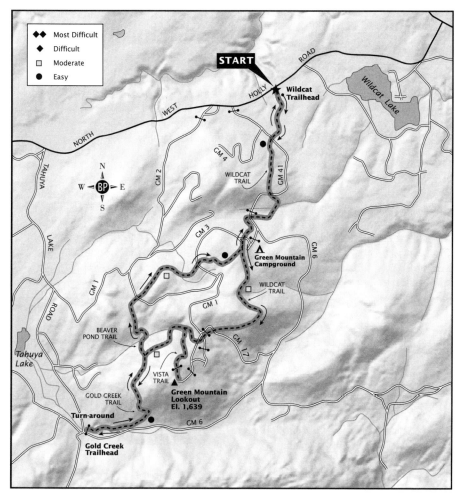

vista (.2 miles). To continue the ride, return to the Green Mountain Vista parking lot and back down the Vista Trail.

Continuing the ride: (mileage now includes Vista stopover)

4.5 Back at the bottom of the Vista Trail, take a left following the sign directing you to the Gold Creek/Beaver Pond Trail.

6.1 Arrive at the junction of the Gold Creek and Beaver Pond trails. Stay left on Gold Creek Trail.

6.4 Pass a short loop trail, staying to the right. Pass a small trail on the right, listening for Gold Creek below.

7.1 Arrive at the base of the Gold Creek Trail and a parking lot. Turn around and head back up the trail.

8.1 Reach the Gold Creek/Beaver Pond trail intersection. Take a right going back the way you came. (You also have the option here to turn left onto Beaver Pond Trail which will lead you back to a junc-

tion with Wildcat Trail at the Green Mountain Campground).

8.4 Continue up, passing the Vista Trail to the viewpoint. Stay straight on Beaver Pond Trail.

9.0 Arrive at the Wildcat Trail (4.3 mile-marker). Come to GM1, cross, and turn right on the trail heading down.

9.6 Cross GM3 again and head up the trail to the left.

11.0 At the junction, follow the trail downhill. The Green Mountain Camp and Picnic area is off to the right. A brief trail offshoot provides a downhill jaunt and avoids an uphill section. Follow the gravel road less than a mile to the Wildcat Trail on the right.

11.9 Take the Wildcat Trail into the woods, over the wooden bridges, across the forest roads and then back up the steep soft, scree section.

12.5 Cross the road and continue downhill.

13.5 Arrive at the Wildcat Trailhead and parking lot.

Cedar Creek
Out and Back

Ride Summary

This picturesque trail provides a great diversion if you're heading east to Winthrop on the North Cascades Highway. Riding between the steep walls of the Gardner and Silver Star Mountains, the first few miles are steady and tough up to Cedar Creek Falls. The trail gets even a little tougher after that, but only briefly. The rest of the route is beautiful singletrack all the way across the valley and back.

Ride Specs

Start: Trailhead #476 from State Route 20
Length: 15.2 miles
Approximate Riding Time: 3 hours
Nearest Town: Mazama
Rating: Moderate
Terrain: Smooth singletrack and two miles of technical singletrack
Other Trail Users: Hikers, horseback riders, and cross-country skiers

Getting There

From Winthrop: Follow State Route 20 west for 17 miles, just past Mazama. Following the sign for the Cedar Creek Trail (on the south side of the highway). Turn left on a gravel road just west of the Early Winters Visitor Center. Follow the gravel road nine-tenths of a mile to the trailhead parking area to the far left of the gravel pit.

Once you've passed the crests of Rainy and Washington Pass on State Route 20, heading east into the Methow Valley (pronounced MET–how), you stumble upon the charming, "Wild West" community of Winthrop. The town is situated at the confluence of the Chewuch and Methow rivers. The great Methow River is an unusually straight and steep-walled river carving its way eastward through the Methow Valley. Both the river and the valley are the product of a glacier on the move during the last ice age.

Winthrop looks like a classically western town—more the result of a 1960s facelift than a natural evolution, but attractive nonetheless. Between the wooden sidewalks and the false storefronts, you feel transported back in time. There's a saloon, a general store, and even hitching posts should you need to tether your horse. But what makes this town special is its people, as friendly and as laid back as any you can imagine. People who come to Winthrop come for its scenery, spectacular weather, and wide open spaces, far away from the pulse of big city life.

The hillsides rising above the Methow Valley are dotted with a few houses and B&Bs and filled with miles of recreational trails. In an effort to insure the integrity of these trails, a very active group called the Methow Valley Sport Trails Association (MVSTA) was formed. The MVSTA is a private, non-profit consortium of skiers, businesses, and families that promote non-motorized trail recreation in the valley. Their goal is to "establish the finest and most interesting year-round trail recreation area in the United States." And they're doing a great job at it. Working with the National Forest Service, and many private landowners, MVSTA is able to build new trails and repair older or abandoned trails in the

national forest and on private property. In many cases, trails on private land connect with the national forest trails making the network in the Methow Valley quite extensive.

When heading to Winthrop for a weekend of mountain biking, a good place to start is Cedar Creek. If you're entering from the west, the Cedar Creek Trail is right on your way. The trail is just a little below Washington Pass—a great place to stop and enjoy the view. Among the tallest peaks nearby are the Early Winters Spires (7,806 feet)—home of the Liberty Bell, a popular and moderately dif-

ficult rock climbing area. The hike to the Early Winters Spires makes for a great, short, side-trip on your way to Winthrop. Head up the Blue Lake Trail, one mile west of Washington Pass. Proceed 1.5 miles up the trail to the open area below the lower slabs of the Liberty Bell.

The Cedar Creek Trail, a little farther east of Washington Pass, is heavily wooded and runs right next to Cedar Creek. In the summer, this ride will be a lot cooler than the trails down in Winthrop. The closer you get to town, the more arid the climate becomes. The first two miles of this ride are great for warming up. The next two, how-ever, are highly technical, due to some incredibly rocky conditions. This short, two-mile section is challenging, especially when it's wet—which is a polite way of say-ing it's not that much fun. At the 1.7-mile point you come to a fantastic, roaring waterfall. You'll want to stop here for a rest before hitting the toughest part of the ride. If you climb down to the river from the trail, be careful; it's a steep embankment. The water crashing against the rocks below

Cedar Falls.

makes it hard to hear anything else once you get down there.

Most people drop out when they reach this section of the ride, but they're missing some of the best trail to come. The next three to four miles are wonderful, with very few rocky sections. The trail ahead is virtually untouched by anyone other than hikers, leaving it peacefully quiet and as smooth as a bike path. There are times when you'll be covered in the shelter and shade of the woods, and others when the trail is in the wide-open, giving a pic-ture-perfect view of the interior of the valley and its steep walls. In the fall, the colors of the trees along the mountainsides are quite spectacular—the bright yellow larch and aspen are easy to spot.

You must turn around and head back just after crossing the river—which is marked—because the trail heads up the mountain and into Wilderness Area (where bicycles are not allowed). The trail on the return trip is a gas, especially the last two miles that were so tough to climb in the beginning.

MilesDirections

0.0 START from the trailhead, up the semi-steep singletrack.

1.8 Pass a pull-off with a view of Cedar Falls on your left.

4.1 The trail opens up into an open meadow. The grove of aspens are gorgeous here in the fall.

4.2 Stay right at the "Y" intersection. The left trail heads to a nice campsite.

5.1 Cross over a small creek crossing.

6.0 Begin a series of creek crossings for two-tenths of a mile.

6.5 Cross a large creek crossing next to Cedar Creek.

6.7 Cross an even larger creek with beautiful falls.

7.6 Turn around here. You are now entering the Lake Chelan-Sawtooth Wilderness—it's closed to bicycles at the ridge top.

Ride Information

Trail Maintenance Hotlines:
- *U.S. Forest Service; (509) 996-4000 or* ***www.fs.fed.us***
- *Okanogan National Forest (509) 826-3275 or* ***www.gorp.com***
- *Methow Valley Ranger District: (509) 997-2131*
- *Report forest fires; 1-800-562-6010*

Local Information:
- *Winthrop Chamber of Commerce Information Station; (509) 996-2125 or 1-888-463-8469*
- *Methow Valley Visitors Center (509) 996-4000*

Local Events/Attractions:
- *The Bone Shaker Mountain Bike Bash (a NORBA sanctioned race), in May, Winthrop, WA; (509) 535-4757*
- *Winthrop Rodeo Days in May and Labor Day Weekend, Winthrop, WA (509) 996-2125*
- *Mountain Triathlon 2nd Sunday in September, Winthrop, WA (509) 996-3287*

- *Methow Valley Mountain Bike Festival in early October, Winthrop, WA (509) 996-3287*
- *"October-West" 2nd weekend in October, Winthrop, WA; (509) 996-2125*
- *MVSTA Ski & Sports Swap November, Winthrop, WA; (509) 996-3287*

Organizations:
Methow Valley Sport Trails Association, Winthrop, WA; (509) 996-3287 or 1-800-682-5787 or ***www.methow.com/~mvsta/ welcome.html***

Local Bike Shops:
Winthrop Mountain Sports, Winthrop, WA (509) 996-2886

Maps:
- *Maptech CD-ROM: Mazama, WA; Silver Start, WA*
- *DeLorme's Washington Atlas & Gazetteer Page 113 D5*

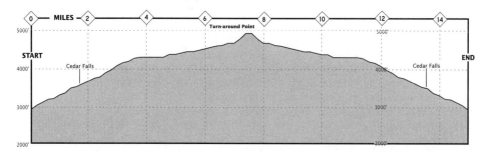

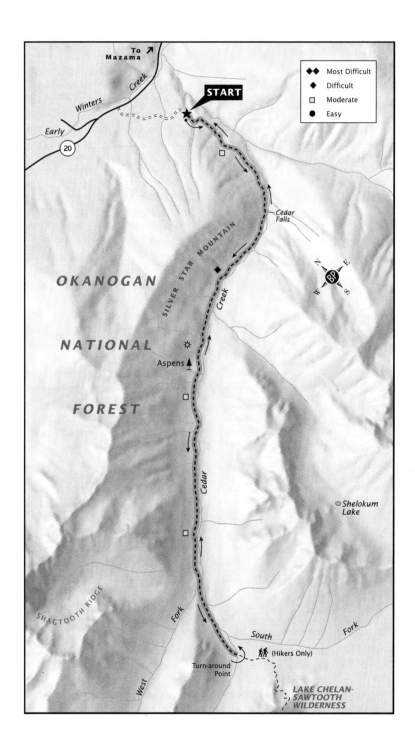

Walker Valley/ Cavanaugh Loop

Ride Summary

If you can't find singletrack to ride in Walker Valley, you're just not looking! Miles of trails meander through 10,000 plus acres of DNR land, an area which is also popular with the ORV crowd. The loop described below is a moderate ride consisting of a short road climb and a rolling attack on the forest. The trails are semi-technical and can be muddy and wet. There are many loop variations, and the trails are marked at most intersections. Some local mountain bikers call Walker Valley the Capitol Forest of northern Washington because its trails and the conditions are similar to those found farther south in Olympia.

Ride Specs

Start: Walker Valley ORV parking lot
Length: 10 miles
Approximate Riding Time: 2-3 hours
Nearest Town: Mount Vernon
Rating: Moderate (difficult singletrack in rainy conditions)
Terrain: Singletrack, doubletrack, and fire roads
Other Trail Users: Motorcyclists

Getting There

From Seattle: Take I-5 North to Exit 221 (south of Mt. Vernon) onto State Route 534 toward Lake McMurray. Turn right at the stop sign, heading east on State Route 534. Follow State Route 534 until it ends—approximately five miles. Turn left on State Route 9 heading north toward Sedro-Woolley. Follow the "S" turns; see Lake McMurray on your right. Continue north, passing Lake Cavanaugh Road. Pass Big Lake on the left. One mile ahead turn right on Walker Valley Road (see the sign for the trailhead and Fire Mountain Scout Reservation) at milepost 46. Go two and two-tenths miles farther, turn right at the ORV park on the gravel road. Stay on the main road. In about a mile come to the Walker Valley ORV parking lot. The trail begins at the end of the parking lot.

Walker Valley is located just east of State Route 9, about 10 miles southeast of the town of Mount Vernon. The 30 miles of trail within Walker Valley's 10,518 acres are well known among the off-road vehicle crowd. The terrain, very similar to that of Capitol Forest below Olympia, is managed by the Department of Natural Resources (DNR) and is used as a "working" forest. Logging continues to change the lay of the trails. New roads appear every so often and will occasionally take over a trail; or in some cases, they may re-route a trail. These logging roads do have a negative effect on the natural workings of things. They fragment forests, destroy trails, and cause erosion problems. The eroded soil ends up in streams and rivers, sometimes blocking the path of spawning fish (the Chinook salmon, for example, is on the endangered species list). Not to excuse irresponsible practices, but it is important to remember that this is a working forest. Timber sales on government lands pay for a lot of things we tend to take for granted.

The trails in Walker Valley are challenging and always a lot of fun. This ride begins in a large parking area that fills up quickly in summer months. The best time to ride here (if you'd like to be free of motorized vehicle noise) is early in the day on weekends or during the week. The route we've charted here climbs gradually, away from the creek near the parking area. A fun offshoot trail is the EZ-Grade Trail, a short section of singletrack offering about a mile of semi-technical riding. Take the JW-1100 road up to the heart of the singletrack—the road is in great condition and provides an easy warm-up grade before hitting the trails. Once in the woods, the trails, like any in the damp northwest, vary from packed dirt to exposed rocks and roots. There will probably be a few large, muddy holes and ruts in which to get sucked. It's a thick forest, so the shade will be especially nice in the summer.

To the north of this ride is the famous Skagit Valley, well known for its tulip and daffodil bounty. Situated along the same longitudinal lines as the Netherlands, the climate in this western region of Washington—warm summers and cool winters—is ideal for growing bulbs. Riding along the color washed roads in springtime, it's as if you've rolled into the end of the rainbow. Every imaginable color of tulip, daffodil, and even iris can be found here.

Bulbs first came to Washington around the turn of the century. In 1889 George Gibbs leased land on Orcas Island (in the San Juan chain) and tried his hand at growing produce. In 1900 he took a turn and tried growing some bulbs he'd procured from the Netherlands. They did well for him, but Gibbs was determined to find the ideal location for bulb production. He tested land farther north and then land as far south as Puyallup. His search finally ended in one of the best bulb growing

regions in the country, the Skagit Valley.

Skagit Valley's bulb fields cover some 1,500 acres. All but 300 of these acres belong to one grower, the Washington Bulb Company. The Roozen family, who own and operate the company, have been growing bulbs for 250 years and actually trace their roots to Holland. Speaking to the rumor that Washington's bulb production has progressed to the point where the Netherlands is placing orders, Richard Roozen, Vice President of the Washington Bulb Company, denies the claim. "The Netherlands grow tons more than we do here," he says, and thus far, the Washington Bulb Company just serves the United States.

To celebrate the change of season and to examine the vibrant festival of color more closely, travel to the quaint town of La Conner, built along the steep hillsides of the Swinomish Channel in the heart of the Skagit Valley. La Conner has always been a point of interest for passers-by. Settled in 1867 as a trading post and named for the wife of its founder (Louisa Ann Conner), this town co-hosts (along with Mount Vernon) the annual Tulip Festival held in April. You can wander through the rainbowed alleyways filled with more tulip and daffodil varieties than one can count—or maybe you'd like to pedal alongside in the official Tulip Bicycle Ride. Tulips, daffodils, and irises last for only a few weeks a year, so check the local newspapers to verify bloom times or call the festival headquarters for times and field maps. La Conner is a growing tourist attraction, especially in spring, so don't count on any tiptoeing through the fields alone. And don't forget your camera.

MilesDirections

0.0 START the ride on the Jam Trail, just left of the outhouses. Immediately pass the EZ Grade Trail on the right. You can take this for some immediate singletrack riding.

0.2 Intersect with a small turn-around area and the other end of the EZ Grade Trail. Follow the Jam Trail to the left.

0.6 Pass three trails.

0.9 The Jam Trail hits Forest Road JW-1100. Turn right on the road, heading up hill. Pass a couple of trails. Cross a bridge. Pass another couple of trails on the left; they all join with the Muddled Meanderings Trail. Keep to the road.

1.7 At the "Y" intersection with SW-JW 1190, stay left. Catch the Walker Valley Trail on the left ahead.

2.6 Intersect with the Scratch N' Sniff Trail on the left. Continue right on the Walker Valley Trail.

2.9 Intersect with a spur road. Stay left on the Walker Valley Trail.

3.2 Come to a "Y" with the Old Toad and Walker Valley Trails. Stay on the Walker Valley Trail—straight.

3.3 Come to another "Y" intersection and head left. The right goes to the road.

3.5 Pass a spur on the right. Stay straight.

3.8 The trail empties onto a new logging road—the trail used to be here. Turn left, heading down the road.

4.3 See the trail on the left heading back into the

woods. Lots of thorny berry bushes in here.

4.5 The trail opens up again onto a logging road. Follow it down to the left.

5.4 See two trails on the left. They are the same trail, so follow one of them up off the road.

6.4 Come to a rocky uphill and see spurs on the left. Keep to the main trail.

6.5 Come to an intersection of SW-B-1040 and B-1000. Turn left onto the road and pick up the Cavanaugh Trail on the right a little ways down.

6.7 On the Cavanaugh Trail now, cross a wooden bridge, ride through a clearcut and hit a logging road "T." Follow the road straight and see the trail again on the right.

7.4 Heading back into the woods.

7.7 Reach a "Y" intersection and turn right. The left trail will take you back into the woods.

7.9 Reach the "Y" intersection of Muddled Meanderings trail. The east (right) heads up. Stay left, going back to the parking lot.

8.1 Cross another bridge.

8.8 Muddled Meanderings Trail finishes its bumpy downhill. Take the little left to get to the road, or take the right trail for more singletrack, eventually hitting the road ahead. Turn right on the road.

9.1 Take the Jam Trail left.

9.8 See the EZ Grade Trail on the left.

10.0 Back at the parking lot.

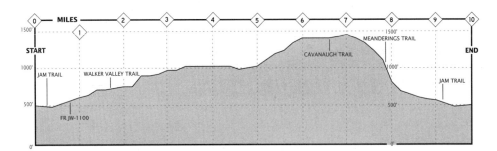

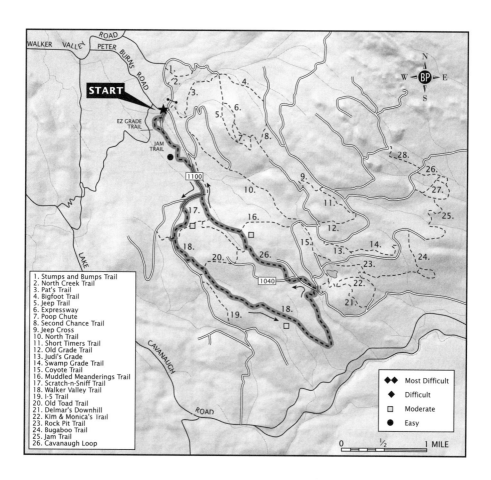

1. Stumps and Bumps Trail
2. North Creek Trail
3. Pat's Trail
4. Bigfoot Trail
5. Jeep Trail
6. Expressway
7. Poop Chute
8. Second Chance Trail
9. Jeep Cross
10. North Trail
11. Short Timers Trail
12. Old Grade Trail
13. Judi's Grade
14. Swamp Grade Trail
15. Coyote Trail
16. Muddled Meanderings Trail
17. Scratch-n-Sniff Trail
18. Walker Valley Trail
19. I-5 Trail
20. Old Toad Trail
21. Delmar's Downhill
22. Kim & Monica's Trail
23. Rock Pit Trail
24. Bugaboo Trail
25. Jam Trail
26. Cavanaugh Loop

◆◆ Most Difficult

◆ Difficult

☐ Moderate

● Easy

0   ½   1 MILE

Ride Information

Trail Maintenance Hotlines:
Department of Natural Resources, Northwest Region: Sedro Woolley, WA (360) 856-3500 or 1-800-527-3305

Local Information:
- *Sedro Woolley Chamber of Commerce (360) 855-1841*
- *Mount Vernon Chamber of Commerce (360) 428-8547*
- *La Conner Chamber of Commerce (360) 466-4778*
- *Darrington Chamber of Commerce (360) 436-1717*

Local Events/Attractions:
- *Skagit Valley Tulip Festival in late March/early April, Mount Vernon, WA (360) 428-5959* **www.tulipfestival.org**
- *Wildflower Festival in June, Darrington, WA (360) 436-1794*

Maps:
- *Maptech CD-ROM: McMurray, WA; Sedro-Woolley South, WA*
- *DeLorme's Washington Atlas & Gazetteer—Page 95 A&B7*

9

Wallace Falls Loop— Out & Back

Ride Summary

A very popular place to hike and mountain bike for many years, Wallace Falls can accommodate the beginner, the intermediate, and the advanced mountain biker. The climb to Wallace Lake advances gradually on singletrack, doubletrack, and minimal logging roads. Beginners will find a challenge in the climb, but will enjoy returning the same way once they reach Wallace Lake. For further adventuring, the route continues on the other side of Wallace River—crossing it is cold and difficult. The trails beyond the east side of the river are more technical, but travel mostly downhill; better suited for intermediate to advanced riders. The descent is sweet and ends up on a paved road, creating a loop that heads back to the State Park trailhead.

Ride Specs

Start: Wallace Falls State Park trailhead
Length: Loop, 19.5 miles; Out & Back, 13 miles
Approximate Riding Time: Loop, 3-4 hours; Out & Back, 2 hours
Nearest Town: Goldbar
Rating: Loop: Difficult; Out & Back: Moderate
Terrain: Doubletrack, singletrack, river & creek crossings, dirt road, and paved road
Other Trail Users: Hikers

Getting There

From Seattle: Take I-405 north to State Route 522 east, toward Monroe/Wenatchee. Turn left at the light onto U.S. Route 2 east. Follow U.S. Route 2 East to Goldbar. Turn left on 1st Street. Go 0.3 miles to May Creek Road and turn right. Follow the signs for Wallace Falls State Park. Stay straight toward the dead-end. Continue to follow the signs for Wallace Falls. The entrance is on the left up the hill. The trail begins from the parking lot by the restrooms.

May Creek.

Two miles northeast of the town of Gold Bar (population 1,200), nestled in the beautiful Skykomish Valley ("sky-KOH-mish" or just "Sky Valley"), is the Wallace Falls State Park. Established in 1977, the park's hallmark attraction—should its name not give it away—is a stunning 265-foot cataract. Visible from U.S. Route 2, the rushing falls are set in crisp relief against the deep green forest of Mount Stickney (elev. 5,367), located in the Mount Baker Snoqualmie National Forest.

The best thing about Wallace Falls is its variety. In the beginning of the ride, the trail is wide and gravelly. Since it's covered in trees, you'll benefit from the shade in the summer months. Views of the waterfall can be seen from below by taking a one mile hiker-only trail. This ride climbs right to the top of the falls by winding up a mildly technical trail.

A few years ago logging returned to this area. About four miles of trail were replaced by gravel road. Though disappointing to those who've ridden Wallace Falls in the past, the road actually elevates you more quickly to Wallace Lake. Once at the lake, explore a little if you have time. This is a good turn-around point if you've had enough riding. If not, cross the bridge and follow the singletrack from here. Flying along on the padded forest floor, you'll arrive at the top of Wallace Falls in no time.

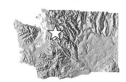

Crossing the river can be difficult—just getting down to the water is a chore. The embankments are steep and covered with wet rocks and slimy green moss and algae. Find a spot where it looks a bit shallow and cross carefully. (Hope you remembered an extra pair of socks.) The river moves swiftly all year long, so the trick to crossing successfully is slow, steady movements. Try not to look down at the water rushing over your feet; this will only make you dizzy. And remember to keep your bike on the downstream-side of you, whether you walk it across or shoulder it. Cross as quickly as possible to avoid hypothermic conditions during inclement weather. If in doubt, TURN AROUND.

Once across, head along the bank down the river toward the falls. You'll have to bush-whack your way up, but once there, you'll feel exhilarated. On this side of the river, the trail is fast and more challenging. Your hands will be tired by the time you get back to the car—but you'll be too pumped to care.

There are full bathroom facilities and camping in the park. The ranger will sometimes provide a hose behind the restrooms for washing off your bike—and your body. The ranger works hard to keep this area open and safe for mountain biking. Please do your part.

If you hail from Seattle, you might consider stopping at one of the local wineries or microbreweries on your way home. The Columbia Winery and the Chateau Saint Michelle

Winery, both in Woodinville, have beautiful gardens and are open daily for wine tasting. The Chateau Saint Michelle offers summer concerts on the lawn. If you prefer a bit of froth, try the Redhook Brewery, next to the Columbia Winery. They have a great restaurant and outdoor seating right along the Snohomish Bike Trail.

MilesDirections

0.0 START the ride on the trail below the power lines.

0.3 Head into the woods.

0.4 Intersect with the Woody Trail, a one-mile trail (open to hikers only) leading to views of the falls.

1.5 Turn left toward Wallace Lake.

2.5 The trail empties onto a logging road. Continue up the road.

4.5 Road divides. Stay straight.

6.3 Turn left onto the Wallace Lake Trail following the sign for Wallace Lake.

6.8 Arrive at Wallace Lake. Ride over the wooden bridge to Wallace Falls (2.6 miles).

6.9 Pass a trail on the left heading back to the lake.

7.3 Pass an overgrown trail to the left for Stickney Ridge. Follow the signs to the falls.

7.5 Pass a trail on right that connects with the logging road you saw a few miles ago.

9.1 Wallace Falls is to the right.

9.5 Arrive at the top of the falls. This is the turning point for the Out & Back. Cross the river for the loop. Head upriver a bit to find an easy crossing.

9.6 Turn right at the intersection. Essentially, take right-hand turns all the way down.

10.6 Arrive at a steep embankment. Cross the creek and climb up the other side.

11.3 Cross another creek bed.

11.7 Keep straight at the intersection. All the left-hand trail spurs are actually loops that go above the washouts on this trail. Stay straight at the switchback.

13.5 Pass a small spur. Stay straight.

13.6 Stay right at the intersection.

13.8 Follow the main dirt road, keeping straight.

14.3 At the "Y" intersection, take the road under the power lines. Don't follow the road running parallel to the power lines. Just cross underneath them, keeping to the right.

14.8 At Reiter Road, turn right.

16.0 At May Creek Road (paved), turn right.

18.9 Turn right on Ley Road up to Wallace Falls State Park.

19.3 Turn left up to the parking lot.

19.5 End of ride.

Ride Information

Trail Maintenance Hotlines:
- *Wallace Falls State Park:*
  (360) 793-0420

Schedule:
  Daylight hours

Local Information:
  Monroe Chamber of Commerce:
  (360) 794-5488

Local Events/Attractions:
- *Old Time Tractor Pull and Threshing Bee in early August, Monroe, WA (360) 659-1682*
- *Fair Days in late August, Monroe, WA (360) 794-4344*
- *Sultan Summer Shindig Logging Show in mid-July, Sultan, WA (360) 793-2565*

- *The Columbia Winery, Woodinville, WA (425) 486-1900*
- *Chateau Saint Michelle Winery, Woodinville, WA; (425) 488-1133*

Local Bike Shops:
- *Monroe Cyclery, Monroe, WA (360) 794-4522*
- *Centennial Cyclery, Snohomish, WA (360) 568-1345*

Maps:
- *Maptech CD-ROM: Wallace Lake, WA; Mount Stickney, WA; Gold Bar, WA; Index, WA*
- *DeLorme's Washington Atlas & Gazetteer Page 80 A&B3*

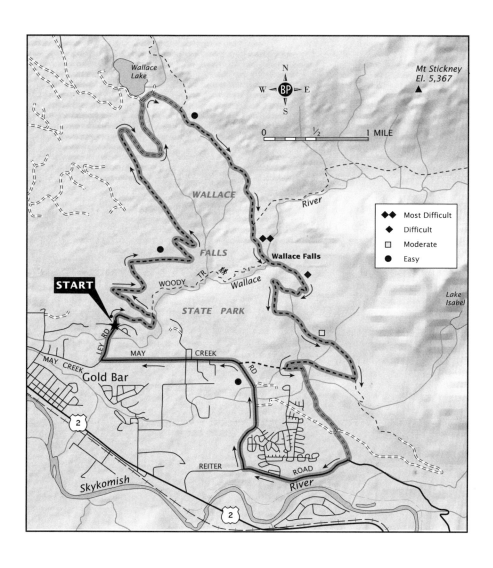

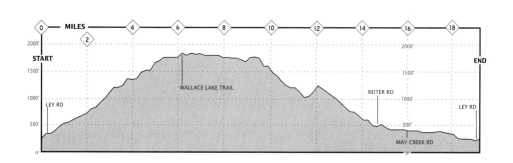

Silver Creek

Ride Summary

This historical trail lures all kinds of people: mountain bikers, hikers, gold panners, miners, geologists, historians... you name it. The trail runs next to Silver Creek on doubletrack that used to be a forest road. Now overgrown and blocked by a huge avalanche field, this road makes a beautiful intermediate mountain biking trail. There are several waterfalls to photograph and a great river to cross, should you dare.

Ride Specs

Start: West side of the North Fork of the Skykomish River, across the bridge from Howard Creek and Index/Galena Road

Length: 12 miles round-trip

Approximate Riding Time: 3 hours

Nearest Town: Index

Rating: Moderate to difficult because of steep, technical ascents and the river crossing

Terrain: Forest Service roads, doubletrack, singletrack, landslide area, and thick brush

Other Trail Users: Hikers

The avalanch field.

Getting There

From Seattle: Take I-405 north to State Route 522 east toward Monroe/Wenatchee. Turn left at the light onto U.S. Route 2 east. Follow U.S. Route 2 east to Index. Turn left, heading north on Index/Galena Road (see the Index Cafe). Follow the road nine miles to Howard Creek. Turn left after crossing Howard Creek onto a one-lane bridge over the North Fork of the Skykomish River. Drive up the dirt road and veer right at the intersection. Park anywhere in this area. You'll be biking up the dirt road, so drive as far up as you like, but this one-mile section of logging road makes for a fun descent on your return.

The Silver Creek ride may not be very long, but it provides a very well-rounded workout within an extremely beautiful landscape. This doubletrack to singletrack route, once a working mining road, comes with short climbs, flat rolling sections, bike portages over landslides, and rock-jumping over Silver Creek itself. There are waterfalls all over the place, too, rushing to meet Silver Creek and eventually the Skykomish River below.

The climb begins on an average grade forest road. This will provide an adequate warm-up for the ride ahead. Arriving at the trail in a little over a mile, you may be surprised at the breadth of the avalanche area you have to cross. This rock slide happened after a flood in 1988, before which time, cars could still drive along what used to be County Road 6335. The trail, which is carved into the side of the slide, is a little daunting: walk your bike over this section.

After the avalanche crossing, the trail is picture perfect for the next few miles. Wide (because it used to carry wagons, and later cars), it's easy to ride side by side, admiring the waterfalls feeding Silver Creek and the mining tunnels along the way. The trail begins to wind up along Silver Creek before finally crossing one of its tributaries. There's no way to avoid getting wet here. There are great boulders along the creek bank for sunning yourself dry.

After you cross Silver Creek, the trail turns into singletrack and immediately begins to scale the hillside toward Hubbart Peak. Long before it reaches the peak, you'll find the trail huddling under thick brush. Most people don't cross the river, so it remains fairly overgrown here. Bushwhacking takes a little time, but getting through the brush is like being greeted by the sun after riding through a tunnel. Once on the other side, you find yourself situated between two incredible peaks: Silvertip Peak (almost 5,000 feet) and Hubbart Peak (at almost 6,000 feet). The river seems very far away up here.

The trail then climbs along the north side of Hubbart. The singletrack looks more like the abandoned road that it is. It intersects with a lovely cascading waterfall streaming from Twin Peaks. (Incidentally, these peaks have nothing to do with the TV show *Twin Peaks* whose credits were, however, shot in Snoqualmie at Snoqualmie Falls, much closer to I-90.) This is the usual turn-around point for heading back down. If you are looking for more adventure, con-

Twin Falls.

sider following the trail yet a little higher to reach the end of the cirque and then hike to Poodle Dog Pass, right by Silver Lake, and then down to Monte Cristo, the historic ghost mining-town.

Monte Cristo was quite the mining boomtown in the late 1880s, but foundations are all that remain of the town now. There used to be trams that carried the galena ore (silver and lead mixture) to a mill in town and then to an Everett smelter. All was running well until a huge flood in 1897 destroyed the Great Northern Railway tracks that ran through the Stillaguamish/Sauk River valleys. The big money investors (which included the Rockefellers) called in their loans, and the town of Monte Cristo quickly died. The Great Northern Railway returned sometime later to haul wood for the sawmills and to occasionally transport miners to the ore mines. Monte Cristo then became somewhat of a tourist attraction, though there are reputedly still active claims with minimal mining going on. Now, it's primarily a great place to hike and mountain bike.

To get there, you can ride your mountain bike up to the crossing of Silver Creek. This trail is rarely used from Monte Cristo down this far and can be tough to negotiate—it makes a more logical hike. After crossing the river, you essentially follow Silver Creek almost all the way up to Silver Lake, keeping to the east of the river. The trail then intersects with a two-mile trail heading to Twin Lakes. Follow the Silver Creek/Monte Cristo Trail straight to Poodle Dog Pass and then down to Monte Cristo. This makes a hefty trip though. It's easier to drive there via The Mountain Loop Highway. Travel east from Everett on State Route 9 north, to State Route 92 east. After passing through Granite Falls, continue east on the Mountain Loop Highway about 26 miles to Barlow Pass where the road turns into Monte Cristo Road.

MilesDirections

0.0 START climbing the gravel road to the right of the intersection (where you parked).

1.4 Pass a spur road on the left.

1.5 Come to a huge avalanche area that falls right into Silver Creek. It's a good idea to walk and carry the bike across this.

1.7 Pass an old mine on the left. And then cross another small washout.

2.0 Nice waterfall on your right across the river.

2.2 Pass another mine on the left.

2.5 Pass a wash-out and a beautiful waterfall.

2.6 Another mine.

2.7 Crossing the second wooden bridge.

2.9 Cross a small avalanche area. The right trail ahead is a camping area close to the river. Check it out and then take the trail up to the left.

3.7 Cross another nice wooden bridge marking a great waterfall on the left.

4.4 Wade across a tributary of Silver Creek to continue on, or turn around and head back for a quick, fun downhill.

4.6 Cross Silver Creek on an old wooden bridge, once the location of Mineral City long ago.

4.9 Continuing on, head into the hills.

5.6 Bushwhacking your way up, continue on trail now to the falls. If the previous winter season has been especially tough, the trail will be in sad repair until late summer. Be prepared for a little more hiking.

6.0 After checking out Twin Falls, turn around and head back for some screaming singletrack descents.

Ride Information

Trail Maintenance Hotlines:
- Mount Baker/Snoqualmie National Forest, Skykomish Ranger District: (360) 677-2414

Schedule:
This trail is open year-round but is best between April and October.

Local Information:
Monroe Chamber of Commerce: (360) 794-5488

Local Events/Attractions:
- Old Time Tractor Pull and Threshing Bee in early August, Monroe, WA (360) 659-1682
- Fair Days in late August, Monroe, WA (360) 794-4344

- Sultan Summer Shindig Logging Show in mid-July, Sultan, WA (360) 793-2565
- The Columbia Winery, Woodinville, WA; (425) 486-1900
- Chateau Saint Michelle Winery, Woodinville, WA; (425) 488-1133
- Red Hook Brewery, Woodinville, WA (425) 483-3232

Local Bike Shops:
- Monroe Cyclery, Monroe, WA (360) 794-4522
- Centennial Cyclery, Snohomish, WA (360) 568-1345

Maps:
- Maptech CD-ROM: Index, WA
- DeLorme's Washington Atlas & Gazetteer—Page 81 A5

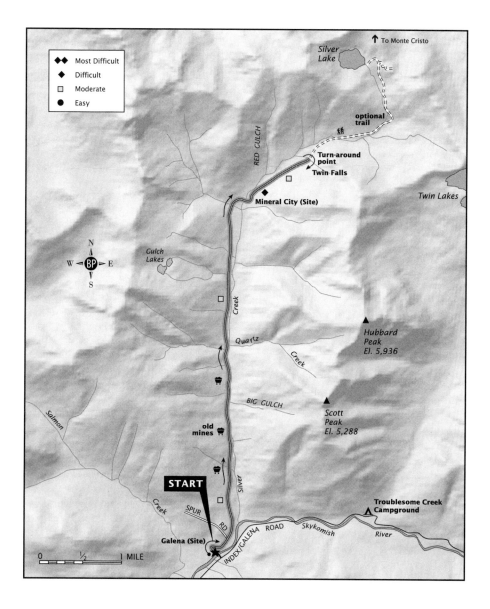

Most Difficult ◆◆
Difficult ◆
Moderate □
Easy ●

To Monte Cristo ↑

Silver Lake

optional trail

Turn-around point

Twin Falls

Mineral City (Site)

Twin Lakes

RED GULCH

Gulch Lakes

Hubbard Peak El. 5,936

Creek

Quartz

Creek

BIG GULCH

Scott Peak El. 5,288

old mines

START

Salmon

Creek

Silver

Troublesome Creek Campground

SPUR

RD

INDEX/GALENA ROAD

Skykomish

River

Galena (Site)

0 ½ 1 MILE

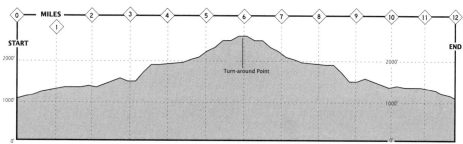

MILES 0 1 2 3 4 5 6 7 8 9 10 11 12

START

END

2000'

Turn-around Point

2000'

1000'

1000'

0'

0'

Nason Ridge Ride

Ride Summary

Nothing beats beginning a difficult ride with a hearty climb. This advanced ridge ride, overlooking Lake Wenatchee, takes you to the panoramic heights of Round Mountain. It's also highly regarded by cyclists who enjoy gonzo-abusive mountain biking. To reduce saddle fatigue, consider turning this loop into a shuttle ride, or possibly shortening the loop.

Ride Specs

Start: Merritt Lake Trailhead
Other Starting Locations: Nason Creek Campground or Nason Ridge Trailhead
Length: 17.6 miles w/shuttle; 30 miles round-trip
Approximate Riding Time: 5 hours
Rating: Difficult due to long, steep climbs and ridge-line riding
Terrain: Steep singletrack, doubletrack, and paved road with the shuttle
Other Trail Users: Hikers and horseback riders

Merritt Lake.

Getting There

From U.S. Route 2 at Stevens Pass: Travel east beyond the Merritt Lake Trailhead (10.8 miles east of the summit) to Coles Corner (about eight miles farther). Turn left, heading north, on State Route 207 to Nason Creek Campground and Lake Wenatchee. Nason Creek Campground is on the left at Cedar Brae Road. Cross the creek and park on either side of the road at the campground. For the shuttle, take the start vehicle back to the Merritt Lake Trailhead (down State Route 207 to Coles Corner; turn right on U.S. Route 2 west to Merritt Lake Trailhead). Turn right onto Merritt Lake Road. Head up to the parking lot about two miles, after passing power lines and a spur road.

Nason Ridge runs parallel to U.S. Route 2 and is smack in between Lake Wenatchee and the Alpine Lakes Wilderness, just east of Stevens Pass. If you're into rockhounding, you might think about hanging out at Lake Wenatchee. Near the Ranger Station toward the end of State Route 207, there is a trail where you can find long green crystals of actinolite, multicolored talc, and soapstone. Lake Wenatchee, now a recreational getaway, just nearly escaped becoming a reservoir. The legislature (with the support of President Taft) passed a bond for construction, but luckily voters vetoed the project. Today Lake Wenatchee is a popular place to mountain bike, hike, fish, and camp. A State Park, beach, and camping on either side of the lake provide ample recreational space.

Covering 306,000 square acres of wilderness in the Mount Baker-Snoqualmie National Forest, the pristine, moon-like Alpine Lakes Wilderness also stretches into the Wenatchee National Forest. At the alpine level, nothing but incredible rocks, lakes, and ptarmigans exist. White-gray rocks of all sizes blend with the sky on gray days, making it difficult to find the hiking trail at times. If it weren't for the cairns marking the trail as it winds around the icy cold, peacefully quiet alpine lakes, it would be quite easy to get lost up there. Be careful not to trip on a ptarmigan—a hearty variety of grouse, with feathers all the way down to

Dirty Face Peak and Lake Wenatchee.

their feet. These rugged, chameleon-like creatures change color according to the season. It can be difficult to spot them at first.

Nearby Stevens Pass was named for John G. Stevens who discovered the Nason Creek route over the Cascades. Crossed by U.S. Route 2, Stevens Pass is also a railroad route across the mountains. Trains don't travel over the pass, but rather, straight through it, via a tunnel carved into the mountains 1,900 feet beneath the summit. It took three years to construct the original two and a half mile-long tunnel in 1900. The tunnel was replaced 29 years later with an eight mile-long version about 900 feet lower than the original!

Stevens Pass has an older sibling—a route just to the north. The old pass is no longer a viable traveling road in most places, but makes for a great road bike ride, with one large river crossing. To ride the old route, start out in Skykomish on the west side of Stevens Pass. Follow the road out of Skykomish that runs parallel to U.S. Route 2 along the Tye River. After about two miles, the road ends at U.S. Route 2. Ride on Route 2 for a little over two miles before crossing over to the north side of the highway, and continue traveling east on the old Route 2. The old road winds up the mountains, which are virtually deserted except for the occasional car where the road is still intact. After crossing the Tye River, the road is in serious disrepair—perfect for biking. The old pass leads right up to the Stevens Pass Ski Area. To return to Skykomish, ride down the newer U.S. Route 2. It is legal—folks do it all the time—and it's screaming fun. Except for the initial gravitational pull of the concrete and

the counterbalancing you have to do because of the ferocious crosswinds, you'll love it. There's an adequate shoulder and plenty of lanes for cars, so you'll have lots of space.

For a thrilling singletrack ride, though, you'll want to go for the Nason Ridge Ride. Now if you are a "super-biker," you can probably ride the initial climb of this ride. Mere mortals will most likely have to push a little. After leaving the parking area at the Merritt Lake trailhead, the climb begins immediately, gaining a lot of eleva-

tion. (We recommend a brief warm-up on the road.) The trail reaches Merritt Lake at 5,083 feet, after about three miles. There is a path around the lake, but this ride takes you up and away from the lake. Because of the incline, the ride can be pretty tough. There are a few short descents in which to catch your breath. After about five miles, the trail gives way to a slightly hairy descent and views of the Nason Creek valley below. Continuing up, the switchbacks will likely be climbers and somewhat technical. The 360-degree view at the Lookout is divine and the descent following to Nine Mile Saddle and Round Mountain is worth the sweat of the climb.

Feeling a mite daunted by the intensity of this ride just by reading about it? Make an easier loop by driving up Forest Road 6910 from the rest stop on U.S. Route 2 to Trail #1529. Begin your ride here, at Trail #1529, making a loop by riding down to Trail #1583 and around Round Mountain to Lake Wenatchee and back. The Lookout is still accessible and the climb will be less harrowing. The most important thing is to have a good time.

Ride Information

Trail Maintenance Hotlines:
- Wenatchee National Forest, Leavenworth Ranger District (509) 548-6977
- Lake Wenatchee Ranger District: (509) 763-3103 or 1-800-452-5687

Schedule:
Open year-round, but best between May and October

Costs:
$3 per car, per day or $25 annual pass

Local Information:
Leavenworth Chamber of Commerce and Visitor Center; (509) 548-5807 or **www.leavenworth.org**

Local Events/Attractions:
- Maifest in May, Leavenworth, WA (509) 548-5807

- Leavenworth Craft Fair in June, Leavenworth, WA; (509) 548-5807
- International Accordion Celebration in August, Leavenworth, WA (509) 548-5807
- Washington State Autumn Leave Festival, September-October, Leavenworth, WA; (509) 548-5807

Local Bike Shops:
- Der Sportsmann, Leavenworth, WA (509) 548-5623
- Leavenworth Ski & Sports, Leavenworth, WA; (509) 548-7864
- Leavenworth Outfitters, Leavenworth, WA; (509) 763-3733 or 1-800-347-7934 **www.thrillmakers.com**

Maps:
- Maptech CD-ROM: Mount Howard, WA
- DeLorme's Washington Atlas & Gazetteer—Page 82 B1

MilesDirections

The ride begins at the Merritt Lake Trailhead and ends at the Nason Ridge Campground. For the two car shuttle, leave one car at The Merritt Lake Trailhead and take the other to the Nason Ridge Campground, or to the Nason Ridge Trailhead to avoid any riding on pavement. For the loop, park at The Merritt Lake Trail and complete the route by riding 13.4 miles back on Road 207 and U.S. Route 2 from the Nason Creek Campground.

0.0 START on The Merritt Lake Trail #1588. The Nason Ridge Trail #1583 is 2.5 miles up, and Merritt Lake is three miles ahead.

2.3 Reach a junction with the Nason Ridge Trail. Rock Lake Trail is to the left. Continue climbing up to Merritt Lake which is at 5,000 feet. Currently the elevation is about 4,800 feet.

2.9 Arrive at Merritt Lake. Follow the trail by the lake, but stay on the main trail to the right heading up the switchbacks to the ridge.

3.2 At the "T" intersection, turn right to continue on to the Nason Ridge Trail #1583 and up to the Nine Mile Saddle Lookout. The left goes to Lost Lake.

4.9 Arrive at a saddle with great views of the valley.

5.8 Begin a series of switchbacks after a narrow, technical descent down the steep hillside. The view is of the Nason Creek Valley. Head up to the ridge top on the switchbacks.

6.4 Encounter the final push up to the junction of the Lookout. Double back on your left for the lookout. It's worth the view. The trail continues around Round Mountain.

6.7 Reach the Lookout for 360 degrees of awesome views.

7.1 Back at the junction, follow the trail straight to Nine Mile Saddle and Round Mountain.

9.7 The trail is now heading around Round Mountain.

10.4 Reach the intersection of Trail #1529. Stay on #1583, taking a left at the intersection—it isn't well marked.

13.5 The trail turns into doubletrack and a gentle climb.

13.7 Turn right as the doubletrack crests the hill.

14.3 Turn left at the intersection, keeping to the Nason Ridge Trail #1583. The road drops down to a saddle and goes off right. The road is RD 114.

16.9 Arrive at the end of the trail. Cruise along the forest floor. Come to a gravel loop and follow it around to the main road.

17.0 Hit asphalt and turn left downhill on Golf Course Road.

17.1 Arrive at a "Y" intersection from the right. Continue downhill.

17.3 Exit Kahler Glen Golf Resort. Turn right.

17.6 Arrive at the intersection with Cedar Brae Road and Nason Creek Campground Road. Head back to your car.

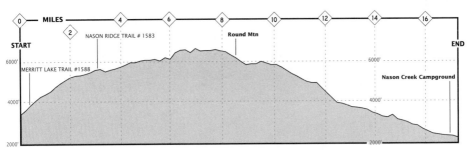

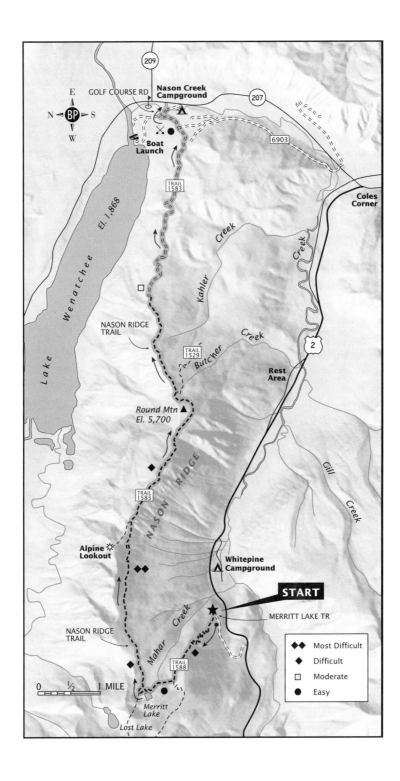

209

GOLF COURSE RD **Nason Creek Campground** 207

E
N ← BP → S
W

Boat Launch

El. 1,868

6903

TRAIL 1583

Coles Corner

Creek

Kahler

Creek

NASON RIDGE TRAIL

TRAIL 1529

Butcher Creek

2

Rest Area

Round Mtn ▲
El. 5,700

NASON RIDGE

TRAIL 1583

Gill Creek

Alpine Lookout ☼

Whitepine Campground

START

MERRITT LAKE TR

NASON RIDGE TRAIL

Mahar Creek

TRAIL 1588

0   ½   1 MILE

◆◆ Most Difficult
◆ Difficult
□ Moderate
● Easy

Merritt Lake

Lost Lake

71

Mountain Home Loops

Ride Summary

Nestled between the steep slopes of the Eastern Cascades, the cross-country trails accessed from Mountain Home Road make great intermediate mountain biking loops in the summer. The forest road climbs are gradual at first, then gain intensity the higher they go. Although the area is still recovering from a series of forest fires, the ponderosa pines still yield some "must-see" views. If you're staying at the Mountain Home Lodge, you can look forward to an incredible meal and a soak in the hot tub at the end of the day.

Ride Specs

Start: Mountain Home Lodge
Length: 12.1 miles
Approximate Riding Time: 2 hours
Nearest Town: Leavenworth
Rating: Moderate with short, steep climbs
Terrain: Doubletrack, logging roads, and single-track
Other Trail Users: Horseback riders, hikers, cross-country skiers, and some motorcyclists

Getting There

From U.S. Route 2 in Leavenworth: Turn south on North Leavenworth Road. Turn left immediately on to Mountain Home Road. Follow for 2.6 miles to the lodge on the left.

View of Leavenworth from Mountain Home Road.

Leavenworth, the Bavaria of the Northern Cascades, is home to anything and everything German—with snow-capped, Alps-like peaks to boot. But Leavenworth hasn't always been that way. In the late 1800s, the promise of the Great Northern Railroad brought life to the small township of Icicle, built along the Icicle River. The town moved to the valley where the railroad tracks would run. Charles Leavenworth, a stockholder with the investment company, spearheaded the relocation. By 1897, the tracks were set and work began on tunneling through the Cascades. But by 1920, the country was heading into the Great Depression, and the railroad packed up and moved out of the valley. Orchards and sawmills saw hard times too, and Leavenworth began to disintegrate. For the next 40 years, the town struggled to survive.

In 1960, Leavenworth citizens re-awakened to the beauty around them, realized their proximity to Washington's larger towns, and decided, in an effort to attract tourists, to go Bavarian. Although it took some time to get off the ground, the "new and improved" Leavenworth began booming oompa music and serving traditional Bavarian fare. And it worked. Leavenworth is now a destination town, a hub for winter and summer recreation. Backpacking, climbing, hiking, horseback riding, and mountain biking are continuing to grow in popularity, drawing a new kind of tourist and economy to Leavenworth.

Anyone would agree that an especially nice reward at the end of a tough day of mountain biking is a big meal and a soak in a hot tub. The Mountain Home Lodge in Leavenworth has both. Much more than a hotel or a simple bed and breakfast, the Mountain Home Lodge is a home away from home. From its massive stone fireplace, both warm and inviting, to its spacious hot tub surrounded by tall, often snowy peaks, the

Toward Icicle Creek and the Enchantments.

Mountain Home Lodge is the perfect place to crash after a long day of pedal pounding. Brad and Kathy Schmidt, the inn's proprietors, are correct both figuratively and literally when they boast that their lodge is 1,000 feet closer to heaven. And this gives you a 1,000-foot advantage when taking off for the hills above.

The going is steady and not at all rough as you begin from the lodge up the Mountain Home Road. The forest of ponderosa pines adorn the roadside like memory lane: some trees are perfect, standing tall, branches reaching out to one another, and others are sadly scorched, ominously reminiscent of the huge and devastating fire that overtook this area in 1994. At the cross-roads, called Four Corners, the route can take off in one of three directions. Heading up and right leads to the helicopter pad, used during forest fires. Turning left, the road leads to a lookout and the singletrack. Riding straight down, the road will eventually run into U.S. Route 97. The directions below will cover both routes—though not the road to the highway.

The climb up to the helicopter pad is steep, and if the road is at all wet, the mud will be thick and challenging to ride through. The views from the helicopter pad make the agony of the muddy climb worthwhile. The hillsides surrounding Leavenworth aren't the rolling kind you see on the western side of the Cascades. These mountains shoot straight up, making most every climb memorable.

After turning around, enjoy the downhill return to Four Corners. Then head up the road to the lookout. It is a steep climb, but the view is wide open. You can see apple orchards and Icicle Creek Road. You'll be able to pinpoint the Enchantments and see cars drive along U.S. Routes 2 and 97. The ponderosa pines stand like silent sentries along the trails.

Getting down to the singletrack is great fun. The trails are well marked, so it's easy to find your way. The Ridge Ride Trail is a serious ridge-runner. Nothing flat about this trail: push up, fly down, push up, fly down. If you can manage to climb each and every rise, your quads will definitely be burning at the top. It's not too long, but it is a workout. The ridge trail travels to a couple of looping trails out behind the Mountain Home Lodge.

This is a good intermediate ride for mountain bikers who don't like to be too far out in the wilderness. The trails are fairly exposed most of the time which is helpful in seeing exactly where you are. And, it's difficult to get lost, even without a map.

MilesDirections

0.0 START from the Mountain Home Lodge. Head down the driveway and turn left onto Mountain Home Road.

3.7 Arrive at the Four Corners crossroads (El. 2,900 ft.) to Boundary Road, the Helicopter Pad, and U.S. Route 97. Turn left for Boundary Butte. For an optional side trip, turn right to the helicopter pad (El. 5,855 ft.).

3.9 Pass a dead-end road on the right. Continue straight for Boundary Butte.

4.2 At the intersection follow the road to the right.

4.6 Pass the intersection leading to the Canyon Crest Trail, continuing straight. At the next intersection turn right for the Boundary Butte Lookout.

6.0 Reach the top of the lookout. See Icicle Creek, the Enchantments, Peshastin, and Leavenworth. Turn around and head back down.

7.4 Reach the bottom of the road from the butte. Turn right at the "Y" intersection and follow the doubletrack down and around to the intersection for the Rat Creek and Canyon Crest trails.

8.2 Arrive at the trailheads for the Rat Creek and Canyon Crest Trails. New signs have been constructed, so it's easy to find your way. Turn right on the Canyon Crest Trail. Continuing straight leads to The Rat Creek Trail.

9.7 Stay straight at the "Y" intersection.

11.2 See the sign for the Mount Stuart Lookout. Stay right at the "Y" intersection.

11.4 Reach the intersection for The Overlook Look and the end of the Ridge Ride Trail. Follow the Overlook Loop straight and then left at the intersection of Wapati Trail (hiker only).

11.9 Watch for a small sign on the right-hand side of the trail for the lodge. Follow it over the meadow and to the lodge. If you miss it, the trail exits onto the private road that is gated at the Mountain Home Road intersection, at which you'll turn right and follow the sign for the lodge.

12.1 Arrive at the Mountain Home Lodge.

Ride Information

Trail Maintenance Hotlines:
  (See Ride Information for Chapter 11)

Schedule: Best between May and October

Local Information:
  • Leavenworth Chamber of Commerce:
    (509) 548-5809
  • Lake Wenatchee State Park:
    1-800-452-5687

Local Attractions/Events/Bike Shops:
  (See Ride Information for Chapter 11)

Accommodations:
  • Mountain Home Lodge, Leavenworth,
    WA; 1-800-414-2378 or
    www.mthome.com
  • Camping on the Icicle Creek Drainage:
    1-800-274-6104
  • Tumwater Campground:
    1-800-280-2267

Maps:
  • Maptech CD-ROM: Leavenworth, WA
  • DeLorme's Washington Atlas &
    Gazetteer—Page 82 D-3

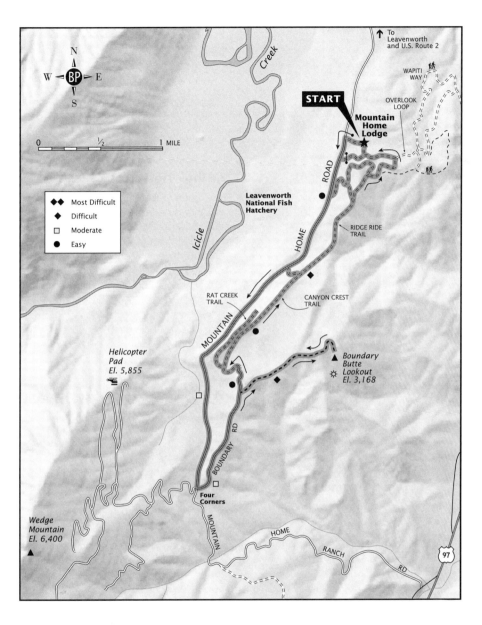

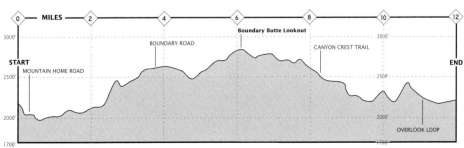

Jolly Mountain

Ride Summary

Hot, dry, and technical describes the climb of this advanced ride to a "T." Thrill-seekers will definitely appreciate the descent from Jolly Mountain. This 18-plus-mile route offers great views of nearby Cle Elum Lake, the Enchantments, and Mount Rainier. For this ride, you'll want to bring along plenty of food and water, and be prepared to ride hard.

Ride Specs

Start: Salmon la Sac campground
Other Starting Locations: Forest Road 4315
Length: 18.2 miles
Approximate Riding Time: 4-5 hours
Nearest Town: Roslyn
Rating: Difficult due to steep, technical single-track
Terrain: Paved road, forest road, and singletrack
Other Uses: Hiking and horseback riding

Getting There

From Seattle: Take I-90 East to Exit 80. Head north from the exit onto Bull Frog Road. Turn left onto State Route 903 to Roslyn. Follow the main road through town into Ronald. Pass The Last Resort Restaurant on the right. Follow State Route 903 for about nine miles to the Salmon la Sac Campground. Drive into the campground and over a narrow bridge. Park at the trailhead, which is close to where the ride finishes. The ride begins on Forest Road 4315, off of State Route 903.

Head back in time, back to a place where simple living is revered and a sense of community has always been in vogue. Eight lanes of interstate narrow to four, forcefully slowing your pace. You then pass through small towns, ones with a delicate western flavor. You may even recognize Roslyn as Cicely, Alaska, the setting for the television show *Northern Exposure*. But Roslyn is more than just a TV celebrity town, it's also a prime location for weekend mountain biking, camping, boating, fishing, and just getting away from it all.

Roslyn was originally settled as a mining town and is actually built on top of a coal field. Coal produced in Roslyn once accounted for half of the coal produced in the state. The mining industry began here in 1884 with the arrival of Nez Jensen. Jensen ran a small mining operation for two years before the Northern Pacific Railroad came to town. Because of existing land deals, it was easy for the railroad to take control of the town and Jensen's coal production. The land deals originated from President Lincoln's days in office. To push the railroads on the West Coast, the U.S. government offered the railroad companies incentive land: 40 square miles of land for every one mile of track. The coal mining areas in and around Roslyn happened to fall within the Northern Pacific's holdings, which is why it was easy for the company to own, operate, and run the town and its coal production.

Working in the coal mines paid well back then. People from all over the world came to Roslyn to get their piece of the action. The names on the headstones in the old cemetery in town illustrate the diversity of the work force: Austrians, Croats, Germans, Italians, Hungarians, Scots, and Swedes. Coal mining itself ended when other, more efficient means of power were discovered, but huge deposits of coal still remain.

Today, Roslyn looks a lot like it did in the late 1800s. The Brick Tavern, (yes, it's "The Brick" from *Northern Exposure*) was built in 1899. It's got an old jail in its basement and a "gutter" spittoon running 23 feet along it's bar, complete with running water! The store on First Street and Pennsylvania still stands as it did in 1889. And many of the old homesteader cabins and houses still exist as well.

North of Roslyn is the small community of Ronald. Named after a mine supervisor, Alexander Ronald. Watch your speed limit while driving through town: 25 miles per hour. About a half-mile outside of Ronald, you can see coal mine tailings on the hill. Six and a half miles down the road, you'll run into The Last Resort Restaurant—which it really is. There are no other restaurants or retail establishments past that point. The food is pretty good, too, especially after a hot and dusty mountain bike ride.

Continuing through Ronald, the road narrows along Cle Elum Lake. Long and blue, this lake stretches for about seven miles and has boat launches and campgrounds on its banks. If you look at a map, Cle Elum Lake, Kachess Lake, and Keechelus Lake all look like they were cut from the same mold. There is a fresh water spring toward the end of the lake—it's easy to miss. And Red Mountain stands at 5,722 feet to the north—it's hard to miss.

Jolly Mountain is located at the northeast end of Cle Elum Lake and Sasse Ridge. The peak is a spectacular point from which to view the natural sites of Central Washington. The climb to this vantage, however, is a tough, dry, and dusty mountain bike ride, with a thrill-seeker's ideal descent. The ride to Jolly Mountain begins with a road climb, the long and steady kind. (The West Fork of the Teanaway ride begins in the same place.) The views of Cle Elum Lake, the Enchantments, and Mount Rainier are breathtaking from the top on clear days, and are well deserved after the last half-mile of ascent—the steepest and toughest part of the climb.

Arriving at the top of the road, you reach the junction with Jolly Mountain, the West Fork of the Teanaway, and the Sasse Ridge Trails. This is where the singletrack begins. There's still a little bit of climbing left to do, interspersed with a few short descents, and then the final climb to the top of Jolly Mountain. All your work won't have been for naught. The steep descent into the Salmon la Sac drainage is an exhilarating experience.

From then on, the trail crosses the Salmon la Sac Creek and travels through the uncut forest, alternating with passes through sparse clearcut meadows. The trail is dry and dusty, except by the creek, before arriving at the road leading back to the Salmon la Sac Campground and Cle Elum Lake. Remember to take a refreshing dip in the lake before you hit The Last Resort.

MilesDirections

0.0 START from the campground and ride over the narrow bridge to State Route 903. Turn right on 903.

1.0 Turn left on Forest Road 4315.

1.8 The road switches back left. Continue on the main road passing a spur road on the right.

2.9 The road switches left, heading east up the basin, then heads north again.

3.2 Pass a gated road on the right.

3.4 Pass a gate again.

3.8 The road switches right. Pass a spur on the left.

4.0 Zig zag up the hill.

4.6 Pass a gated road on the left and Spur Road 121.

6.2 Keep heading up. Pass a spur road that heads down.

7.6 Round a bend—get a great view of Mount Rainier and Lake Cle Elum, Mount Stuart, and The Enchantments.

7.7 Pass another spur on the right and climb up the spine of this ridge. Trail #1340, Sass Ridge, heads off to the right. Continue up the road, which will become Trail #1340 later. There will again be a trail marked #1340 that you'll pass shortly before the end of the road.

8.1 Wind up the edge of a clearcut. Stay right on the main road.

8.3 Come to the saddle and get a great view of the Enchantments and Mount Rainier. Head over the rise and see the trail on your left.

8.5 Pass the Sasse Ridge Trail on your right. Ride to the end of the road, onto the Teanaway Trail.

8.9 The climb tops out and drops a little to the trail junction of Jolly Mountain Trail #1307, and in a little bit, the West Fork of the Teanaway Trail (on the right).

9.0 Head up to Jolly Mountain for a view.

9.3 Pass a junction on the right. Stay left to Jolly Mountain (one mile).

9.8 The trail to Jolly Mountain rounds the top of a drainage and gives you some incredible views of Mount Stuart and The Enchantments.

10.0 Pass the junction of Jolly Creek Trail #1355 on the left. Stay straight on the Jolly Mountain Trail #1307. Ditch the bikes and travel 0.7 mile to the top (6,443 feet) for a panoramic look at Ellensburg and the Stuart range. Turn around for the descent and go back the way you came.

11.2 Arrive at the junction with the West Fork of the Teanaway Trail. Continue straight.

11.5 Turn right on the Jolly Mountain Trail.

14.0 Reach the junction with the Paris Creek Trail #1307A. Continue straight on the Jolly Mountain Trail.

14.7 Cross a tributary of Salmon la Sac Creek.

15.4 Great downhill ends at a clearcut. Look for the trail about 30 yards below. Rock cairns show you the trail on the left.

16.0 Cross the logging road. The trail is marked; just follow it across the road.

16.7 The trail crosses a spur road.

16.9 Back into the trees again. The river is just off to the left.

17.5 Come out at the top of Cayuse Horse Camp. See the trail signs. Follow the main road straight. Pass many spur roads. Take the trail off to the right for a bit more singletrack. It drops to a creek with a short hike-a-bike climb into the horse camp and the trails for Jolly Mountain and the other trails.

17.9 Hit the paved road and turn right, heading back to Salmon la Sac Campground and your car.

18.1 Come to the campground intersection and turn left.

18.2 Arrive back at the parking lot.

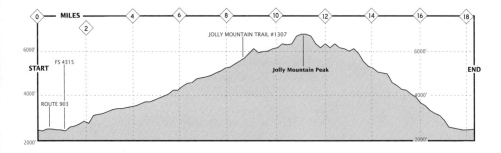

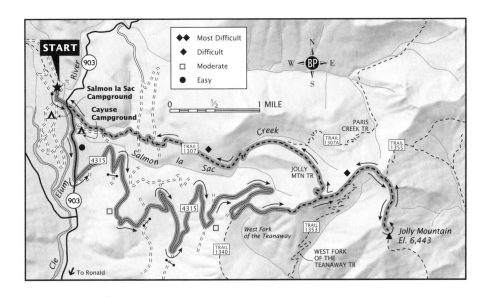

Ride Information

Trail Maintenance Hotlines:
- Wenatchee National Forest, Cle Elum Ranger District: (509) 674-4411
- Wenatchee National Forest Headquarters, Wenatchee, WA (509) 662-4335

Schedule:
This trail is open year-round. Best April to October when snow levels are low.

Costs:
$3 per car per day or $25 for an annual pass.

Local Information:
- Cle Elum Chamber of Commerce: (509) 674-5958 or http://www.ohwy.com/wa/c/cleelucc.htm
- Ellensburg Chamber of Commerce: (509) 925-3137

Local Events/Attractions:
- Pioneer Days in July, Roslyn, WA (509) 674-5958
- Sweet Pea Festival in July, Roslyn, WA (509) 649-2758
- Croatian Picnic in July, Roslyn, WA (509) 649-2714
- Roslyn Miner's Celebration and Wing Ding Paradee in August, Roslyn, WA (509) 649-2795
- Whisky Dick Triathlon in July, Ellensburg, WA; (509) 925-3137
- Ellensburg Rodeo in August, Ellensburg, WA; (509) 962-7831 or 1-800-637-2444

Local Bike Shops:
- Recycle Bicycle Shop, Ellensburg, WA (509) 925-3326
- Central Sundries (also Roslyn's de facto Visitor Center), Roslyn, WA (509) 649-2210

Maps:
- Maptech CD-ROM: Davis Peak, WA
- Green Trails: Kachess Lake No. 208 and Mount Stuart No. 209
- DeLorme's Washington Atlas & Gazetteer—Pages 65 A8 & 66 B1

14

Kachess Ridge

Ride Summary

Located just east of Snoqualmie Pass, this ride offers a convenient adventure for Seattle-area mountain bikers. This route has a long, steep climb along a forest road before hitting the singletrack. The trail begins along a quickly eroding hillside, then hits some marvelous trail, jettisoning you across meadows and streams. The finale comes with steep, tight switchbacks. If you have the control, this race course-like trail is furiously fast and drops you into the parking area just a mile or so from where you began.

Ride Specs

Start: Kachess Lake area

Other Starting Locations: Anywhere along Forest Service Road 4818

Length: 19.7 miles

Approximate Riding Time: 3-4 hours

Nearest Towns: Easton, Roslyn, Snoqualmie Summit

Rating: Moderate

Terrain: Forest road, singletrack, and creek crossings

Other Trail Users: Hikers and horseback riders. ORVs are not allowed on this particular trail, but they do use the area adjacent to this ride.

Getting There

From Seattle: Take I-90 east over Snoqualmie Pass to Exit #70 at Lake Easton State Park. Turn left over the overpass to Sparks Road. Turn left onto Kachess Dam Road heading west (a feeder road of I-90). Go 0.4 miles and turn right. Take the 4th right to Forest Road 4818 (see sign for "Boeing Overnight Camp"). Head straight toward the power lines. Turn right on Spur Road 203 under the power lines. Follow to any offshoot and park.

Summers on Snoqualmie Summit are perhaps only slightly surpassed by spring and fall on the east side of the Cascade range. Located a few miles east of Snoqualmie Pass, Kachess Ridge is situated neatly beneath the rain shadow of the Cascades, making this a drier trail than other rides on the neighboring western slopes.

Along the I-90 corridor, nature and man have been at odds for some time. The forests surrounding this corridor resemble a colossal checkerboard, especially apparent when flying overhead. Squared sections of forest-land, thick with trees, lie quietly next to other squared sections stripped bare. A product of pure economics, the checkerboard exists not because of some devastating arboreal disease, but from years and years of logging. The checkerboard effect now threatens the life of the forest and the trails recreationalists enjoy.

In 1864 President Abraham Lincoln offered 40 million-plus acres of federal land to the Northern Pacific Railroad (now part of the Burlington Northern system) in an effort to see that rail was extended west of Lake Superior to the Puget Sound. As it was figured, for every mile of track Northern Pacific laid, the federal government gave 40 square miles of land. The land grant was divided into alternating square-mile sections, mostly along the 2,000 miles of track. The Plum Creek Timber Company, a subsidiary of Burlington Northern, has,

in the years since the agreement, logged a large percentage of their first holdings—bringing the checkerboard to life.

When the federal government began creating the national parks, large portions of land had to be traded between the government and the railroad. Large portions of parks like Mount Rainier National Park were owned by the Northern Pacific Railroad. In order to secure the land, the government had to exchange what were markedly tree-less tracks around Mount Rainier for perfectly lush federal lands along the western Cascades. Northern Pacific then harvested the new squares of federal lands and promptly extended their railroads to the park systems to carry tourists.

When you fly over the I-90 corridor, which travels

east to west, you'll see where the Plum Creek Timber Company has logged this sprawling area for years. The alternating federal lands, now controlled by the U.S. Forest Service, have also seen their share of logging. Spirited discussions continue between loggers and environmentalists, and with every new proposal there's still hope that before the Pacific Northwest's last 15 percent of old-growth forests are cleared, a peaceful balance between consumption and conservation can be found.

Responsible bicycling is mandatory in the area around Kachess Ridge. Walk carefully around areas where erosion is already taking its toll. As mountain bikers, we must do what we can to preserve these vanishing landscapes for future use and enjoyment. If that means walking our bikes every once in awhile, then that's the least we can do. Enjoy the incredible views, challenging terrain, and peaceful quiet. It's hard to believe you're so close to the big city.

The ride begins north of the parking area up Forest Service Road 4818. The climb starts on Forest Road 4824, eventually leading to overlooks of Lake Kachess ("kachess" meaning "many fish" or "more fish"). Anglers will certainly appreciate knowing that the neighboring lake Keechelus means "fewer fish."

Finishing the rigorous climb, there is still a short, steep section of hike-a-bike to shoulder your bike down and then back up to reach the saddle. Once at the top, the true screaming-fun singletrack begins. You'll fly through meadows and pass over a couple of creeks for seven miles or so. Moving onto switchbacks running through the woods, you'll really pick up the pace. Technically challenging, these trails are more easily negotiated by the advanced mountain biker. When you hit the trailhead at the bottom, you're done. Just follow the dirt road back out to the power lines and to your car.

MilesDirections

0.0 START riding from the parking area back to Forest Service Road 4818 along the dirt road. Turn right onto Forest Road 4818.

2.2 Pass Spur Road 111.

4.1 Pass the Boeing Overnight Camp.

6.0 Turn right on Forest Road 4824.

7.6 The road switches back to the right, with an intersecting road on the left. Keep right.

8.0 Veer left at the switchback. Pass through the logging gate.

9.1 At the dirt spur road, continue on the left fork up the more noticeably traveled road.

10.0 Take the right fork up a really short, steep section.

11.0 Arrive at the saddle. Follow the road to the right. Look for the Kachess Ridge Trail #1315, the singletrack trail on your left—it can be difficult to find. If you get to the parking area at the end of the road you've gone too far. Looking due-south, there is another small saddle below the rocky crag. That is your destination. The trail intersection from the left is the Kachess Trail coming off Thorp Mountain. Keep right.

11.5 Hike-a-bike!

14.8 Cross Silver Creek.

17.9 Take another switchback down left into the trees. (There is a blocked trail intersection here. If you take it you'll dead-end at a viewpoint of the I-90 corridor.)

18.5 Finish more switchbacks heading down into the drainage.

19.0 Reach the end of the Kachess Ridge Trail #1315.

19.7 Stay on the main dirt road. Ride south back to the power lines. Turn right and head west to your car.

Ride Information

Trail Maintenance Hotlines:
- North Bend Ranger Station, North Bend, WA; (206) 888-1421

Schedule:
June through November (depending on snowfall.)

Local Information:
- Snoqualmie Pass Visitor Info Center: (425) 434-6111
- Upper Snoqualmie Valley Chamber of Commerce, North Bend, WA (425) 888-4440

Local Events/Attractions:
- Grundig/UCI World Cup Race and State Championships in June, The Summit at Snoqualmie, WA (509) 535-4757 or (425) 434-7669

- Snoqualmie Days and Bike Ride in August, Snoqualmie, WA (425) 888-4505
- Snoqualmie Falls, Fall City, WA (425) 396-5200

Local Bike Shops:
- Valley Bike Rack, Snoqualmie, WA (425) 888-4886
- Recycle Bicycle Shops, Ellensburg, WA (509) 925-3326

Maps:
- Maptech CD-ROM: Kachess Lake, WA
- DeLorme's Washington Atlas & Gazetteer Page 65 B7

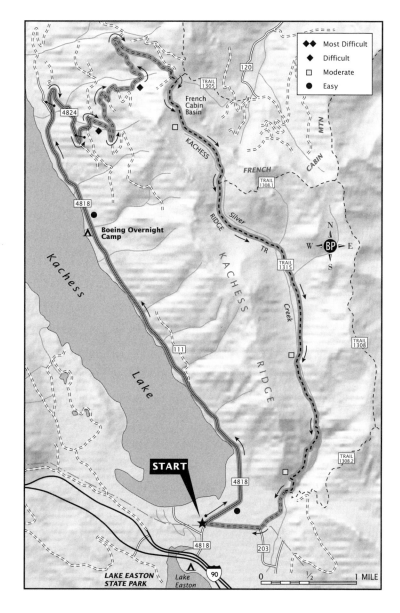

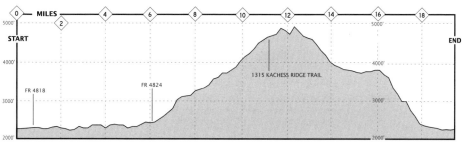

West Fork of the Teanaway

Ride Summary

In the same neighborhood as the Jolly Mountain Ride, this route along the West Fork of the Teanaway River has something a little different going for it—water. There are about a dozen creek crossings to contend with on this advanced ride, each a refreshing break on super hot days. The first third of the route begins with a road climb before hitting the trail. The trail ride down to the river is steep, narrow, and challenging. Following along the river, the singletrack passes a canyon filled with cool, inviting pools of water. Then the singletrack turns back onto a forest road about nine miles southeast of the start. As a shuttle or a round-trip, this is a ride you'll definitely want to try.

Ride Specs

Start: Forest Road 4315 parking area
Other Starting Locations: Ronald or along Cle Elum Lake
Length: 25.5 miles
Approximate Riding Time: 5-7 hours
Nearest Town: Roslyn
Rating: Difficult due to steep terrain
Terrain: Forest road, singletrack, and paved road without a shuttle
Other Trail Users: Hikers and horseback riders

Getting There

From Seattle: Take I-90 East to Exit 80. Head north from the exit onto Bull Frog Road. Turn left onto State Route 903 to Roslyn. Follow the main road through town into Ronald. Pass The Last Resort Restaurant on the right. (Leave one car here for the shuttle.) Follow State Route 903 toward the Salmon la Sac campground. At eight-and-a-half miles, turn right onto Forest Road 4315 and park on the shoulder or farther up at the designated parking area.

The towns along the central Kittitas Valley are as interesting to explore as the mountains that surround them. Spend a little time in Roslyn, the home of the Emmy-award-winning television show *Northern Exposure*, or drive farther south to visit Cle Elum, where you can indulge in baked goods from its 1906 bakery. Or travel even farther still to Ellensburg, host to Washington's finest rodeo.

Ellensburg is actually the largest town in the area. It was named in 1871 for Ellen, the wife of John Shoudy, a man actively involved in improving the route over Snoqualmie Pass (the top of I-90). In 1889, when Washington became a state, Ellensburg was in the running for the capital city position—as were Yakima and Olympia. Although Ellensburg and Yakima initially received more votes from Washington's citizens, Olympia won in a runoff election. A financially strong farming community, Ellensburg is well known in Washington for its crop production, especially its timothy hay—the primary feed for racehorses all over the world. Ellensburg hosts the oldest and most popular rodeo in the state, held every year over Labor Day weekend.

Logging was also a major industry on this side of the Cascades. Until 1917, loggers used to float their felled trees down the Teanaway River to mills farther south in Yakima during springtime floods. This practice stopped after farmers complained and lawsuits ensued because the river frequently left big trees in their fields. Log transportation moved to rail after that, and the river is now left to its own devices, providing a refreshing backdrop to the trails running alongside it.

The trail along the West Fork of the Teanaway offers summer solstice cycling at it's best. No matter how heated you become, the river will be there to cool you off. There are approximately 13 to 15 splashing opportunities along this ride as it crosses the West Fork of the Teanaway and its tributaries.

Mount Stuart.

This route should not be mistaken for an easy river trail. This is an advanced mountain bike ride. If possible, make this a shuttle trip. There are many convenient spots along Cle Elum Lake to leave a car while you take the second car to the top of the trailhead. Without a shuttle though, there will be a nine-mile paved road ride to contend with.

Oftentimes, after especially windy or snow-filled winters, the trail has more than its fair share of deadfall. The newly imposed trailhead fees should help eliminate this sort of hazard, but a quick call to the Ranger District before heading out will verify if this trail has been cleared sparing you the time it takes to hike over logs and debris.

This day-long ride begins with a long, steady climb that eventually becomes a steady, intensely-steep climb. In the summertime, add a little dust, heat, and elevation to the mix, and you've got a recipe for heat exhaustion. Bring plenty of food and water along, or at least a dependable water filter—you should NEVER drink straight from a river.

Ride Information

Trail Maintenance Hotlines:
- Wenatchee National Forest, Cle Elum Ranger District: (509) 674-4411
- Wenatchee National Forest Headquarters, Wenatchee, WA (509) 662-4335

Schedule:
This trail is open year-round. Best April to October due to snow levels.

Costs:
$3 per car per day or $25 for an annual pass.

Local Information:
- Ellensburg Chamber of Commerce: (509) 925-3137
- Cle Elum Chamber of Commerce: (509) 674-5958 or http://www.ohwy.com/wa /c/cleelucc.htm

Local Events/Attractions:
- Pioneer Days in July, Roslyn, WA (509) 674-5958
- Sweet Pea Festival in July, Roslyn, WA; (509) 649-2758

- Croatian Picnic in July, Roslyn, WA (509) 649-2714
- Miner's Celebration and Wing Ding Parade in August, Roslyn, WA (509) 649-2795
- Whisky Dick Triathlon in July, Ellensburg, WA; (509) 925-3137
- Ellensburg Rodeo in August, Ellensburg, WA; (509) 962-7831 or 1-800-637-2444

Local Bike Shops:
- Recycle Bicycle Shops, Ellensburg, WA (509) 925-3326
- Central Sundries (Roslyn's de facto Visitor Center), Roslyn, WA (509) 649-2210

Maps:
- Maptech CD-ROM: Cle Elum Lake and Teanaway Butte, WA
- Green Trails: Kachess Lake No. 208, Mount Stuart No. 209
- DeLorme's Washington Atlas & Gazetteer—Pages 65 A8 and 66 B1

Like most road climbs, this seven to eight-mile leg burner is a steady, semi-tough, granny-gear to middle ring event, but the views do a great job of distracting you from the pain in your legs and lungs. The last half-mile of the climb, before the singletrack, is the toughest section because of its steep grade. As you approach the crest of the climb, the Sasse Ridge Trail is to the right. Portions of this trail are defunct—the road now runs where the trail once roamed. The Sasse Ridge Trail is still alive farther up ahead, though, and starts again where the road intersects with it and the West Fork of the Teanaway Trail.

The singletrack of the West Fork Trail begins with a short hike-a-bike then levels out and drops to a saddle. Following the saddle are some steep, descending switchbacks to the river which are very technical as the path travels along the narrow and steep hillside. There are an equal number of short climbs along the river, too. Remember, this is not a beginner's ride. Along the way there are many rewards for your work. The river canyon, for instance, has several refreshing pools for the weary, heat-riddled mountain biker.

After tearing yourself away from the river's edge, the singletrack finally leads to a forest road climb and onto the road descent back to Cle Elum Lake. From there it's to your car—either catch your shuttle or you've got nine miles to ride back to your parking spot. Don't forget the bakery in Cle Elum on the way home.

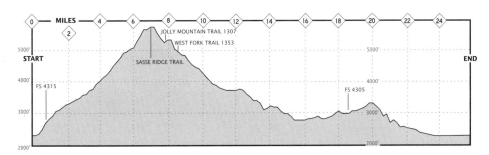

MilesDirections

0.0 START on Forest Road 4315 with a gentle climb.

0.2 Pass Spur Road 112 on the left.

0.3 Take the road heading up.

0.8 The road switches back left, still heading up. Stay on the main road.

1.6 Stop and enjoy views of the Enchantments to the north, Kachess Ridge to the west. Right behind is Sasse Mountain and Sasse Ridge.

2.0 Enjoy a little bit of a downhill here.

2.2 Pass a gated spur road on the left.

2.4 Cross a gate and a small trail on the left.

2.8 The road switches back right—still climbing. Pass a logging spur.

3.5 Pass Spur Road 121 as you switchback left.

4.9 Pass a left switchback and another spur, keeping to the main road and heading up.

5.2 Pass a little spur on the left. Steep granny-gear climbing!

5.8 Hit a short and sweet downhill. The trail elevation is about 5,200 feet here.

6.5 After curling into the Salmon la Sac drainage, the trail switches back and around the Cle Elum Lake side of Sasse Ridge. See Mount Rainier and Cle Elum Lake.

6.7 Pass a spur road heading down to the right. Stay straight and continue up to the ridgeline. Fifty yards ahead, see a Forest Service marker #1340, Sasse Ridge Trail—a strenuous trail. Keep to the road.

7.0 The road curves to the right on the edge of a clearcut. Pass a couple of spurs to the left and then to the right. Stay on the main road.

7.5 Reach the end of the road—the Sasse Mountain Trail #1340—about 5,300 feet of elevation. A sign indicates that the Sasse Mountain Trail, West Fork Trail, and the Jolly Mountain Trails are ahead.

7.9 Start a white-knuckle descent into the next saddle where the Sasse Mountain Trail #1340 joins with the Jolly Mountain Trail #1307.

8.3 Riding the ridge-top, arrive at the junction of the West Fork Trail #1353 and the Jolly Mountain Trail #1307 (one mile ahead). Take the West Fork trail.

8.5 Descend into a meadow. The sign posted on a huge fir tree indicates you are still on the West Fork Teanaway Trail #1353. Spring Creek Road is 10 miles back from this point.

10.4 The trail crosses the West Fork of the Teanaway. You may get your feet wet.

10.8 Cross a tributary of the river. Meander through the brush.

11.5 Cross another feeder creek of the river.

11.9 Cross the West Fork again and get your feet wet.

12.3 Hanging at the creek side, you'll cross again to the east side of the river. Cross another tributary.

12.5 Cross the river, yet again, to the west side.

12.9 Steep climbing on the west side of the river now. Keep going.

13.1 Cross another tributary. Keep going.

14.0 Cross another creek draining into West Creek.

14.5 Cross the West Fork and a rocky chasm.

14.9 Promontory viewpoint overlooking the waterfall on the West Fork.

15.2 Cross over to the West Fork's west side.

16.8 Cross the West Fork of the Teanaway River for the last time!

18.1 Cross over the creek but stay on the left bank.

18.6 Reach the end of the West Fork of Teanaway Trail. Turn right on FR 4305.

18.9 Continue on FR 4305 to a small clearing on your right. Cross the clearing and drop down to a dry wash and another creek. Continue up the road directly across, which may be blocked. If so, just go around the berm. Head up the road for about a half-mile.

19.6 Pass a spur road on your left. Continue up the main road. Pass several spurs, keeping to the main road.

23.5 Reach the main paved road. At this point, you can meet your shuttle, or ride the road back to the parking lot on Forest Road 4315.

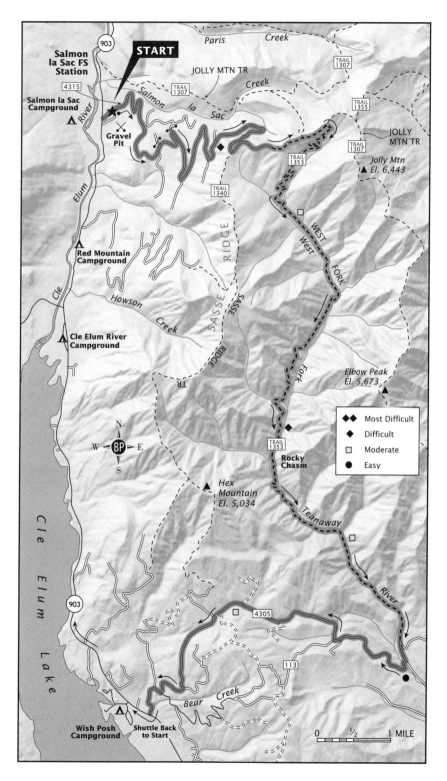

START

Salmon
la Sac FS
Station

903

4315

Salmon la Sac
Campground

JOLLY MTN TR

TRAIL
1307

Paris Creek

TRAIL
1307

Creek

TRAIL
1355

JOLLY
MTN TR

TRAIL
1307

Jolly Mtn
El. 6,443

Gravel
Pit

Salmon   la   Sac

TRAIL
1353

TRAIL
1340

WEST   FORK

West   Fork

Elum   River

Red Mountain
Campground

Cle

Howson   Creek

Cle Elum River
Campground

SASSE   RIDGE

SASSE   RIDGE   TR

Elbow Peak
El. 5,673

◆◆ Most Difficult

◆ Difficult

☐ Moderate

● Easy

TRAIL
1353

Rocky
Chasm

N
W ←BP→ E
S

Hex
Mountain
El. 5,034

Teanaway

☐

Cle   Elum   Lake

903

River

●

4305 ☐

113

Bear   Creek

Wish Posh
Campground

Shuttle Back
to Start

0   ½   1 MILE

Honorable Mentions

Northwest Washington

Compiled here is an index of great rides in the Northwest region that didn't make the A-list this time around but deserve recognition. Check them out and let us know what you think. You may decide that one or more of these rides deserves higher status in future editions or, perhaps, you may have a ride of your own that merits some attention.

(A) Lake Padden Park

Located near Bellingham and loaded with trails, this area offers rides for all skill levels. Warm up on the easy lake loop, following a wide gravel path for close to four miles. Or, increase the workout by heading up the trails into the hills, passing power lines along the marked trails. For an example of an especially challenging route, travel about one mile down the singletrack from the trailhead. Turn right at the intersection to follow a series of steep, banking switchbacks that are sure to test your technical skills. Always within a few miles of the parking lot, it's difficult to get lost.

Take I-5 to Bellingham. Exit at N. Lake Samish Road. Turn right on Samish Way, heading north away from Samish Lake. Travel for two and a half miles to the east entrance of Lake Padden Park. Turn left into the park. Follow the road to the end to the trailhead. For more information, there is a large, outdoor park map, or contact Bellingham Parks and Recreation at (360) 676-6985. See *DeLorme's Washington Atlas & Gazetteer: Page 109, C5.*

(B) Bellingham's Interurban Trail

An easy, seven-mile trail, the Interurban is a refurbished railroad grade that travels from the waterfront of Bellingham to the beaches at Larrabee State Park. This popular course is open to skaters, walkers, and joggers. In town, you can pick up the trail at Fairhaven Park, or farther east at Arroyo Park. Follow the trail, running parallel to Chuckanut Drive, on mostly level pathways all the way to Larrabee State Park, then turn around and head back.

Take I-5 north to State Route 11 north into Bellingham. Turn right into Fairhaven Park. Call the Larrabee State Park at (360) 676-2093. See *DeLorme's Washington Atlas & Gazetteer: Page 109, C5.*

(C) Cranberry Lake in Anacortes

2,200 acres of community forest land surround Cranberry Lake (funded by local Anacortes tax payers), offering a great spot to stretch your legs while you wait for the ferry during the San Juan Islands' summer rush. Be aware that some trails prohibit bikes, so please heed the signs. Several moderate to advanced trails create loops ranging in length from a couple of miles to 20. The connecting trails are perfect for improvising your own route. From the Anacortes-Sidney, B.C. ferry terminal, ride a couple of miles up Oak Street (which turns into 12th). Turn right at Georgia Avenue and right onto West 4th Street. Follow that up to Cranberry Lake. For more information, contact Bob Vaux, Operations and Forest Lands Manager of Anacortes Parks and Recreation (360) 299-1953. Maps and info packets are available at many local businesses on Main Street, including Anacortes Cyclery and the Anacortes Chamber of Commerce Visitor Center. See *DeLorme's Washington Atlas & Gazetteer: Page 94, A3.*

(D) Sadie Creek

This area has two loop options, one that's moderate and another that's a little more difficult. After driving out past Port Angeles, time may dictate which loop you take. The longer, more difficult loop is about 18 miles long. Start at the parking area and take the trail heading into the forest. Turn right down to Sadie Creek, crossing the creek at the bottom. Turn right on the old road for a half-mile, then pick up the trail again on the left. Turn right at Forest Road 3040 where the trail ends and then turn left on Forest Road S1150 toward the Sadie Creek Trail, following the signs. Veer right with the path and begin the climb. Keep right at the "Y" intersection, riding up steep, rocky doubletrack. Come upon harrowing switchbacks and veer right again at the next "Y" in the road. Arriving at the ridge after only four miles, the trail continues along the ridge over at least a dozen summits. After another four miles, veer right at the "Y" intersection and begin to descend, finally. Turn left of Forest Road PA 100. Turn right on Forest Road 1450. After a mile, turn left following a trail down the valley into the woods. Turn left on the old road. At the end, turn left up the logging road. At the "Y" intersection, stay straight, following the old road. Turn left on the steep course descending to Susie Creek. Cross the logging road and follow the power lines. Turn left at the top, pass a spur and head down, staying right at the intersection. Continue on Forest Road PA 1000 and ride ahead, crossing Forest Road 3040 and onto the trail into the woods. Veer right to the parking lot and the end of the ride.

To ride the shorter, more moderate, 11-mile loop, begin at the same trail from the parking area. Cross Forest Road 3040 on Forest Road PA 1000. Stay left at the "Y" in the road and again at the spur. Climbing, veer left again where the road divides. Turn right onto the old road. Stay straight, cross Susie Creek, and ride up the valley. Turn right where the road ends, then right again back to the old road. Catch the trail on the right climbing just ahead. Turn right when the path ends, continuing up the logging road. Turn right back onto Forest Road PA 1000. After about two miles, the road divides. Follow the left fork, even though it looks much less traveled. Two miles ahead, turn left at the intersection, cross Forest Road 3040 and follow the trail back to the parking area.

From Port Angeles, head west on U.S. 101 then west on State Route 112 to Forest Road 3040. For more information, contact the Department of Natural Resources in Forks at (360) 374-6131 or 1-800-527-3305. See *DeLorme's Washington Atlas & Gazetteer: Page 92, D2.*

(E) Tahuya River Ride

Lots of racing goes on in Tahuya State Forest. Miles of trail await the beginner, intermediate, and advanced mountain biker. For a 10 to 12-mile moderate loop, take the Tahuya River Trail north from the campground to Twin Lakes Road and turn left. Quickly join the Howell Lake Trail on the left. Follow this rolling route all the way to the Howell Lake Loop,

crossing both Bennettsen Lake Road and Belfair-Tahuya Road. Ride out to Howell Lake and continue until reaching Belfair-Tahuya Road again. Turn right on the road briefly and catch the Tahuya River Trail again, descending for about two miles back to the campground.

From Bremerton take State Route 304 to State Route 3. Follow to State Route 300 at Belfair keeping to the north side of Hood Canal. Turn right on Sand Hill Road and left onto Goat Ranch Road. Continue to Tahuya River Road and park at the campground. For detailed maps, call the Department of Natural Resources at (360) 825-1631 or 1-800-527-3305. See *DeLorme's Washington Atlas & Gazetteer: Page 78, D1&2.*

(F) Tolt Pipeline Trail

One of the few in-city rides, the Tolt Pipeline Trail actually follows the Seattle waterline along a service road before branching off into a rather brief section of singletrack. About 14 miles round-trip, this is easily considered a moderate ride. From the parking lot, follow the Sammamish River Trail to the right, then turn right again onto the Tolt Pipeline Trail. Follow this over a couple of roads to the end. Turn right onto the singletrack. The course crosses a few more roads and a couple of streams before ending at an overlook of the Snoqualmie River, at which point, simply turn around and head back.

From Kirkland take I-405 to Monroe/Bothell, exiting onto State Route 522. Take the Woodinville exit for State Route 202. Turn right onto 131st Avenue NE and again at 175th. Turn left onto State Route 202, see the Sammamish River Park on the left. For more information, contact King County Parks and Recreation at (206) 296-4136. See *DeLorme's Washington Atlas & Gazetteer: Page 79, B&C7.*

(G) Mad Lake

Bring plenty of water on your trek to Mad Lake. The 20-plus miles of advanced trails are usually hot and dusty and only open during the summer months. The ride begins by climbing up Chikamin Ridge on Trail #1561. Turn right at the "T" intersection onto Trail #1409.1. Ride past Marble Meadow, eventually reaching Mad Lake via a short trail to the right at the top of Mad Meadow. From there, turn around and head back, or wander off on your own adventure to Klone Peak, or loop around to Two Little Lakes.

From Lake Wenatchee, take State Route 207 north to Chiwawa Loop Road. Veer right after the Wenatchee River. Turn left onto Chiwawa Road and cross the Chiwawa River. Turn left onto Road 62. Follow that for about 10 miles to Road 6210. Turn right onto 6210, and park about eight miles up at the trail intersection. For more information contact the Lake Wenatchee Ranger District in Leavenworth at (509) 763-3103. See *DeLorme's Washington Atlas & Gazetteer: Page 82, A3.*

(H) The Summit at Snoqualmie/Ski Acres Trails

This steep, rocky area is convenient to Seattle (only about an hour away), and the Ski Acres cross-country trails are great for mountain biking. There are many loop options, but the route around Mount Catherine is particularly good, encompassing beginner, intermediate, and advanced trails. Take the easy way up on the chair lift and turn left on Trail #1A, following it to Trail #15. The routes to the left (#14 and #16) are easy to intermediate; the trails to the right (#15 and #6) are advanced. All circle around the mountain and connects with intermediate trail #17, so take your pick and have a blast.

From Seattle, take I-90 east to any one of the exits to The Summit. Continue on the summit road a mile or so to Ski Acres on the right. For more information, call The Summit at Snoqualmie at (425) 434-7669, ext. 3372. See *DeLorme's Washington Atlas & Gazetteer: Page 65, A5.*

Ⓘ Money Creek Road #6420

Washington has thousands of logging roads, both abandoned and in-use, which make great rides in and of themselves, or they lead to incredible singletrack. This is one such area. From the Money Creek Campground, ride up Forest Road 6420 (Money Creek Road) to Lake Elizabeth.

From U.S. Route 2 in Skykomish, head west to the Money Creek Campground. For more information, call the Skykomish Ranger District at (360) 677-2414. See *DeLorme's Washington Atlas & Gazetteer: Page 81, C5.*

Ⓙ Mill Creek Valley

The Stevens Pass Nordic Center is a great area to ride and explore. From the Nordic Center you'll find the Walker Trail and many roads used for skiing in the winter that are smooth and fast for mountain biking.

From U.S. Route 2, head to Stevens Pass. Just to the east of the pass is the Nordic Center, on the south side of the highway. For more information, call the Stevens Pass Nordic Center (360) 973-2441. See *DeLorme's Washington Atlas & Gazetteer: Page 81, B&C8.*

Southwest Washington

Honorable Mentions

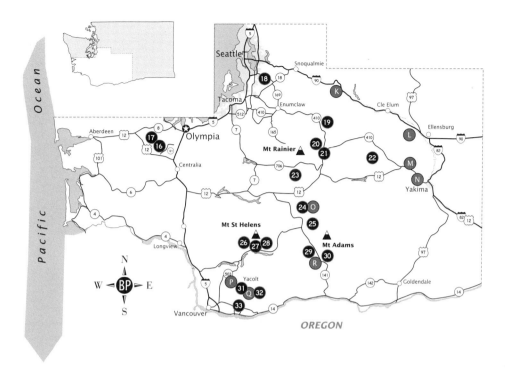

From Tacoma to the Columbia River and as far east as Yakima, the southwest corner of Washington state is a geologic playground and home to our own local chunk of mountain biking heaven. Three mighty volcanoes reside south of I-90: Mount Rainier, Mount St. Helens, and Mount Adams. In between them all, there are hundreds of miles of trails, years upon years of history, and Native American legends to explore.

Mighty and tall, Rainier will always be a point of reference and reverence. Magically evoking deep emotional pangs in the heart of every human who sees it, Mt. Rainier remains, to locals and to tourists, the most majestic landmark in western Washington. The national park that surrounds Mt. Rainier is off-limits to mountain biking, but around its periphery outside the park's boundaries, lie trails galore all giving incredible views of this glacier-covered behemoth.

Mount St. Helens, the hyper-active little sister of Rainier and Adams, awoke from her deep centuries-long slumber with a mighty eruption on May 18, 1980. Never before has the word make-over been used to such an extreme. Almost 20 years later, life has returned to this place, and Mount St. Helens is now officially a National Volcanic Monument. New trails have been built around all sides of this mountain enabling visitors to witness history in the making as the environment recovers.

Mount Adams, the loner, 50 miles east of St. Helens, is the second tallest mountain within the Washington Cascade chain. Virtually undiscovered when compared to its "sibling" volcanoes, Adams keeps to himself, a sentry keeping watch over southern Washington. The trails around this mountain are marvelously fun for mountain biking, and the weather is more dependable—more sunshine and less rain—than found farther north. Holding neither national park nor monument titles, Adams is pristine, remote, and the perfect place to "get away."

Mount St Helens

For years it was said that Mount St. Helens had no rival in the Cascade range when it came to beauty—just as mythology's Helen had had no rival in all of Greece. Ranked a modest fifth in height among Washington's landmark peaks, the volcano derived its allure not from age or size or vertical achievement but from its flawless symmetry and its graceful, glacier-trimmed slopes. It was proudly dubbed the Mount Fuji of America. And then one day, rather unexpectedly, the sleeping beauty began to rumble. Geologists rightly feared that the volcano was about to blow and set to warning the surrounding communities. The gravity of the geologists' concern could not have been imagined by Washingtonians, since no living soul had ever witnessed a Cascade eruption. For two months the mountain was rocked with nearly 10,000 localized earthquakes and hundreds of steam explosions. The pressure had swollen the north flank by more than 270 feet. On the morning of May 18, 1980 (8:32 a.m.), the once serene volcano awoke to a magnitude 5.1 earthquake. The swollen north flanks immediately collapsed, in mass, amounting to the largest recorded landslide in history. Within seconds the mountain blew. The eruption lasted, without pause, for 9 hours. But it was the initial lateral blast, which lasted only the first few minutes, that cause the most destruction. Steam and rock debris shot from the mountain at 670 miles per hour, leveling 150 square miles of forest and killing virtually everything in its path—a number of pocket gopher actually survived the blast. All told, the mountain shed 1,312 feet off its crown, killed 57 people and countless animals, destroyed 96,000 acres of timber (a good deal of it old-growth), and deposited 490 tons of ash on 22,000 square miles of land.

Pla

Ape Canyon

Lava Dome

Sasquatch Steps

braham

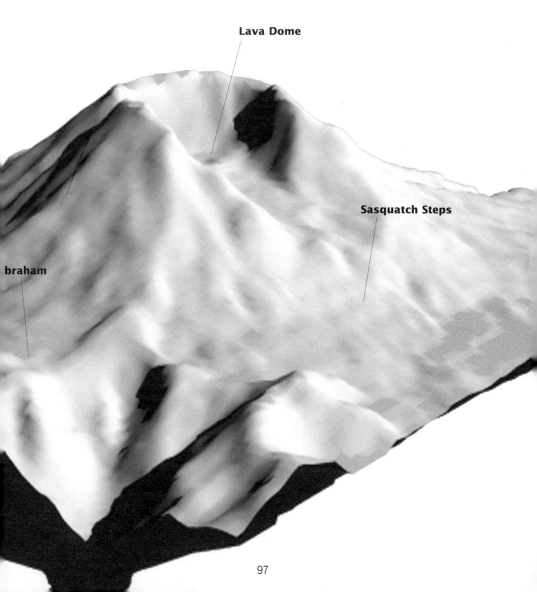

97

Capitol Forest— Lost Valley Loop

Ride Summary

This trail is especially nice for riders moving into the intermediate mountain biking skill level. Rolling along Capitol Forests' hillsides, this loop is fast, fun, and non-technical. With a variety of side trails to explore, you can tailor the mileage of this ride to suit any time or fitness constraints.

Ride Specs

Start: Mima Falls Trailhead
Length: 21.2 miles
Approximate Riding Time: 3.5–4.5 hours
Nearest town: Tumwater
Rating: Easy to moderate
Terrain: Singletrack, logging roads
Other Trail Users: Hikers and horseback riders. No motor vehicles

Getting There

From I-5 in Olympia: Take Exit 95 onto State Route 121 west to Littlerock. Follow to the "T" intersection of Waddell Creek Road (to the right) and Mima Road (to the left). Turn left on Mima Road. Turn right on Bordeaux Road, then right again onto Marksman Road. Continue to the Mima Falls Trailhead and Campground.

Capitol State Forest assumes some 90,000 acres of the Black Hills of western Washington. Micro-fossils found at the top of Capitol Peak (2,658 ft.) remind us that the better part of Washington State spent some time under the waters of the Pacific Ocean. It's taken about 50 million years, through numerous fluctuations in the water level, for these "hills" to reach the heights to which they stand today. And so it's funny to think that these once water-soaked Black Hills got their name when the region's first settlers found the area blackened by forest fires. Where's water when you need it?

Scattered throughout the southwest side of the Black Hills, where the hills turn to prairie, are the mysterious Mima Mounds—"mysterious" because no one can say with any surety how they got there. Some suspect that they are Indian burial mounds (though excavations have only revealed gravely soil). And in equal measure, there are those who insist that these mysterious earthen piles were left by prehistoric gophers (apparently the size of a Buick). Less radical theorists assume that they are gravel-filled deposits from the last glacial melt. Though the glacier theory seems perfectly reasonable, the mounds occur in areas that were never glaciated. At any rate, these mounds have excited enough interest to earn designation as a Natural Area Preserve. The mounds range from five to 10 feet tall and 15 to 25 feet in diameter and spread out across several hundred acres of the Black Hills. The best time to visit is from April through June when the wildflowers are in full bloom. Self-guided tours are available.

Cedar Creek.

Capitol Forest is a working forest. Logging has been active here for a number of years, and continues even today. A good number of the trails, rivers, and creeks within the forest are named for historical figures who worked in the logging industry during the late 1800s and early 1900s. Porter Creek and the Porter Creek trails are named for a man who ferried commuters across the Chehalis River. There was also a small logging community called Porter, as well, complete with its own mill. Up Bordeaux Road, just past the entrance to the Lost Valley Loop ride, is where the French born Bordeaux brothers (Joe, Tom, and Leo) started their family logging business in 1890. Incorporated under the name Mason County Logging Company, the Bordeaux brothers remained in the business for 40 years.

The town of Bordeaux was situated just below the junction of the Big Mima and Little Mima Creeks. The Bordeaux family was well known and respected among their peers in the industry, and their sons, reared into the business, took over when their fathers retired. In the early 1920s, the family business grew steadily until logging in general hit hard times. By the 1940s, the forests were stripped of all the old-growth trees, and forest fires began to rage, devastating the Black Hills. Bordeaux, once a prosperous logging town, quickly became a ghost town. The Bordeaux entrance of Capitol Forest still has a few reminders of the logging heyday of the early 1900s. The old concrete vaults mark the site of the Mason County Logging Company store where the Bordeaux's payroll was kept. The original Bordeaux home still stands nearby but is privately owned.

View of Mount Rainier from Mima Mounds area.

This is a great loop for the beginner to intermediate mountain biker. There's only a moderate amount of climbing, and the trails are in good shape. The singletrack begins as a smooth, wide trail, shared only with hikers and horseback riders. There are a few rooty sections, but on the whole, this is a well-maintained, fun ride. There are several optional loops, too. Contact the Department of Natural Resources (DNR) for a free copy of the latest Capitol Forest recreation map.

MilesDirections

0.0 START from the Mima Falls Trailhead, up Mima Porter Trail #8.

0.4 The trail turns into doubletrack and intersects with Greenline #6. Sign reads: "Capital Peak 14.1 miles; Porter Creek Camp 23.5 miles; Wedekind 18.2 miles." Continue left on the Mima Porter Trail #8 toward Mima Falls.

0.5 Keep straight on Mima Porter #8. The Greenline #6 is accessed off to the right.

0.7 Reach the intersection for Mima Falls 1.7 miles ahead.

2.1 Arrive at the intersection of Trail #10 and Mima Falls, 0.5 miles ahead. Stay on Trail #8.

2.4 Reach Mima Falls—check out the view!

3.0 Cross Road D-6000, the trail begins on the other side.

3.5 Cross Road D-6700 going down to Mima Creek.

4.4 Cross Mima Creek on a wooden bridge.

4.8 Come to the intersection of Road D-5000, climbing up out of Mima Creek.

5.9 You're almost at the top; check out the valley views.

6.3 Cross the road continuing on Mima Trail #8.

6.8 Cross Road D-4000.

7.1 Arrive at West Mima Road. (See the sign for D-4000.) The trail is at the top of the "T" intersection. Keep straight on the Mima Porter Trail #8.

7.7 Turn left at the intersection of Lost Valley Trail #20 at the "T," staying left on Mima Porter Trail #8.

10.1 Arrive at the intersection of Mima Porter Trail #8. Turn right. Right goes to D3000.

12.9 Cross a creek and start heading up #6. #8 heads north over D-3000. Continue east on #6, crossing Road D-4300.

15.5 Reach the intersection with Trail #20. Stay on Green Line Trail #6. Turning right leads back to the trail you came out on.

15.8 Reach an intersection with Roads D-4200 and D-4000. Stay east on the Green Line Trail #6, passing a sign about no motorized vehicles. Bikes are OK.

16.3 The trail hits Road D-4200 again and continues on the other side.

16.8 Cross Road D-4200 to a great downhill. See a great view of Mount Rainier.

17.0 Cross the road again.

17.1 The trail jumps onto the road again. Stay left.

19.2 Come to the junction of Trail #6 and #10. Stay on Green Line #6.

19.7 Come to the intersection with Trail #6A; McKinney Camp is to the left one mile on #6A; Mima Trail is ahead 2 miles. Stay on Green Line #6.

20.1 The trail crosses D-6000.

20.3 Again, the trail crosses D-6000. Arrive at the intersection of the Waddell Loop Trail and Green Line #6. Follow Green Line #6 to the right, toward the Mima Falls Campground.

20.8 At the next intersection, a trail comes in from behind to the left and joins up with Trail #6. Continue straight.

21.1 The trail crosses a small road section. Continue on the trail across the road to another road crossing cut during recent logging. Just ignore it.

21.2 Come to the intersection of Green Line #6 and Mima Porter #8 and the trail back into the campground parking area.

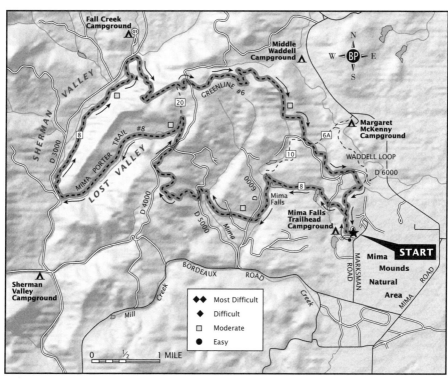

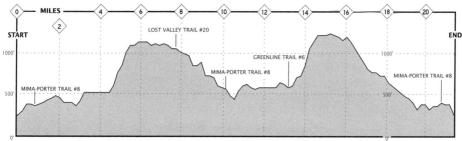

Ride Information

Trail Maintenance Hotlines:
Department of Natural Resources:
(360) 748-2383 or 1-800-527-3305

Local Information:
- Tumwater Chamber of Commerce
  (360) 357-5153
- Olympia/Thurston County Chamber of Commerce; (360) 357-3362

Local Events/Attractions:
- Mima Mounds Interpretive Area, near Tumwater, WA
  www.ohwy/wa/m/mimamnap.htm
  (For more, see Ride Information Ch. 17)

Local Bike Shops:
(See Ride Information for Chapter 17)

Maps:
- Maptech CD-ROM: Little Rock, WA
- DeLorme's Washington Gazetteer & Atlas—Page 45 A7&8

Capitol Forest—
Larch Mountain Loop

Ride Summary

The mainstay for mountain biking on the western side of the Cascades, Capitol Forest will always be a popular site for recreation. This ride starts with a hefty forest road climb and moves into rolling single-track at the top. There are many trails out here, so follow the signs and our directions to avoid getting lost.

Ride Specs

Start: Rock Candy Mountain entrance to Capitol Forest

Length: 20.5 miles

Approximate Riding Time: 2-4 hours

Nearest Town: Tumwater

Rating: Moderate

Terrain: Fire roads, singletrack, frequently muddy, moderate ascent with semi-technical descents

Other Trail Users: Motorcyclists, mostly on week-ends

Getting There

From I-5 in Olympia: Take Exit 104 onto U.S. Route 101 north, then pick up State Route 8 west toward Aberdeen. Follow State Route 8 for just over 10 miles. Turn left on Rock Candy Mountain Road (small sign). This road turns into gravel. Turn right at the fork and follow the main gravel road for 0.1 mile to the parking lot.

Throughout the year riders flock to Capitol State Forest, all anxious to get away to Nature and the challenging trails of Larch Mountain. And yet, as popular as this area is, especially to Seattlites, you'll rarely come across another rider on the trails—even when the parking lot suggests otherwise. This is chiefly because there are so many trails to explore—which means you'll need a compass and a good map. The trail options may even overwhelm you. Weather is a big fun-factor at Capitol Forest. If it has rained at all in the last 48 hours, you'll more than likely encounter thick, sticky mud. But rain or shine, these wonderful trails provide a great workout.

This ride begins on a logging road with a gradual incline, partially canopied by the forest. The side roads along the way may tempt the curious, but we recommend staying to the main road, for now. At the saddle is a junction of road, hills, and power lines. The signs here will tell you where you are and where you're heading (the Department of Natural Resources is good about keeping you informed). The road takes you to a large clearing resembling a gravel parking lot (it's actually just a large intersection of roads). At the apex you'll see a hillside that seems to be missing a chunk of land. The singletrack trail starts here, across from the parking area, and the loop portion of the Larch Mountain ride begins.

Short climbs and descents, with patches of rooted trail, carry you along as other trails shoot off in a variety of directions, inviting those with a sense of adventure to explore. By the time you're heading down again, you'll hardly realize you've gone 10 miles. Following Capitol Forest's excellent signage, complete the loop and head downhill in the direction of the forest road. If you're up for more, spur off onto more singletrack. It's not all downhill, but you'll still get back pretty quickly.

Capitol Peak in the distance.

Capitol Forest is situated next door to Washington's capital city, Olympia. Home to some 37,000 people, Olympia has a surprisingly small-town appeal, with friendly faces, elegant homes, and tree-lined streets. Settled in 1846 by Edmund Sylvester and Levi Lathrop Smith (and briefly called Smithfield), Olympia had a meteoric rise to fame. In 1853 it was named the capital of the newly formed Washington Territory. But nearly forty years would pass before Olympia could rest comfortably with the title. Seattle, North Yakima, Port Townsend, Centralia, Vancouver, and Ellensburg all vied for the position. A rather presumptuous Ellensburg even went so far as to build a state capital building. It wasn't until 1889, when Washington became the 42nd state, that the case was finally settled. The White House sent a telegraph to Olympia informing them of their official title and welcoming the state into the Union. Rather unceremoniously, however, they sent the wire collect. Olympia couldn't read the message until the charge was paid. Welcome to the U.S., indeed.

The area in and around Olympia was far from uninhabited prior to Smith and Sylvester's claim. Coastal tribes such as the Chinook, Nisqually, and Puyallup had lived in the region for years. Allowing for this, the U.S. government, with its so-called noble intentions, planned to relocate the tribes (in bulk) to the Olympic Peninsula. The treaties of 1854-55 saw to this, giving the Indians the right to fish, hunt, and gather at all of their "traditional" locations in exchange for U.S. ownership.

Many of the tribes chose to fight rather than sign these treaties. The very next year saw such tribes as the Puyallup and Nisqually still battling American volunteers and the U.S. army. In August of 1856, another compromise was drawn. Sadly though, this agreement was not much different from the Medicine Creek Treaty of 1855. It's remarkable, then, if not gratifying, to see so many of these tribes still living along rivers and towns which bear their names.

In a grove of trees by Medicine Creek stands the "Treaty Tree"—the site on the Nisqually Delta where the Medicine Creek Treaty of 1855 was signed. Contained in a no-access area of the Nisqually Wildlife Refuge, you can see this tree from a protected area within the wetlands. Take Exit 114 from I-5 and follow the signs for the refuge. There are five and a half miles of walking trail through the delta that are open during daylight hours year-round. Bikes and dogs are not allowed and there is a $2 admission fee per family.

Ride Information

Trail Maintenance Hotlines:
Department of Natural Resources:
(360) 748-2383 or 1-800-527-3305

Schedule:
Trails closed to ORVs and horses from
November 1 to March 31

Local Information:
Tumwater Chamber of Commerce
(360) 357-5153
Olympia/Thurston County Chamber of
Commerce; (360) 357-3362

Local Events/Attractions:
• Coffee Fest and Swap Meet in March,
Olympia, WA; (360) 753-8380
• Art Walk in April, Olympia, WA
(360) 753-8380
• Swede Day in June, Rochester, WA
(360) 786-5595
• Lake Fair in July, Olympia, WA
(360) 943-7344
• Capital Lakefair in mid-July, Olympia,
WA; (360) 943-7344
• Harbor Days in August, Olympia, WA
(360) 352-4557

• Music in the Park, Saturdays in August,
Rochester, WA; (360) 786-5595
• Washington State Capitol Museum,
Olympia, WA; (360) 753-2580
• Longhouse/Evergreen State College
Campus, Olympia, WA
(360) 866-6000

Local Bike Shops:
• Deschutes River Cyclery, Tumwater, WA
(360) 352-4240
• Bike Stand, Olympia, WA
(360) 943-1997
• Bike Tech, Olympia, WA; (360) 754-2453
• Cobb Works, Olympia, WA
(360) 352-7168
• Falcon Schwinn, Olympia, WA
(360) 943-2091
• Sports Warehouse, Lacy, WA
(360) 491-1346

Maps:
• Maptech CD-ROM: Little Rock, WA;
Capitol Peak, WA
• Washington Gazetteer & Atlas:
Page 45 A7&8

MilesDirections

0.0 START from the Rock Candy entrance, heading up B-Line Road west.

0.2 Follow B-Line past B-8000.

0.7 B-8000 forks left. Stay on B-Line.

1.5 Pass the North Rim #1 Trail crossing.

2.3 Pass a road to the left. Follow the main road.

2.5 Reach Porter Pass, intersecting with B-5000. Stay on B-Line through the saddle. See the North Rim Trail. Ride through the saddle and turn left on B-1000—toward Capitol Peak.

3.1 Turn left on C-4000. B-1000 follows to the right.

5.0 Stay left following C-4000 at the "T."

5.9 Come to an intersection of C-4700 (Army Road). Stay right on C-4000.

6.9 Pass a gravel pit on the left.

7.0 Begin the Larch Mountain Loop. Look for the trail to the left of C-4000 that runs straight through this intersection. The trail goes down into the woods and the loop will take you to the east side of Larch Mountain and back on the west to this very same point. Follow the trail a little ways to the sign reading "Mount Molly Porter #3 for Bordeaux Camp and Mount Molly Camp." At the first intersection, follow Mount Molly Trail #4. Take the right fork. (The left fork is Trail #20, which you'll take back to Rock Candy).

7.3 The trail hits C-4000 briefly. Follow the trail.

8.9 At the Intersection, Trail #40 head south to Bordeaux. Follow the right-hand trail, #30, up toward Capitol Peak.

9.3 Arrive at C-4000—stay on the trail.

9.9 Take Road C-4400 briefly to the rock pile at the main intersection. C-4400 continues left. Turn right up the hill. One hundred yards ahead is a sign for Trail #30. Follow Trail #30.

11.4 Cross a logging road. Keep to the trail.

11.9 Follow Trail #30 straight. The other trail (#3) goes west to Porter Creek Camp.

15.0 Turn left at the junction. The trail straight ahead leads to C-4000. The left trail follows C-5000.

15.3 The Larch Mountain Loop comes back to join C-4000 and C-5000. This is where the singletrack began earlier. Head back down the trail turning left instead of right. Follow the signs for Trail #20 down the east side of Rock Candy Mountain. One hundred feet into the trail the left leads to Trail #40 and then to Trail #20.

15.6 Turn left on Trail #20 at the intersection.

17.1 After crossing C-4700, the trail continues across the road about 20 feet away.

17.9 Cross entrance. Continue down toward Rock Candy.

19.0 See the North Rim #1 Trail. Stay left, keeping the road on your left. Access the trail about 100 feet down the road.

19.3 Come to an intersection. Stay right on the narrower trail.

19.4 Cross a small creek.

19.5 Hit a slight junction. Keep to the main trail on the right.

19.8 Cross B-8000, but stay on the trail heading down.

20.4 Cross B-8000 again, staying to the trail.

20.5 Hang a left and head toward the parking lot.

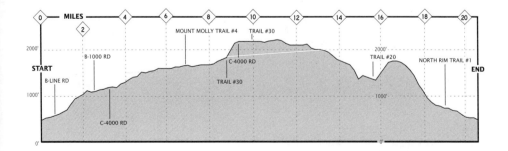

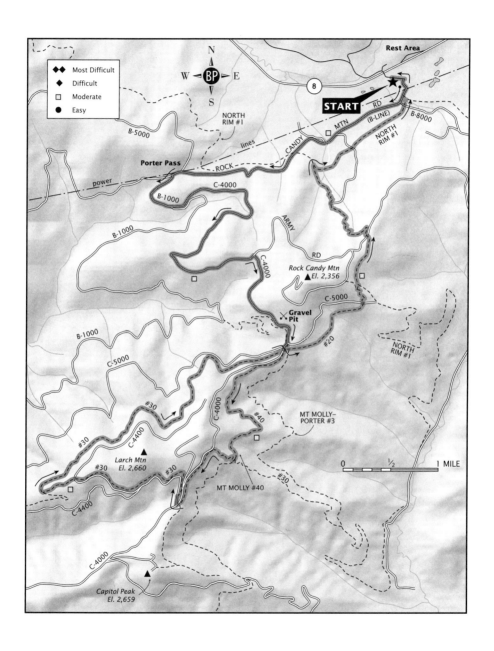

18

Tiger Mountain

Ride Summary

One of the few neighborhood trails in the Seattle area still open to mountain bikers, this mountain is very popular and has a lot to offer. The forest roads lead up to the singletrack. In turn, the singletrack leads to the woods, over technical trails darkened by the thick canopy of trees overhead. The singletrack at Tiger Mountain is a great training ground for those learning how to ride wet terrain, through muddy bogs, and over rocks and roots.

Ride Specs

Start: Tiger Mountain parking lot
Length: 11.5 miles Preston/NW Loop; 4 miles for the Short Loop
Approximate Riding Time: 2 hours for Preston/NW loop; 0.5 to 1 hour for the Short Loop
Nearest Town: Issaquah
Rating: Preston/NW Loop, Moderate; short loop, Easy
Terrain: Logging roads and singletrack
Other Trail Users: Hikers and horseback riders

Getting There

From Seattle: Take I-5 to I-90 east. Take Exit 25 onto State Route 18 west toward Auburn and Tacoma. Travel 4.5 miles to the summit and turn right into the parking lot of Tiger Mountain State Forest.

A common trail hazard.

So you've come to Seattle to check out the sights and go for a couple of radical mountain bike rides. You'll need a little elevation training, right? Just pack up the car and head east on I-90; Tiger Mountain is waiting to kick your unsuspecting butt. Part of what are known as the "Issaquah Alps"—a range that's even older than the Cascades—the Tiger Mountain area is one of Washington's most popular hiking and mountain biking destinations (if not *the* most popular). Greenbelt areas connect it to nearby parks, creating a seemingly endless system of trails—explaining how the town of Issaquah came to be called the "Trailhead City."

This particular trail is great because it's challenging and not too long. You can ride these trails in any direction depending on the workout you want to achieve. Most trails can be individually covered in a couple of hours—locals use them for after-work night rides. During rainier times, it's likely to be muddy and slick. The occasional mud-bogs can be very deep and some instances do require a bit of hike-a-biking.

Most of the trails, like this one, start out with a road climb on fire roads no longer open to vehicles. The roads can be rather steep. On the way up, you'll pass a couple of trails, which you should definitely explore if you've got the time. After about three miles of climbing, you'll reach the Preston Railroad Trail. It's a bit dark and ominous when the sun is hidden, but you'll be having too good of a time to be bothered by it. The trail is well worn, so there are many exposed roots to catch you if you aren't paying attention. No matter what time of year, there always seems to be standing water somewhere along the way. Just beware, you never really know how deep some of those holes are.

On the southeast side, you'll catch the Northwest Timber Trail, which is comfortably smooth. It takes you into a ravine-like section with a couple of fun surprises. Watch out for

hikers, in particular, along this trail. Since it's in such good condition, it seems to be a favorite of hikers. There are horses to contend with as well, so be courteous. Some of these horses are unfamiliar with mountain bikes and can become skittish. Always dismount and stand between the horse and your bike as you pass.

This is one of the few remaining trails still open to mountain bikers in the Seattle area. The Backcountry Bicycle Trails Club (BBTC) has been fighting for some time to keep the Tiger Mountain trails open to mountain bikers. Thus far, they've been successful, but biking in this area always seems to hang in the balance. The BBTC and the Sierra Club will have the most current information about which trails in the area are open, closed, or under construction.

Except for the road climb up, the trails are protected by thick forest. It gets dark rather quickly at the end of the day. Make sure you are prepared for bad weather—around here you just never know when it will hit. This area is known as a convergence zone, where low pressure zones from Alaska and Canada, which rise counter-clockwise, converge with high-pressure zones from the mid-Pacific, which fall clockwise. As the two come together over the region in and around Seattle, they produce cloudy conditions and…you guessed it…rain!

Don't let a little rain get you down though. There's plenty of Gore-Tex to go around. And after your ride, you can always go for a little of Seattle's liquid sunshine. Depending on your taste, you could go for a coffee or a beer or some juice—Seattle aims to please. There are plenty of juicebars and great coffeehouses in virtually every neighborhood—this is the home of the Starbucks Revolution, after all. And there are just as many local brewpubs and breweries, many of which offer daily tours. You might try the Redhook Ale Brewery (where they've redefined the term "micro"), the Rainier Brewery, or the Pyramid Ale House—just to name a few.

If you're into festivals, Seattle is the place to be, especially in the summertime. It seems like just about every weekend in the summer there's a festival or fair going on somewhere, and many have become very popular annual events.

Between mid-May and early June, you'll want to catch the Seattle International Film Festival, featuring high art, slapstick, and shorts. Also in May is the University District Street Fair, offering crafts, live music, art, and food. The Northwest Folklife Festival is the highlight of the month. Held during Memorial Day weekend, this festival features music, dance, and traditional arts. Clearly Seattle's biggest fair, the three-week long Seafair hosts dozens of events held all over the city, from an opening fun-run and parade to boat races and an air show featuring the Blue Angels. Along the waterfront, Navy ships are usually docked and opened for tours. If you really want to get a taste for Seattle (quite literally), try the Bite of Seattle in mid-July where local restaurants, microbreweries, wineries, and coffee shops show off their talents. And for the summer finale, there's Bumbershoot, a two-day arts extravaganza held over Labor Day weekend, featuring live musical, dance, and theater performances, as well as countless other activities to keep you entertained all day long.

Ride Information

Trail Maintenance Hotlines:
Department of Natural Resources:
(360) 825-1631 or 1-800-527-3305
Backcountry Bicycle Trails Club (BBTC):
(206) 283-2995 or bbtc@cycling.org
www.dirtnw.com/bbtc/bbtc.html

Schedule:
Open April 15 through October 15—
closed in winter

Local Information:
Seattle/King County Convention and
Visitors Bureau: (206) 461-5840
Issaquah Visitor Information Center:
(425) 392-7024

Local Events/Attractions:
• Seattle International Film Festival in
mid-May to early June, Seattle, WA
(206) 324-9996
• University District Street Fair in May,
Seattle, WA; (206) 547-4417

• Northwest Folklife Festival, over
Memorial Day weekend, Seattle, WA
(206) 684-7300
• Bite of Seattle in mid-July, Seattle,
WA; (206) 684-7200
• Seafair from mid-July to mid-August,
Seattle, WA; (206) 728-0123
• Bumbershoot, over Labor Day week-
end, Seattle, WA; (206) 684-7200

Local Bike Shops:
The Bicycle Center of Issaquah,
Issaquah, WA; (425) 392-4588

Maps:
• Maptech CD-ROM: Hobart, WA;
Fall City, WA
• DeLorme's Washington Atlas &
Gazetteer—Page 64 A1

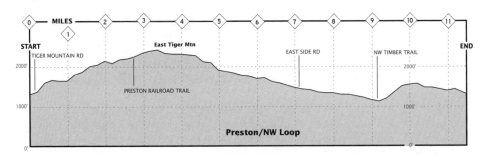

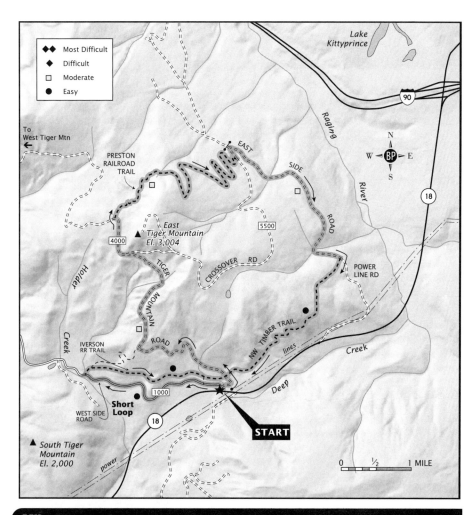

MilesDirections

Preston/NW Loop (Moderate)

0.0 START from parking lot and take the Tiger Mountain Road on the far right.

2.8 At the "T" intersection, turn left onto Road 4000, toward West Tiger Summit. Sign reads: "East Tiger Summit 1.4 miles to the right."

3.2 Turn right onto the Preston Railroad Trail.

4.7 Switchback left. There are old trails dying in the woods. Keep to the main trail.

5.2 Switchback right.

5.7 Switchback left.

6.0 Switchback right again.

7.0 Arrive at Road 5500/Crossover Road. Turn left heading downhill.

7.1 Turn right at the "T" intersection onto Eastside Road.

9.1 Arrive at the NW Timber Trail, turn right at the fence.

11.5 Reach the bottom of NW Trail at the Tiger Mountain Road. Turn left for the parking lot.

Short Loop (Easy)

0.0 Head up the West Side Road to the left of the gate at the end of the parking lot.

1.5 Turn right on the Iverson Railroad Trail.

3.5 Turn left at the NW Timber Trail to head back to Tiger Mountain Road, or turn right onto West Side Road. At Tiger Mountain Road turn right toward the parking lot.

Ranger Creek

Ride Summary

On a quest for the quintessential mountain bike ride? You just might find what you're searching for at Ranger Creek. Combining every element of the "ideal" ride, this course includes a couple of creek crossings, a long road climb, and technical singletrack with lots of roots, rocks, switchbacks, drop-offs, thread-the-needle gaps, and steep sides. Some trail sections are smooth, while others are a little rough. Stunning scenery, elevation gains, and an incredible descent are just a small selection of what you'll get with the Ranger Creek Ride northeast of Mount Rainier.

Ride Specs

Start: Forest Road 72
Length: 23 miles
Approximate Riding Time: 4-5 hours
Nearest Town: Greenwater
Rating: Difficult due to high elevations and challenging singletrack downhill
Terrain: Forest service road, singletrack, and short paved road section
Other Trail Users: Hikers and horseback riders

Getting There

From Puyallup: Take State Route 167 to State Road 410 East. Follow 410 for 38.2 miles to Forest Road 72. Turn left and go 50 yards. Park on the side of the road at the "Y" intersection. The ride begins to the right up Forest Road 72.

I f you're looking for a long, technically challenging ride, with a good road climb and hair-ball descents, then you'll love Ranger Creek. Roots, rocks, switchbacks, drop-offs, thread-the-needle gaps, steep sides—this trail has it all. While some sections are carpet-smooth, others will rattle the bolts right out of your joints. And as always, you can bank on stunning scenery: an array of Douglas fir, western red cedar, and western hemlock, all intertwined with glacier-fed creeks and rivers and all in the shadow of the magnificent Mount Rainier.

Forest Road 72 takes you up the first three miles of the ride. You'll encounter challengingly steep inclines, with the exception of a small descent traveling south to north along the first ridge. Lightning Creek intersects your path a few times in the first few miles. The road up is fairly smooth, packed with dirt and gravel. The elevation tops out around 5,500 feet. Bring appropriate clothing in case the weather decides to take a turn. Packing an extra shirt is a good idea, too. After crossing Ranger Creek, several rather steep switchbacks will initiate your final descent.

If you take out a state map, you'll notice a lot of land in this region tagged "Wilderness Area." You may not realize it, but mountain bikes are not permitted within these areas. The reason for this is the Wilderness Act of 1964, signed into law by President Lyndon Johnson.

"A wilderness, in contrast with those areas where man and his own works dominate the landscape, is hereby recognized as an area where the earth and its community of life are untrammeled by man, where man himself is a visitor who does not remain..."

(from the Wilderness Act of 1964)

This act spawned a program called the National Wilderness Preservation System. The charge of this system, to a certain degree, is to keep "man" out of prescribed areas, so that the wilderness may remain wild. Forbidden are the building of roads, the logging of trees, and unfortunately, anything mechanized—from mountain bikes to chainsaws.

Washington has 4,287,875 acres of designated wilderness areas—724,700 acres of which are in the Mount Baker-Snoqualmie National Forest. The Norse Peak Wilderness Area—one of eight in the Mount Baker-Snoqualmie National Forest—has 51,300 acres of high ridges, mountain lakes, and forested valleys— and approximately 52 miles of hiking trails. This Wilderness is home, in part, to the famous Pacific Crest Trail which stretches a staggering 2,600 miles from Mexico to Canada—through four of Washington's national forests and two of its national parks. Recreational miners might want to venture into the Norse Peak Wilderness to take a stab at panning for gold (Morse and Crow Creeks are said to be fruitful locations).

With such a definite presence in this area, we would be remiss to not say just a little about the fourth tallest mountain in the lower-48, Mount Rainier. From the start of this ride, you're only five miles, as the crow flies, from the northern edge of the Mount Rainer National Park. By car, it's a little farther. With over 230,000 acres of glacier-filled crevasses, flower-studded prairies, old-growth forests, and cascading waterfalls, Mount Rainier is an adventurer's paradise. Though relatively quiet for the last 2,500 years, Mount Rainier's volcanic core is hardly tame. But scientists say the mountain's greatest threat to man is not its molten core but rather its potential for mudslides. To put a gauge on a mudflow's destructive power: 5,700 years ago, triggered perhaps by an earthquake, Mount Rainier shed an unwanted 2,000 feet off its summit, sending mud and debris racing through the White River Valley to just shy of the Puget Sound, completely inundating what today are the towns of Buckley, Enumclaw, Puyallup, and Kent.

A Word of Caution Concerning Bees...

Whether hiking or mountain biking along wooded trails, avoid disturbing fallen trees. These decaying logs are nurseries for new trees, but more importantly they are home to bee colonies, snakes, and all sorts of varmints. If you come in contact with a hive of bees in particular, the scenario that ensues will most likely not be pretty.

The most obvious thing to do if you've upset a hive of bees is to run like crazy. In some cases you may have to leave your bike behind—as we did once. You'll want to wait at least a half-hour before retrieving it. At a safe distance, examine your sting(s) to make sure there are no bees clinging to your clothing. And above all, remember to relax. Drink some water and collect yourself. Being stung by one bee can be annoying but being stung by a swarm of bees can be downright frightening. Emergency treatment for stings begins with the stinger, which needs to be removed very gently if it is still in the skin. Then, apply a paste of baking soda, a cold, wet cloth, or ice cubes to reduce the pain and swelling—mud works great out in the woods. If you remembered to bring an antihistamine, take it—this will slow down your reaction to the venom.

About one in 10 people are allergic to insect stings. For some, being stung by a bee or another insect can be life-threatening and can cause an anaphylactic reaction. If you're not sure whether or not you're allergic to bees, some of the symptoms may include: a swollen tongue or throat; swelling about the eyes and lips; difficulty breathing; coughing or wheezing; numbness; cramping; hives; slurred speech; anxiety; mental confusion; nausea or vomiting. If anaphylactic symptoms occur, get the victim to a hospital as quickly as possible. You should know before heading into the woods if you are allergic. Consult your physician. He or she might suggest that you carry an emergency epinephrine injection called an Epi-Pen (which costs about $50).

Ride Information

Trail Maintenance Hotlines:
- U.S. Forest Service White River Ranger District, Enumclaw, WA (360) 825-6585
- Department of Natural Resources: (360) 825-1631 or 1-800-527-3305

Schedule:
This trail is open year-round depending on snow levels.

Costs:
There may now be a $3 per car per-day charge. ($25 for an annual pass.)

Local Information:
- Enumclaw Visitor's Center: (360) 825-7666

- Radio AM530, Enumclaw, WA—the latest weather and road conditions, plus mountain area information.
- Mount Rainier National Park Service, Ashford, WA; (360) 569-2211—call for maps and brochures.

Local Events/Attractions:
- King County Fair in July, Enumclaw, WA (360) 825-7666
- Pacific Northwest Highland Games in July, Enumclaw, WA; (360) 825-7666

Maps:
- Maptech CD-ROM: Sun Top, WA
- DeLorme's Washington Gazetteer and Atlas—Page 64 D4

MilesDirections

0.0 START from the "Y" intersection where you parked, heading up Forest Road 72.
1.5 Pass Road 7290.
2.4 Pass an unmarked road on the right. Stay straight, crossing Lightning Creek a couple of times.
3.5 Cross Boundary Creek at 3,750 feet—you've covered about 1,500 feet already.
4.1 Cross around the west end of the ridge, and begin heading southeast.
5.2 Pass spur roads on the right and left. Continue straight on the most traveled road.
5.3 Another spur road is on the right. Keep straight. See the Viewpoint sign ahead of the intersection.
5.5 Pass a viewpoint on the left side of the road, with views of Mount Stuart, The Enchantments, and Mount Pilchuck.
5.6 Pass another unsigned spur on the right.
6.4 Pass a spur from behind on the right. The sign for Forest Road 72 assures that you're on the correct route. Continue climbing.
6.8 Pass another spur from behind on the right. Head downhill a bit around the next drainage.
6.9 Pass another spur.
7.1 Pass signed Spur Road 138.
7.4 Road 72 begins to descend. Take Road 7250 on the right, climbing up.
7.7 Pass spur Road 102 on the right. Stay left on Road 7250 through a road cut.
8.6 At the "Y" intersection, stay to the right continuing on 7250. The left is Spur 110.
9.6 Come to a four-way intersection. Stay straight, gently climbing up Spur Road 210. The right goes down. The left doubles back behind you and ends shortly.
10.2 Forest Road 210 ends at the Dalles Ridge Trail #1173. Climb up the trail into the ridge.
10.7 Look for the sharp right-hand turn for Ranger Creek Trail #1197—it's hard to catch so beware. The Dalles Ridge Trail continues straight ahead. The Ranger Peak viewpoint is 3.0 miles ahead; the White River Trail, 6.0 miles; and SR. 410, 7.0 miles. Hang onto your brakes; there are some quick switchbacks coming up.

11.9 Arrive at Ranger Creek Shelter. The trail is to the left in the back. In the front is the Palisades Trail #1198. Follow Ranger Creek Trail #1197 left behind the cabin, downhill.
14.2 Come to a junction for Ranger Peak viewpoint. Continue down the Ranger Creek Trail.
16.8 At the 3-way intersection, take the hard right, down the White River Trail. Don't go straight unless you want to take SR. 410 back now.
16.9 Come to a new spur down to SR. 410. Continue along the trail paralleling SR. 410 northwest.
17.0 The White River Trail #1197 comes right up on SR. 410. Since they've widened 410, the trail runs right next to the highway. Ride along #1199, toward Camp Shepherd (2.0 miles ahead). The trail basically parallels the highway. Keep the highway on your left.
17.3 Pass a small wooden bridge over a creek. Continue rambling next to SR. 410.
17.6 Cross another creek.
18.2 Come to a junction with the Buck Creek Trail #1169 on the left. To the right is Snoquera Falls Trail #1167. Skookum Flats is across the highway. Continue straight on the White River Trail.
18.5 Reach the junction with the Snoquera Falls Loop (closed to bikes) at a 4-way intersection.
18.6 Cross a bridge and come to a 4-way intersection. Go straight. The left heads to SR. 410, the right goes to the falls.
18.7 Come to another 4-way at Camp Shepherd. Take the soft right, staying right of the camp. If you start climbing too much you're not on the correct trail. Or, you can head left to SR. 410 and ride back.
18.8 - 18.9 Cross three clearing sections.
19.4 Come to another 4-way. Stay straight. The Snoquera Falls Trail is looping into the White River Trail again here.
19.8 Pass Dalles Creek Trail #1169 back from the right. Go straight, following down the side of the drainage. Turn right on Powerline Way, heading to SR. 410.
20.0 Turn right on SR. 410 for a paved, gentle downhill back to FR. 72.
23.0 Turn right on FR. 72.

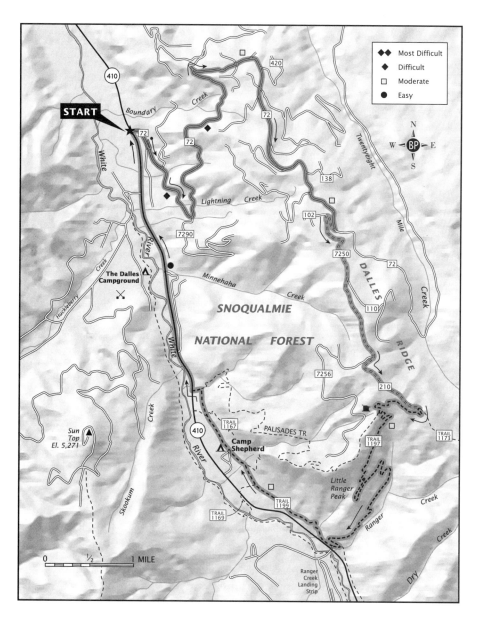

Most Difficult ◆◆
Difficult ◆
Moderate ◻
Easy ●

START

410

Boundary ... Creek

420

72

72

72

138

102

7250

72

110

DALLES

RIDGE

7290

The Dalles
Campground

Huckleberry

White ... River

Creek

Minnehaha ... Creek

SNOQUALMIE

NATIONAL FOREST

7256

210

Sun
Top
El. 5,271

Skookum ... Creek

410

TRAIL
1167

PALISADES TR

Camp
Shepherd

TRAIL
1197

TRAIL
1173

Little
Ranger
Peak

Ranger ... Creek

TRAIL
1169

TRAIL
1199

Dry ... Creek

Ranger
Creek
Landing
Strip

0   ½   1 MILE

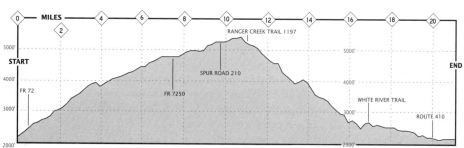

MILES

RANGER CREEK TRAIL 1197

SPUR ROAD 210

START

FR 72

FR 7250

WHITE RIVER TRAIL

END

ROUTE 410

Skookum Flats

Ride Summary

Across the highway from Ranger Creek, this popular trail runs along the riverside in a virtual dance with the drainage that requires a lot of effort in the technical skills department. Rolling along, this trail doesn't gain any elevation, but you will still have to contend with lots of roots and rocks. It's a great ride to build your skills, and if necessary, there are several points at which to leave the trail for higher routes, or to return to the start.

Ride Specs

Start: Skookum Flats Trailhead #1194
Length: 14.9 miles
Approximate Riding Time: 4-5 hours
Nearest Town: Greenwater
Rating: Moderate
Terrain: Singletrack and paved road
Other Trail Users: Hikers and horseback riders

Getting There

From Puyallup: Take State Route 167 to State Route 410 East. Follow 410 for 39.1 miles. Take a right on to Forest Road 73. Go over the bridge and follow 0.4 miles to the parking lot on the right. The Skookum Flats Trail #1194 is on the left side of the road.

N ative American influence is strong in the Pacific Northwest. Although tribal names and words are easy to learn, their translations are often difficult to decipher. Skookum, the name used in this ride, comes from Chinook jargon, an Indian trade language—a particular way of speaking created by different tribes to "talk business" between themselves. Skookum has been translated to mean "strong" or "strength." In some translations, this word also means "ghost," "evil spirit," or "demon." Such heavy words make one curious, but according to one expert at the University of Washington's Northwest Special Collections Library, it's important not to read too much into this cobbled language. What you see is what you get.

The White River, glacially fed from Mount Rainier's icy crown, runs through the Skookum Flats. Following the river's course from the northeastern base of Mount Rainier to its western terminus, Commencement Bay in Tacoma, there are more than a few sights to see.

Mount Rainier is the most impressive site, by far, along White River. At Rainier's base, the White River Campground is a great location for hiking near the glaciers. Mountain biking is prohibited in national parks, but being so close to the goliath Rainier is an experience unparalleled in the Northwest, where there are many trails and campgrounds from which to choose.

Following the White River northward from the mountain is the town of Greenwater just a few miles from the start of the Skookum Flats mountain bike ride. A small town, Greenwater is home to the Catherine Montgomery Interpretive Center. The center showcases Washington's flora and fauna within the Federation Forest State Park's 612 acres of virgin timber. Greenwater is also close to the starting point for an historic route that Native Americans once traveled to cross the Cascade Mountains. This route, Naches Pass, can only be accessed on foot. Travel 10 miles east from Greenwater along Forest Road 70 to a trailhead just past Pyramid Creek for a short five-mile (one-way) hike to the pass.

From Greenwater the river flows west toward Enumclaw, a town named in 1885 by Frank Stevenson after a nearby mountain. Native Americans used this word to refer to the mountain, too, believing that the Thunderbird, who lived in a cave in this mountain, changed a tribesman into thunder. Enumclaw has been translated to mean "loud rattling noise" or "thundering mountain."

Although Enumclaw Mountain can't be seen from State Route 410, evidence of the town's prominent industries can. Timber mills and dairies have been in operation since the 1800s in Enumclaw. Passers-by will easily notice the logged roadsides and the lumberyards just as they are sure to take notice, with only a whiff, of what the locals call their "Dairy Air."

The White River joins with the Puyallup River in Tacoma (which is known for its pulpy aroma). Home to about 170,000 people, Tacoma is Washington's third largest city, behind Seattle and Spokane, and began as a settlement sur-

rounding a sawmill. Built in 1852 by Swedish immigrant Nicholas Delin, Tacoma's first sawmill stirred interest in the region as a future port, for both ships, and later, rail. Commencement Bay, deep and wide, proved to be a better shipping center than Seattle's Elliot Bay to the north.

A city tour of Tacoma wouldn't be complete with seeing the revitalized Union Station. Built in 1911, the building is now a courthouse, located on S. 19th Street and features a marvelous collection by internationally renowned local glass master Dale Chihuly. Next to Union Station is the interactive Washington State History Museum which opened in August 1996 and is heralded as "the best history museum west of the Mississippi."

After the in-city tour, head to Point Defiance Park, a 700-acre oasis of old-growth forest. Home to many attractions, the park has miles of trail open to bicycles and features a wonderful zoo and aquarium. From Tacoma, take I-5 to State Route 16 north. Turn right on Pearl Street before the Tacoma-Narrows Bridge.

Water and erosion from the White River creates a challenge for mountain bikers who ride the Skookum Flats Trail. A root-riddled experience, the Skookum Flats trail winds up and down drainages alongside the river. The mileage is short and the elevation gain is nil, but this ride is extremely technical and challenging. The trail follows the river for about four miles until it crosses a suspension bridge, at which point mountain bikers can bailout if necessary.

The singletrack continues down the Buck Creek Trail on the opposite side of the White River, along similar rooty terrain, for another four-and-a-half miles until it too intersects with a bailout option to State Route 410. To complete the final third of the Skookum Flats ride, take the White River Trail; it's easier to negotiate than the other two trails. The trip ends with a three-mile ride on State Route 410 back to Forest Road 73.

Ride Information

Trail Maintenance Hotlines:
- U.S. Forest Service White River Ranger District, Enumclaw, WA; (360) 825-6585
- Department of Natural Resources (360) 825-1631 or 1-800-527-3305

Costs:
There may now be a $3 per car per day charge. ($25 for an annual pass.)

Local Information/Events/Attractions:
- Washington State History Museum, Tacoma, WA; (253) 272-3500

(Also see information in Chapter 25)

Maps:
- Maptech CD-ROM: Sun Top, WA
- DeLorme's Washington Gazetteer and Atlas—Page 64 D4

MilesDirections

0.0 START at the Skookum Flats Trail #1194.

1.1 Pass a small trail coming in from the right. Follow the river.

1.3 Begin traversing a series of wooden bridges for the next two-tenths of a mile.

2.2 Cross a stream—trying not to get wet.

3.5 Notice the huge trees on this section of trail.

3.7 Pass over a wooden bridge with rails.

4.1 Come to a trail intersection with a sign that reads: "Road 73: 4.1 miles; Skookum Falls: 2 miles." To the left is the suspension bridge crossing the White River. Take a moment to check it out, then continue along Trail #1149. (This is a potential **Bail-Out Point:** Cross the bridge and take Buck Creek Trail up to State Route 410, and then back to the start.)

5.5 Turn left and continue along the White River. Pass an uphill spur and Forest Service Road 7160 on the right.

5.6 Come to a "Y" intersection. Turn left up the river.

5.8 To the right of the airstrip is Silver Springs Campground along the White River.

5.9 Pass the right-hand spur leading to Ranger Creek State Airport.

6.2 The river curves to the left and the trail is a little rough for a couple hundred yards.

6.5 Pass Ranger Creek Camp off to the right. Arrive at a "T" intersection. The trail to the right goes to the campground. Turn left heading toward the White River and the trail after the washout.

6.7 Reach an intersection with the old washed-out trail.

7.1 Pass a horse camp and a forest service road. Turn right along Forest Road 210 and follow it to the concrete bridge, paralleling the airstrip.

8.3 At the top of the airstrip turn right toward the Skookum Flats Trail, White River, and State Route 410.

8.5 Come to State Route 410. Turn left, heading toward Enumclaw. Take the White River Trail #1199 on the right, paralleling the road. (The Ranger Creek trail is behind you.)

10.1 Intersect with the Buck Creek Trail #1169 and the Snoquera Flats Trail #1167—one mile ahead. Continue straight.

10.4 Reach an intersection for Snoquera Falls Loop Trail #1167 (closed to horses and bikes). Stay straight on the White River Trail #1199. Cross a bridge up ahead.

10.5 Turn right at the "Y" intersection. The lower trail goes to Camp Shepherd. Continue straight past a spur trail.

10.8 Cross an open clearing—look for big elk. Cross a couple of clearings ahead.

11.3 Arrive at a four-way intersection with Snoquera Flats Trail #1167, the Powerline, the trail to State Route 410, and Buck Creek Trail #1169. Stay on the White River Trail #1199.

11.7 Reach the junction of the Dalles Creek Trail #1198, plus many other trails to the right. Stay straight.

11.8 Reach the junction of Power Line Way. Follow the trail as it curves down to State Route 410.

11.9 Arrive at State Route 410. Turn right and continue along State Route 410 back to Forest Road 73.

14.4 Turn left on Forest Road 73.

14.5 Stay left at the "Y" intersection.

14.7 Cross a bridge over the White River.

14.9 Arrive at the parking lot.

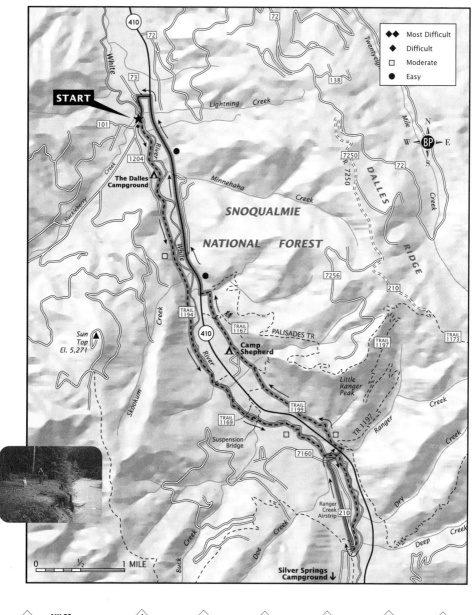

Most Difficult
Difficult
Moderate
Easy

410
72
72
White
73
138
START
101
River
Lightning Creek
Twentyeight
Mile
Creek
1204
N
W BP E
S
The Dalles
Campground
Minnehaha
7250
R 7250
72
DALLES
Huckleberry
Creek
SNOQUALMIE
Creek
NATIONAL FOREST
RIDGE
White
7256
210
Creek
TRAIL 1194
410
TRAIL 1167
PALISADES TR
TRAIL 1197
TRAIL 1173
Sun Top
El. 5,271
River
Camp Shepherd
Little Ranger Peak
Skookum
TRAIL 1199
TR 1197
Ranger
Creek
TRAIL 1169
Creek
7160
Suspension Bridge
Dry
Ranger Creek Airstrip
210
Creek
0 ½ 1 MILE
Buck Creek
Doe Creek
Silver Springs Campground ↓
Deep Creek

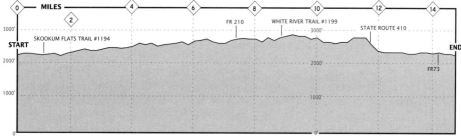

MILES
0
4
6
8
10
12
14
2
3000'
FR 210
WHITE RIVER TRAIL #1199
3000'
STATE ROUTE 410
START
SKOOKUM FLATS TRAIL #1194
2000'
END
2000'
FR73
1000'
1000'
0'
0'

Crystal Mountain Loop

Ride Summary

Of all the rides along the Cascade Range (situated on one of Washington's most popular ski resorts) this is the "must-do" course for Washington mountain bikers. Featuring an extremely aerobic advanced climb up forest road and singletrack, a 7,000-foot view of three volcanoes, and world-class singletrack downhill, few rides compare to the rush this route can provide. There are more moderate, alternative routes that will get you to the top, too, and as long as you get there, you'll find it very difficult not to have a sensational day on the mountain.

Ride Specs

Start: Forest Road 510 parking area
Other Starting Locations: Crystal Mountain Resort and trailhead
Length: 14.5 miles
Approximate Riding Time: 4 hours (shorter hour-long option with chair lift ride up to the top)
Nearest Town: Greenwater
Rating: Difficult ascent/Moderate descent
Terrain: Singletrack, doubletrack, fire roads, sand, creek crossings, and a short section of paved road
Other Trail Users: Hikers and horseback riders

Getting There

From Puyallup: Take State Route 167 to State Route 410 East. Follow 410 for 47 miles to the Crystal Mountain Road. Turn left and travel five miles to Forest Road 510 (a dirt road). Turn right between mile markers 4 & 5. Follow down into the parking lot.

Crystal Mountain Ski runs

State Route 410 is one of the main avenues to Mount Rainier, with many incredible trails and sights along the way. A few miles south of the turnoff for Crystal Mountain Road, along State Route 410, is Cayuse Pass. This portion of the highway closes in the winter because of snow. In the summertime, however, the drive up to Cayuse Pass is as breathtaking as seeing an eagle soar or a sunset over the Pacific Ocean.

At the top of Cayuse Pass and with a quick turn to the left, State Route 410 takes two deep switchbacks up and over Chinook Pass, between Sourdough Gap and Dewey Lake. Trailheads for both the gap and the lake are on either side of Chinook Pass. The hike to Dewey Lake is a popular trail because it has an easy grade and follows the Pacific Crest National Scenic Trail. Camping is permitted along the trail. The hike to Sourdough Gap is great for backpacking. The trail passes Sheep Lake and travels along the Pacific Crest Trail, too. Mountain bikes are prohibited on the Pacific Crest Trail which also crosses into wilderness areas. But Crystal Mountain does allow bikes, and it's relatively close by.

There are three ways to tackle Crystal Mountain in the summertime. First there is the heart-pumper route: up Forest Road 184 and the Silver Creek Trail for a relatively short, steep climb; and then down the Crystal Mountain Trail for a world-class downhill experience. This is not the easiest way up, by any means, but it offers a challenging, exhilarating, cardiovascular workout. Of course, there is the "traditional" route, too. By climbing up the Crystal Mountain Trail and coming down the Silver Creek Trail through the ski resort, more of the technical trail is saved for the descent. Just follow our instructions in reverse, starting

at the trailhead in the parking lot. The third option involves a meager fee. Take the chair lift up and ride down the Crystal Mountain or Silver Creek Trails, or even down the absurdly steep cat tracks. Our way is harder, but we feel it's worth the effort.

Share the Trail.

When temperatures rise, this ride can get pretty warm. Scaling the gravel road up into the trees, there is little escape from the sun. The Crystal Mountain Resort lies to the right—you should be able to see the chair lifts from here. (Just keep telling yourself that this grueling climb is saving you $10.) The singletrack traverses the bunny slope and leads into the woods where the trees give much needed relief from the unrelenting sun. As if the sun weren't bad enough, expect on your typical summer day to confront a welcoming committee of biting flies. Without some form of insect repellent, these inhospitable hosts will keep your rest stops to a minimum.

Well into the hills, the trail passes the abandoned Silver Creek Mine —a highly unadvisable side-trip. It is here that the terrain breaks from super steep to super technical. The deep ruts come from the hard pounding this portion of the trail used to get when it was host to an annual cross-country mountain bike race. (Races are no longer held on the mountain.) Some of these sections are tough enough to negotiate when you're going downhill, but heading up, the way we take you, they are almost unbearable—almost.

After completing the toughest and most technical portion of the ride, the trail leaves the forest and rounds a bluff, coming face to face with the bowls carved into the side of Crystal Mountain. Crossing a few cat tracks along the way, the trail encircles one of the bowls and begins the slow traverse up the hillside into some gnarly, rocky terrain. At the top, just below 7,000 feet, the Summit House and outdoor picnic tables are a welcome sight. The Summit House happens to be the highest restaurant in Washington and offers a picturesque setting for any meal of the day.

Leaving the crest of the mountain, head down along the ridge, over the large boulders in the direction paralleling Mount Rainier. It's best to walk over the boulders (unless you're Hans Rey). The singletrack picks up at the bottom of the boulder field and then just screams. It's a blast the entire way down. You'll pass meadows and overlooks, Mount Rainier and Mount Adams, and sometimes even Mount Hood's crystalline peak. The views along the ridgeline of the Crystal Mountain trail are truly entrancing, and the trail surface couldn't be more perfect.

MilesDirections

0.0 START from the parking lot at the trailhead on Forest Road 510 and ride back up to Crystal Mountain Road.

0.4 Turn left onto Crystal Mountain Road (also called Forest Road 7190).

0.8 Turn right onto Forest Road 184, the first intersection with a dirt road.

1.1 Pass the Norse Peak Trail that heads into Wilderness Area and is closed to bikes.

3.1 At the four-way intersection, the road goes left. Stay straight to the doubletrack on the Silver Creek Trail #1192, toward the Crystal Mountain Trail #1163.

3.5 The doubletrack ends and the singletrack begins to the right. Follow the trail signs and the singletrack, leading under a chair lift.

3.6 On the left a bridge crosses the creek at the abandoned Silver Creek Mine.

4.5 Reach a junction with a spur trail that leads to Bullion Basin and the Pacific Crest Trail. These trails are hiker-only trails. Cross over the creek to the right, heading toward the ski resort.

4.8 Veer right at the fork, following the signs.

5.0 Turn left at the junction.

5.1 Arrive at Henskin Lake. Stay on the main path curving around Henskin Lake. Keep the lake to the right.

5.2 Reach the intersection of the Bear Gap Trail

and the Crystal Mountain Trail #1163. Stay on #1163.

5.7 Stay right at the intersection. The left path heads up to a small lake.

6.2 Cross the creek to the right, heading toward the chair lifts.

6.3 Cross the cat track and continue up.

6.5 Encounter a short, flat meadow and ride under two chair lifts.

7.5 Skirting the southwest side of a bowl in the mountain, you'll encounter a long switchback up to the saddle.

7.6 There is a healthy climb from the saddle to the top of the mountain. You can follow the lesser climb on the left.

8.1 Turn right up the dirt, doublewide track toward a large boulder field. You can see the Summit House Restaurant at the top a few yards away.

9.5 Begin the descent over the boulder field. The junction to the left makes a steeper downhill, but the trail in front of you meets with the left hand trail in just a of couple yards.

11.2 For close-up views of Mount Rainier, head left to the edge of the ridge. Continue along the switchbacks of the Crystal Mountain Trail.

14.5 Arrive at the trailhead and parking area on State Route 510.

Ride Information

Trail Maintenance Hotlines:
- *Crystal Mountain Ski Area;*
  (360) 663-2265 or 1-888-754-6199
  www.crystalmt.com
- *U.S. Forest Service: (360) 825- 6585*
- *U.S. Dept. of Natural Resources;*
  (360) 825-1631 or 1-800-527-3305

Schedule:
Ride after snow melt in June to October; Lift operates Memorial Day to Labor Day

Costs:
Chair lift is $10 for the day

Local Information:
- *Campground reservations;*
  1-800-280-2267
- *Radio AM530 in Enumclaw gives latest weather, road conditions, and mountain area information*

Local Events/Attractions:
Summit House, Crystal Mountain, WA
(360) 663-2300

Maps:
- *Maptech CD-ROM: White River Park, WA; Norse Peak, WA*
- *DeLorme's Washington Atlas & Gazetteer—Page 49 A5*

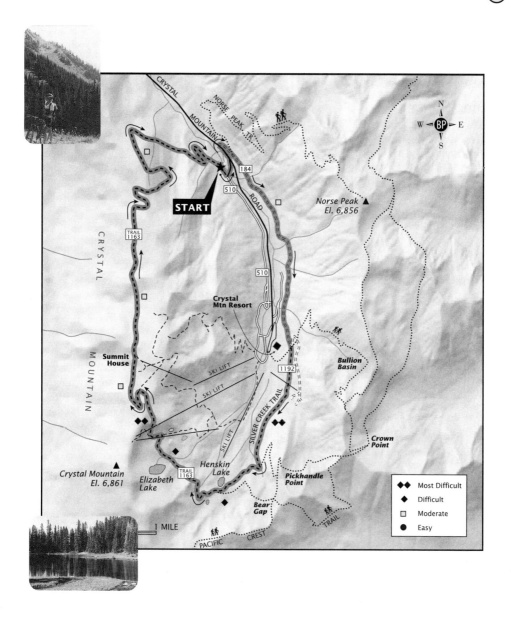

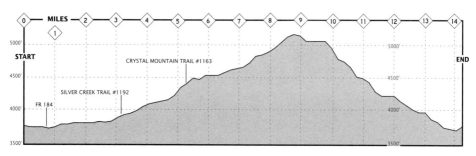

Fife's Ridge

Ride Summary

Located in the middle of a prime recreational area, Fife's Ridge is within "arm's reach" of Mount Rainier, camping spots, a slew of rivers, and Bumping Lake. Heading up one of the most scenic forest roads in the state, this ride begins with a smooth nine-mile climb that's not too strenuous. Skirting the edges of a Wilderness Area, it's important to keep to the designated, ridge trail. The views are stupendous, and the singletrack is impressive and fun with brief, moderately-technical sections.

Ride Specs

Start: Crow Creek Campground at Forest Road 1902
Length: 14.4 miles
Approximate Riding Time: 3 hours
Nearest Town: Cliffdell
Rating: Moderate with steady ascent and technical descents
Terrain: Singletrack and forest road
Other Trail Users: Hikers and horseback riders

Getting There

From Chinook Pass: Head east on State Route 410 to Forest Road 19 north toward Little Naches Campground and Horsetail Falls. Pass Forest Road 1901 to Quartz Creek. Follow signs for Raven's Roost #14. Turn left on Forest Road 1902. Cross the bridge over the river. See Road 1920 Fife's Ridge sign ahead. Park in adjacent camping areas along the river.

Heading down from Fife's Ridge.

R emnants of volcanoes dating back 40 million years have been found along the lower edges below Mount Rainier. This trail along Fife's Ridge runs atop a vestige of the second volcanic episode Mount Rainier experienced. Although it doesn't look like one, neighboring Fife's Peak is a volcano as well. It is believed to have erupted about 25 million years ago. Rocks found around Mount Rainier contain fossil plants, like palms and other warm climate trees, which are evidence that, at one time, temperatures here were on the balmy side.

Over the last 20 million years, Mount Rainier has had some time to cool off, and now shoulders 26 glaciers. Rising to 14,411 feet, Mount Rainier has been, and will continue to be, a landmark from which to navigate and a beacon for aspiring mountain climbers. Each year this mountain draws nearly 8,000 eager climbers who use ropes and ice axes for their two-day ascent. Day One gets climbers to Camp Muir where they rest, eat, and prepare to continue to the summit. Between midnight to 2 a.m. of the following day, climbers depart Camp Muir and continue to Rainier's peak for a 14,000-foot sunrise view of the world, which also gives them enough time to descend during daylight hours.

Permits are required to climb Mount Rainier and are issued at the mountain ($25 per person currently). The park service allows a rather large number of people per day to head up, but on the weekends, climbers should get there early. The National Park Service recommends that prospective climbers be educated in crevasse rescue and ice ax arrest (stop-

Looking east from the top of Fife's Ridge.

ping a slide by using an ice ax.) No matter how good the other climbers are, you'll want to know what to do if they get into unexpected trouble.

Climbing Mount Rainier fascinated early European settlers, but not the local Native Americans. They believed that attempting the summit would anger the mountain spirit—though Native American legends speak of medicine men, and others, reaching the peak. In August of 1870, General Hazard Stevens and Philomen Van Trump made the first successful summit attempt. An Indian named Sluiskin led Stevens and Trump to within a day of the summit, but turned back at the last minute, citing the "evil spirit who dwelt in a fiery lake on the summit" as reason enough. The first women to summit Mount Rainier were Kay Fuller in 1890, and 13 year-old Susan Longmire in 1891.

Captain George Vancouver of the Royal British Navy discovered Mount Rainier in 1792 and named it after his friend Rear Admiral Peter Rainier. Mount Rainier became the nation's fifth national park in 1899. James Longmire, owner and operator of Mount Rainier's first "tourist attraction," is credited with exciting the popular interest in the mountain that ultimately lead to its protected park status. It was while leading his third successful summit climb of Mount Rainier in 1883 that Longmire, resting for the night next to steam vents for warmth, discovered hot mineral springs. He quickly filed a mineral claim and developed the area into the mountain's first mineral hot springs resort, called Longmire Springs (also known as Longmire's Medical Springs).

The Longmires are well known for their explorations on Mount Rainier. Martha Longmire named Paradise Valley—the most famous of all sites on the mountain—in 1885. And the Longmire family is credited with identifying and naming hundreds of places along the mountain, as well as creating miles and miles of trail. There are over 300 miles of hiking trails now, which in winter can have up to 30 feet of snow.

This area around Mount Rainier offers some spectacular mountain biking terrain. The Fife's Ridge Ride is one that anyone with a little determination can complete. The climb is fairly long, but it isn't that strenuous. The road itself is in great condition—hardly a washboard wrinkle to be found. The trail situation seems to be a bit unsettled, though, in that certain trails, once open to mountain bikers, are now considered part of the Norse Peak Wilderness Area—where mountain biking is prohibited. Some of the trails you'll really want to explore now happen to be within the Wilderness Area. Leave your bike, or carry it, and hike along the ridge for a couple of miles to catch the excellent views of Mount Rainier's eastern face. From the ridge you can climb out onto some rock formations for the best views—a great spot for lunch, too!

The ridge trail is in good condition. Horses and motorcycles do leave some sections chewed up, but for the most part, it is fast and a ton of fun. Conditions range from packed dirt to sand, with a few technical, rocky sections. It then descends onto doubletrack with huge motorcycle ruts—a slight challenge to navigate. These trails will lead you right back to the campground.

Ride Information

Trail Maintenance Hotline:
- Wenatchee National Forest Headquarters; (509) 662-4335
- Naches Ranger District; (509) 653-2205

Schedule:
This trail is open during summer months.

Costs:
$3 per car per day or $25 for an annual pass.

Local Information:
- The Mountaineers, Seattle, WA (206) 284-6310
- Rainier Mountaineering Inc., Halls Lake, WA; (253) 627-6242

Maps:
- Maptech CD-ROM: Goose Prairie, WA; Old Scab Mountain, WA
- Green Trails: Bumping Lake No. 271 and Old Scab Mountain No. 272
- DeLorme's Washington Gazetteer Page 49 A6
- Naches Ranger District Map

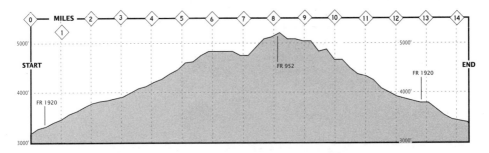

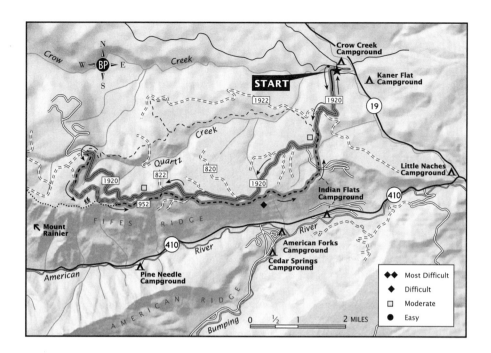

MilesDirections

0.0 START from the Crow Creek camping/parking area and turn right up Forest Road 1920, which begins with pavement and turns into gravel almost immediately.

1.3 Pass Forest Road 1922 the on right and Spur Road on the left. Continue up the gravel road.

1.7 Pass a side trail. Continue up the road.

2.1 Pass Spur Road 94 on the left.

2.7 Pass Trail #955. This is the junction for the West Quartz Creek Loop. Stay straight up the road.

3.4 Pass Trail #955. Continue ascending.

4.1 Pass Spur Road 820 on the right. Still climbing.

5.5 Pass Spur Road 822 on the right. Continue traversing the contours of this ridge.

6.5 Rounding a drainage on the ridge, look off to the right, north and northeast, to the Manashtash Ridge, Panther Ridge, and Peaches Ridge—all in one long succession. The tallest peak is Quartz Mountain.

8.2 Intersect with Trail #952, the West Quartz Creek Trail, and Forest Road 828. Forest Road 828 takes you into Wilderness Area. Take Trail #952 left to the top of the ridge. (Or turn right for a six mile downhill.)

9.3 Arrive at the top. See the Wilderness Area signs and the trail #954 to the right (hiker only). Stay left on #952

10.0 Cross Road #823.

10.3 Keep straight at the intersection, closest to the drainage. Pass a road cut on the left.

10.5 Pass road crossing of Forest Road 1920.

11.5 Trail #955 crosses over the ridge to State Route 410.

11.6 Cross Forest Road 824.

12.9 Arrive at the intersection for the loop of trail 952 and Forest Road 1920. Turn right on 1920.

13.4 Reach the intersection of Forest Road 1920.

14.4 Arrive at the Crow Creek Campground.

In Addition:**Bicycle Camping**

If you consider your mountain bike saddle the most comfortable seat in the house and crave an opportunity to prove your self-sufficiency, try bicycle camping. It does require more planning and preparation than a standard day trip, but the particular satisfaction gained from reaching a campground or a remote outdoor destination on two wheels, knowing you're ready for a cozy night outdoors, makes the extra effort worthwhile.

If you plan on doing a lot of bicycle camping/touring, it's a good idea to invest in quality equipment. Everyone should have a pair of medium-to-large size panniers that can be mounted on a rear rack (if you are planning a long trip, you might consider a front rack). A lightweight backpacking tent, sleeping pad, and sleeping bag can be attached to the rear rack using two or three bungie cords. We all have a tendency to over-pack, but the extra weight of unnecessary equipment may cause you to tire more easily. Here are some tips to help you find the appropriate amount of gear:

- Bring a multi-purpose tool that has a can opener, bottle opener, scissors, knife, and screwdriver.
- Pack only one extra change of clothes, plus any necessary layers such as a polypropylene shirt and tights, polar fleece, wool socks, and rain gear. If you are on a multi-day trip, bring extra shorts and t-shirts, and if it's winter, bring an extra pair of polypropylene tights and shirt, as well as a few extra pairs of wool socks.
- Bring a tin cup and spoon for eating and drinking and one lightweight pot for cooking.
- Invest in a lightweight backpacking stove, tent, and sleeping bag.
- Bring along freeze dried food. You can buy many pre-packaged rice and noodle mixes in the grocery store for half of what you'll pay at backpacking stores.
- Bring the minimum amount of water needed for your intended route. Anticipate if there will be water available. Invest in a water filter that can be used to filter water from water sources along the trail.

There are several reasonably priced outdoor gear companies. If you order by mail, you can generally save 10-40 percent. Check out some of the companies listed below:

Bike Nashbar
4111 Simon Road
Youngstown, Ohio, 44512
Phone: 1-800-627-4227
FAX: 1-800-456-1223
www.nashbar.com

Performance
P.O. Box AW
Beckley, West Virginia, 25802-2845
Phone: 1-800-727-4177
www.performanceinc.com

Recreational Equipment, Inc. (R.E.I.)
1700 45th Street East
Sumner, Washington, 98390
Phone: 1-800-426-4840
www.rei.com

SUPERGO
501 Broadway
Santa Monica, California 90401
Mail Orders: 1-800-326-BIKE
Information: (310) 576-6633
Order FAX Line: (310) 576-6665

Purchasing good, quality outdoor gear is worth the investment. The list below will give you an idea of what you might expect to pay for some of the items you'll need:

Large panniers — $150 - $200
Lightweight tent — $100 - $200
Sleeping Bag — $75 - $150
Rain gear — $50 - $200

Stove — $35 - $85
Sleeping pad — $20 - $50
Rack — $20 - $40
Cook set — $25 - $60

If you don't want to pay full price you can scan the classified ads in your local newspaper, or you can often find used equipment at garage sales.

Equipment List

Use the checklist of equipment below when you are planning for a single or multi-day trip. You can develop your own equipment list based on the length of your trip, the time of year, weather conditions, and difficulty of the trail.

Essentials

bungie cords
compass
day panniers
duct tape
fenders
pocket knife or multi-purpose tool
rear rack
front rack
trail map
water bottles
water filter
tool kit
patch kit
crescent wrench
tire levers
spoke wrench
extra spokes
chain rivet tool
extra tube
tire pump

Clothing

rain jacket/pants
polar fleece jacket
wool sweater
helmet liner
bicycle tights
t-shirts/shorts
sturdy bicycle shoes/boots
swimsuit
underwear
bike gloves
eye protection
bike helmet/liner

First Aid Kit

bandages (various sizes)
gauze pads
surgical tape
antibiotic ointment
hydrogen peroxide or iodine
gauze roll
ace bandage
aspirin
moleskin
sunscreen
insect repellent

Personal Items

towel
toothbrush/toothpaste
soap
comb
shampoo

Camping Items

backpacking stove
tent
sleeping bag
foam pad
cooking and eating utensils
can opener
flashlight/batteries
candle lantern
touring panniers
pannier rain covers
zip-lock bags
large heavy duty plastic garbage bags
citronella candles (to repel insects)
small duffels to organize gear

Miscellaneous Items

camera/film/batteries
notebook/pen
paperback book

> **Tool Tip**
>
> Zip-lock bags are a great way to waterproof and organize your gear. Large, heavy-duty plastic garbage bags also make excellent waterproof liners for the inside of your panniers.

Osborne Mountain

Ride Summary

This is another advanced mountain biking loop that can be categorized in the gonzo/abusive realm. The "climb that never ends" really does find a stopping point—it just takes a while. And, gads! The scenery is spectacular. Right between Mount Rainier within the Sawtooth Ridge, this route is both challenging and rewarding. The descent is filled with switchbacks and requires a lot of technical skill, wiping out any unsuspecting mountain bikers if they aren't careful.

Ride Specs

Start: Big Creek Campground
Length: 24.4 miles
Approximate Riding Time: 6 hours
Nearest Town: Ashford
Rating: Difficult due to steep, unrelenting climbs
Terrain: Singletrack, paved road, and forest road
Other Trail Users: Hikers and horseback riders

Getting There

From Ashford: Head east on State Route 706 toward the southwest entrance of Mount Rainier. (See Osborne Mountain ahead, dominating the skyline. High Rock Lookout is on the other side of the mountain.) Turn right onto Forest Road 52 into the Gifford Pinchot National Forest. Head toward Big Creek Campground and Forest Road 85 on the right as the road curves left. Turn right toward Osborne Mountain Trail #250 on Forest Road 29. Parking is available in the campground or any other pull-off.

L ong before there were any modern modes of transportation, State Route 706 and the roads leading east out of Ashford to Mount Rainier were Native American trails laid out by tribes traveling east to the Yakima country. By the 1880s, as homesteads began springing up and sawmills became the primary employers of the area's residents, the trails quickly became wagon roads.

Homesteading began in the late 1800s in this region. The community of Ashford was established in 1891. The National Mill operated near Ashford, serving as the region's primary employer, and specialized in the production of especially long and especially large timbers. It might have taken a man days to find trees that were tall enough for their purposes. But in those days, the turn of the century, there were still plenty of old-growth trees to choose from. The Ford Motor Company reportedly purchased three enormous planks of wood from the mill for their mid-west factory. Each timber measured 3'x3'x150'—all from one tree! To see old-growth forest of this size, visit the Grove of the Patriarchs on the eastern flank of Mount Rainier National Park. From Paradise, follow the Stevens Canyon Road east, almost all the way to State Route 123. The grove is open between the end of May (or after snowmelt) to mid October (or before snowfall).

Timber companies pumped out a lot of cut lumber in those days. The largest timbers were used as factory roof supports. Steel beams were used occasionally, but when the heat rose, the steel beams got hot enough to actually burn the roofs they supported. Heavy, wooden beams were used in place of steel because they could absorb more heat.

Ashford became a terminal for the railroad around 1907 and actually was a decent sized shipping center and service area for travelers heading up to visit Mount Rainier from the

Paradise entrance on the southwest side of the mountain. Following the steps of early settlers, it's a short drive up to Paradise, where visitors can have a face-to-face with Mount Rainier and its several glaciers. Once there, forest rangers at the national park's visitor center can provide information on the best views, the wildlife, Mount Rainier's history, and much more. There are also a few superb, short hikes that leave from the Paradise Visitor Center up to the glaciers. Glacier Vista is a three-mile round-trip hike, perfect for getting a taste of the mountain. A worthy reminder: dogs and bicycles are not allowed on national

Mount Rainier from High Rock Lookout.

park trails. But, they are allowed on the trails at Osborne Mountain.

Heading east from Ashford the road leads to a marvelous area for mountain biking in the foothills of Mount Rainier. Just outside the national park boundaries is Rainier's neighbor, Mount Osborne, where mountain bikers can expect to get one of the most difficult rides of their cycling career. Beginning at Big Creek Campground, the road climb is fairly easy. Climbing gently up a paved road, the forest canopy provides a shady cover for most of the way. The saw blade ridge of the Sawtooth mountains cuts sharply into the sky ahead as the road beneath you changes from asphalt to gravel on the way up to High Rock Lookout. But the trail is where all the action is. It is the singletrack that brings the most challenge to this ride, offering a great place to practice your technique. Littered with switchbacks, the trail is steep. Its rolling route traverses bowls and around mountain lakes on a very technical path that seems to go on forever. Rapidly descending the mountain, you may smell the rubber from your brakes heating up and feel the metal begin to quiver beneath your deteriorating brake pads. As you continue to succumb to gravity's pull, your fingers may crimp and your forearms moan, echoing the scream from your calves and your quads begging for relief. And then, all of a sudden, you'll arrive back at the Big Creek Campground.

Native Names...

Many tribes have lived along the base of Mount Rainier: the Nisqually, Puyallup, Upper Cowlitz, Muckleshoot, and Yakima. The Native Americans tribes had other names for Mount Rainier, like Takhoma and Ta-co-bet. Translations of these names include "big mountain," "snowy peak," or "place where the waters begin." The name Little Tahoma has been preserved as a place name for the conspicuous rock outcropping seen on the east side of Mount Rainier.

Sawtooth Ridgeline.

Ride Information

Trail Maintenance Hotline:
Gifford Pinchot National Forest,
Packwood Ranger District
(360) 494-0600

Costs:
$3 per day per car or $25 for an annual pass; appropriate campground fees for overnight camping

Local Information:
• Mount Rainier Visitor Center,
Paradise, WA; (360) 569-2211

• Mount Rainier Scenic Railroad, Elbe, WA
(360) 569-2588
• Forest Service Outdoor Recreation
(206) 470-4060

Local Bike Shops:
The Sports Hut, Packwood, WA
(360) 494-7321

Maps:
• Maptech CD-ROM: Sawtooth, WA
• Green Trails: Randle, WA No. 301
• Washington Gazetteer Page 48 C2

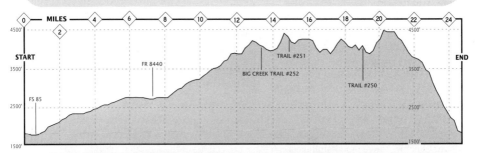

MilesDirections

0.0 START from Big Creek Campground. Head back out and cross the bridge to paved Forest Road 52 and turn left toward Ashford. As the road curves right, turn left onto Forest Road 85 following the sign for Osborne Road.

0.1 Cross a one-lane bridge.

1.0 Pass a spur road: No trespassing.

1.4 The climb begins on the paved road.

2.5 Pass an unmarked spur on the left.

5.0 See one of the points of the Sawtooth Ridge directly in your line of vision.

6.2 Pass the remains of a spur road on the left.

6.3 There may be water over the road at this point.

7.3 Reach the intersection of Forest Road 8440 (to High Rock Lookout) and Forest Road 85 (to Randle). Turn left toward High Rock Lookout (5 miles ahead). The road has turned to gravel.

9.5 Pass Spur Road 064.

10.6 Intersect with Spur Road 54 on the right. Switchback to the right up the ridge. The road will switchback a few times up ahead.

12.5 Arrive at Towhead Gap where the road curves to the left. See High Rock Lookout, the upward jutting rock overlooking Mount Rainier. Goat Rocks Wilderness is ahead of you. At this time, you can take the 2.6 mile round-trip hike to

the top of High Rock Lookout. It's worth it. Descend into the big right-hand turn.

13.4 Round the turn and turn left onto Big Creek Trail #252, climbing up to the saddle.

13.9 You're now on singletrack, climbing up through a nice section of old-growth.

14.2 The trail switches back again and intersects with old overgrown doubletrack. The trail heads off to the left. You're almost to the top of the gap.

14.3 Just as you push up this last section, Mount Rainier jumps into view. The trail descent is steep, narrow, and tends to be overgrown.

14.8 Trail Intersection: Take Trail #251. The sign reads: "Granite Lake 2 miles, Bertha May Lake: 3 miles." Begin to climb again.

15.1 The climb tops out at a sharp corner underneath High Rock.

15.6 The climb tops again for the descent to Granite Lake.

16.3 The descent stops and the trail starts climbing again around a saddle.

17.2 Climbing out of the cirque is a long, arduous process. When the trail is in the woods, it's clean, but a first gear grind. Out in the open, the trail is covered in briar bushes.

17.6 Reach Granite Lake. The trail heads toward a saddle and Bertha May Lake.

(continues)

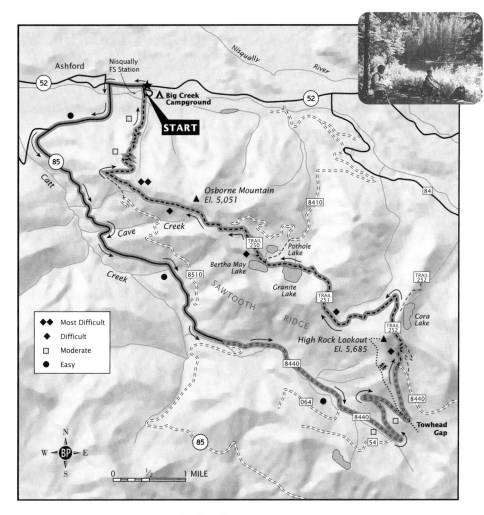

(continued)

18.2 Come down to Bertha May Lake—an emerald green mountain jewel. The trail winds away from the lake on the other side. Go around the lake.

18.6 Reach the junction of Trail #251, which drops down to the road and Pot Hole Lake. Climb up from the junction, now on Trail #250.

18.7 The trail opens up to almost doubletrack. Cross an old road cut, then head into a sandy gully that turns steep.

18.9 Here, the super steep gully section turns into nice singletrack—a first-gear climb.

19.3 The singletrack comes out next to a road that curves up and right. Brush by the road. The trail turns away a little to the left.

19.5 Trail #250 comes to Road 8410. The trail across it peters out, so turn left up the road and climb a little.

19.8 Take the trail to the left that comes up shortly, heading into the saddle, as the road switches back right. The trailhead is signed on your left and the trail, somewhat faint at first, traverses a clear-cut of Osborne Mountain.

20.1 The trail heads back into the trees.

20.3 The singletrack becomes well groomed. The trail now meanders through a few clearcuts on the west side of Osborne Mountain.

21.7 After some excellent downhill, come to Cave Creek Trail #911A (or #255). Switchback right and continue heading down Osborne Mountain.

23.5 Cross a drainage, making sure you cross to the right side. You'll switch back and forth on the way down.

24.3 Cross a wooden bridge.

24.4 End of the ride. Back at the campground.

Tongue Mountain

Ride Summary

The super fast trail lies in the heart of timber country. Ridden as a loop or a shuttle, the climb up forest road is gentle, but the singletrack above is challenging. A quick jaunt will take you to a view on the mountain itself, while the trail actually circles around before heading down. The descent is steep and relatively smooth. This ride can be done fairly quickly by advanced riders, and is frequently the finale of the Juniper Ridge route that connects to the Tongue Mountain Trail to the south.

Ride Specs

Start: Forest Road 29, or Spur Road 2904 for the shuttle

Other Starting Locations: Intersection of Cispus Road and Spur Road 2801

Length: 11.1 mile shuttle ride; 17 miles round-trip

Approximate Riding Time: 2-3 hours

Nearest Town: Randle

Rating: Moderate climb and difficult singletrack descent

Terrain: Singletrack—some smooth, some technical; forest roads; optional pavement (round-trip return)

Other Trail Users: Hikers, horseback riders, and motorcyclists

Getting There

From Chehalis: Take U.S. Route 12 east to Randle. Turn right onto Woods Creek Road/ Forest Road 25, and then left on to Cispus Road. Follow Cispus Road over the Cispus River. Park along the Spur Road 2801 to the left for the round-trip ride, or leave one car here and continue for almost a mile to a "Y" in the road. Turn left on Forest Road 29. Follow about three miles to any pull-off or on to Spur Road 2904 to begin the ride.

The view from Tongue Mountain. Tower Rock is on the right.

One of the most scenic driving tours in Washington is the loop around our famous lady volcano, Mount St. Helens. There are two loop routes, both originating from the town of Randle on U.S. Route 12. Loop One is 75 miles and heads south from Randle down Forest Road 25. Winding southward on paved forested roads, this loop takes Forest Road 26 and Forest Road 99 to the perch of the awe inspiring Windy Ridge Viewpoint, facing the great mountain and Spirit Lake. From Forest Road 99, head back to Forest Road 2560 leading back to Forest Road 25 northward to Randle. Loop Two is over twice as long, heading west on U.S. 12 to I-5 south. Exit at Woodland #21, and travel east on State Route 503 to Cougar, picking up Forest Road 90 to return northward to Randle on Forest Road 25. There are all kinds of photo opportunities along this route, as well as a slew of hiking and mountain biking trails.

Surrounded by mountains, the town of Randle is located on what used to be an ancient glacial lake that once stretched for 30 miles. A town of farmers and loggers, Randle saw its first sawmill go into operation in 1866. To the west and east of Randle are the towns of Morton and Packwood, both of which were settled in the late 1800s. Pioneering farmers from Kentucky and Tennessee populated these towns after growing weary of their south-

eastern homelands. Coming West in droves, they hoped to find homes in which to raise their families, where fish and wildlife were plentiful and where there was room to grow.

Packwood was named after William Packwood, a well-known explorer who traveled the Cascade Range with James Longmire in the 1850s in search of a better crossing over the mountains from the Oregon Trail to Puget Sound. Together they cut the trail for Cowlitz Pass on the east side of Mount Rainier. In Packwood you'll find Hotel Packwood which has been operating since 1912. President Theodore Roosevelt stayed here while attending the christening ceremonies of Mount Rainier National Park. This cozy hotel has nine rooms, two with private baths, and is furnished in antiques. It's open year-round, and rooms are from $20 to $38. Across the street is the Timberline Library. Built during the same time period, this small log library is set in a grove majestic Douglas firs alongside a city park.

Tongue Mountain rising up ahead.

Southeast of Randle down Forest Road 25 is the Tongue Mountain Trail. One of the many ridge-top trails in the Gifford Pinchot National Forest, the trail to Tongue Mountain is at the north end of an epic ridge-runner along Juniper Ridge. Included in this book as an

One of the many tight switchbacks.

Honorable Mention, Juniper Ridge is a longer and tougher route. The Juniper ride circles east of four peaks along the Cispus River before climbing up to the ridgeline and around Jumbo, Sunrise, and Juniper peaks, finishing out with the trail to Tongue Mountain—all in one ride.

The Tongue Mountain ride begins by climbing a well graded forest road up the Lambert Creek drainage. The road climb is only four miles to the Juniper Ridge Trail at 2,200 feet. (The trail climbs to 3,600 feet.) Logging trucks tend to run pretty fast out here, so be on

Hovering above the super-fast Tongue Mountain Trail.

the lookout. The climb can be made longer by starting lower on the logging road. It's not a tough climb so doing this ride as a loop is a good option if you're looking for more miles.

After climbing about three miles, the first peek at Tongue Mountain comes into view before hitting the singletrack. Remember, this is a ridge ride. The trail is steep at first and has intermittent downhills. There are several small climbs before the real descent begins after about four-and-a-half miles. The descent can be incredibly fast due to its steep grade in places. Under the cover of the dense forest canopy, the trail is technical and deeply rutted in places. Horseback and motorcycle riders also use this trail, so it does have its choppy moments. The last few miles of trail make an incredible mountainside descent. At the intersection with FR 2801, it's all downhill on forest road to the Cispus River. A couple of pull-offs along the river make for nice picnic spots.

MilesDirections

Shuttle Ride starting on Forest Road 2904:

0.0 START the ride by heading up Forest Road 2904.

1.2 Start crossing the drainage and traversing to the other side of the valley.

1.9 Pass Spur Road 604 on the left.

3.0 Round the corner to see Tongue Mountain in full view.

4.1 Intersect with the Juniper Ridge Trail #261 on the right and the Tongue Mountain Trail #294 on the left. Turn left onto Trail #294.

4.5 Ride along the ridge, downhill to the next saddle and then into another climb.

5.6 Climb to the next ridge of Tongue Mountain. From there it's all downhill!

5.7 Take an eight-tenths mile hike up to a viewpoint at the top of Tongue Mountain, or continue straight toward Forest Road 2801.

5.8 Pass a small trail berm off to the right. From here you can see Tower Rock and the whole ridge ahead of you.

6.2 Intersect with the Highbridge Trail #293A on your left. Turn right at the "Y" intersection, staying on Tongue Mountain Trail #294.

6.7 Just finishing an A+ section of downhill—fast.

7.6 Encounter a super tight switchback—be careful.

8.9 The trail starts a long descent down the ridgeline of Tongue Mountain: sweet, smooth downhill with little humps.

9.7 Reach Forest Road 2801, and turn left to continue to your shuttle point.

11.1 Reach shuttle point at Cispus Road and Forest Road 2801.

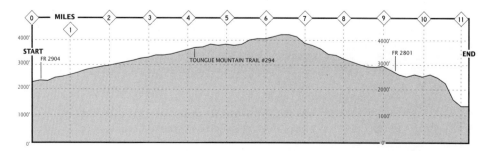

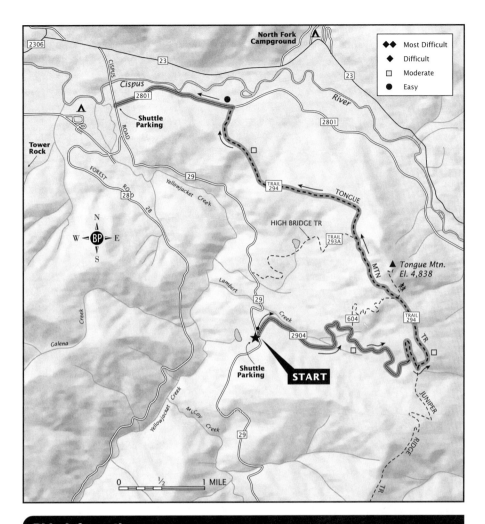

Ride Information

Trail Maintenance Hotlines:
- Gifford Pinchot National Forest, Randle Ranger District; (360) 497-1100

Schedule:
June through October

Costs:
$3 per car per day or $25 for an annual pass; appropriate camping fees at the campgrounds

Local Information:
- Forest Service Outdoor Recreation Information; (206) 470-4060
- Hotel Packwood, Packwood, WA (360) 494-5431

Maps:
- Maptech CD-ROM: Greenhorn Buttes, WA
- Green Trails: McCoy Peak No. 333
- DeLorme's Washington Atlas & Gazetteer Page 34 A2
- Gifford Pinchot NF Randle Ranger District Map

Chain of Lakes
Figure Eight

Ride Summary

This fantastic loop covers rolling singletrack and a forest road descent while weaving around an actual chain of lakes. Although Mount Adams rarely comes into view, two river crossings and great singletrack make this moderately difficult ride one you will want to do again and again.

Ride Specs

Start: Chain of Lakes Campsite
Other Starting Locations: Takhlakh Lake Campground
Length: 16.5 miles
Approximate Riding Time: 3-4 hours
Nearest Town: Randle or Trout Lake
Rating: Moderate due to semi-technical single-track and intermediate climbs
Terrain: Singletrack, Forest Service road, and short pavement
Other Trail Users: Hikers and horseback riders

Getting There

From Chehalis: Take U.S. Route 12 east to Randle. Turn right onto Woods Creek Road/ Forest Road 25, and then left on to Cispus Road. Follow Cispus Road to a "Y" intersection just before crossing the Cispus River. At the "Y," follow Forest Road 23 to the left. Follow Forest Road 23 south at least eight miles to the "Y" with Forest Road 21. Veer right to stay on Forest Road 23 for about 10 miles to the intersection for Takhlakh Lake and Forest Spur Road 2329.

Mount Adams and Takhlakh Lake.

Mount Adams. Now this is the place to mountain bike. Though remote when compared to its high-traffic sister volcanoes, Mount St. Helens and Mount Rainier, Mount Adams offers spectacular trails, interesting geologic traits, and warm, dry weather—not to mention plenty of elbow room. Since Mount Adams has no national park designation, mountain biking is allowed just about everywhere (except in the Wilderness Areas, of course). For those who are willing to venture a little off the beaten path, Mount Adams is an exquisite oasis for all kinds of fun.

Standing at 12,276 feet, Mount Adams is Washington's second highest peak and home to the second largest glacier in the Cascade Range, the Klickitat. Though Mount Adams has been dormant for about 10,000 years, there are acres of evidence, easily spotted along this ride, to suggest that the mountain has not always been so well bahaved. As you ride the Chain of Lakes loop, look for the ancient basalt surrounding the mountain's periphery, especially on the descent to Adams Creek. The black clumps of rock are hard to miss. Also, keep on the lookout for hawks and ravens riding the warm air currents of the mountain thermals.

Of all the Cascade volcanoes, Mount Adams is probably the least understood, due in part to its attention-getting neighbors, but also due to its remoteness. The few geologic studies that have been conducted draw some interesting conclusions. David Alt and Donald Hyndman, authors of *Roadside Geology of Washington*, describe the mountain as being "broadly squat in form, which looks distinctively different from every direction..." which is different from the other volcanoes, indicating that there is more to Adams than meets the eye. One theory to explain the difference in shape is that Mount Adams may be made up of more than just one volcanic cone—quite possibly several. This is of no real consequence to

your safety, but geologists find it interesting and enjoy speculating about the shape of the mountain's lower half.

Mount Adams may be dormant on the inside, but there's certainly a lot of activity on the outside. The entire area surrounding Mount Adams has a labyrinth of awesome trails—however, not all are open to mountain bikes. The weather is dry and warm on summer days and cool and crisp at night, making this a fantastic place to ride and camp. Even in August you can ski, climb, and snowboard on the frozen, white fields above the treeline. The forests are dense with hemlock, Douglas fir, and some silver fir. These dry, needle-bedded forests are considerably different from the lush, wet forests west of the Cascades.

The Chain of Lakes trail officially begins at the Chain of Lakes Campground, a secluded area next to one of the placid mountain lakes in the chain. There are only a few camping pull-offs and an outhouse up the road. The High

Down the singletrack from the lakes to Adams Creek.

Lakes Trail laces its way around a few small lakes connecting with the Chain of Lakes Trail at the Chain of Lakes campground. After a moderate climb into the woods and around a few more small lakes, the scenery changes upon entering what looks like a graveyard of igneous rock deposits. The trail tightly hugs the hillside and drops quickly to Adams Creek, a fairly large creek. You will probably get wet at some point along this ride—either here or farther up the trail. There are no bridges along this portion of the ride, just a downed log over Adams Creek, and nothing else over the stream ahead.

Climbing up from the creek requires strong legs and a bit of tenacity. Fortunately, the trail is smooth. It's a long climb, though, flattening briefly before arriving at Killen Creek. Much smaller than Adams Creek, Killen Creek is still a great place to dunk your head to cool off. After crossing the creek, the ride is pretty easy. Continue to Keenes Horse Camp around Horseshoe Lake, and the singletrack ends shortly thereafter. At the horse camp there's a gravel forest road that winds down along the Wilderness Boundary of Mount Adams all the way back to Takhlakh Lake.

Camping is available at either Takhlakh or Chain of Lakes. There are three peaceful sites at Chain of Lakes ($6 a night per site). There is no running water and only one outhouse, a short walk from the lake. Takhlakh Lake sites ($9 a night per site) do have running water in a few central areas and room for RVs. It can get a bit crowded at this campground, but it's right on the lake facing the mass of Mount Adams. You just can't beat the view.

Killen Creek.

141

MilesDirections

0.0 START from Road 022 at the Chain of Lakes Campground, ride back up the gravel road to Forest Road 2329 toward Lake Takhlakh.

1.0 Turn right on Forest Road 2329.

1.5 Turn right on Forest Road 5601.

1.6 Pass Squaw Creek Trail #265 on the left.

1.7 Turn right on High Lakes Trail #116 (See mile marker #6). Chain of Lakes is two miles ahead on this trail.

3.2 Complete a short descent heading to the Chain of Lakes, passing one on the left. Follow the trail left toward the lake and arrive at the camping area; or, follow the right turns and cross Forest Road 022 to the connecting trail across the road.

3.6 The lake trail ends at the campsite. Turn right on the road and pick the trail up on the left a few hundred feet up. Take the High Lakes Trail #116. Elevation is 4,350 feet.

5.3 Cross Adams Creek. There should be a log to walk over.

6.3 Wade across Killen Creek.

7.0 Intersect with Trail #115 and Keenes Horse Camp Trail. Follow the Keenes Horse Camp trail to the right.

7.1 Pass a spur to the right leading to the lake. Ahead 50 yards, pass signs for Horseshoe Camp. Take Trail #116 on the left, or bail to the road if you've had enough.

7.6 Turn right onto Trail #120. Follow it toward Keenes Horse Camp. In one-tenth of a mile, at the "Y" intersection, turn left heading up.

8.1 Cross a wooden bridge

8.3 Cross another wooden bridge.

8.5 Cross another wooden bridge into Keenes Horse Camp. Leave the horse camp to the right heading to Forest Road 2329. Turn right on Forest Road 2329. There are a few trails off to the right of the road that you can take for extra singletrack riding.

9.7 Pass Killen Forest Camp on your right.

10.2 Pass Killen Creek Trail on your left.

11.6 Cross the East Fork Adams Creek, elevation 4,300 feet.

12.3 Cross the Middle Fork Adams Creek.

12.5 Cross the West Fork Adams Creek.

12.8 Pass Divide Camp Trail #112 on the left.

13.7 Pass Takh Takh Meadow. The trail is open to hikers only.

14.9 Come to an intersection with Forest Road 26. Continue straight.

15.2 Turn right on Forest Road 22 to the campground.

16.5 Arrive back at the Chain of Lakes campground.

Ride Information

Trail Maintenance Hotlines:
- Gifford Pinchot National Forest, Randle Ranger District (360) 497-1100
- Mount Adams Ranger District, Trout Lake, WA; (509) 395-2501

Costs:
$3 per car per day or $25 for an annual pass; appropriate camping fees at the campgrounds

Local Events/Attractions:
- Arts Festival & Volkssport Ride & Walk in July, Trout Lake, WA (509) 395-2294
- Community Fair and Dairy Show in August, Trout Lake, WA (509) 395-2241 (or 395-2289)
- Huckleberry picking in August all over the Mount Adams area. Ask at the Trout Lake Ranger Station for a permit and map of the legal areas in which to pick.

Local Bike Shops:
- Dick's Bicycle Center, Vancouver, WA (360) 696-9234
- Excel Fitness, Vancouver, WA (360) 834-8506
- Discovery Bicycles, Hood River, OR (541) 386-4820
- Mountain View Cycles & Fitness, Hood River, OR; (541) 386-2888

Maps:
- Maptech CD-ROM: Green Mountain, WA
- DeLorme's Washington Atlas & Gazetteer—Page 34 B4
- Gifford Pinchot N.F. Mt. Adams Ranger District Map (Pacific Northwest Region)

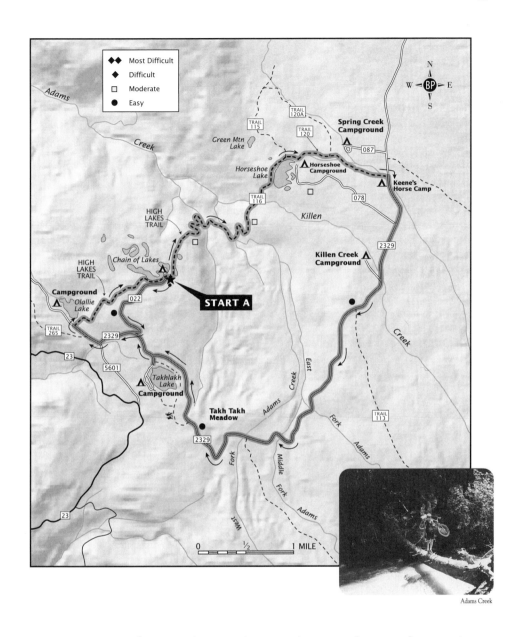

Symbol	Difficulty
◆◆	Most Difficult
◆	Difficult
□	Moderate
●	Easy

Adams Creek

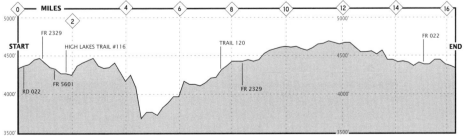

Mount St. Helens
McBride/Kalama Loop

Ride Summary

This popular route skirts the base of Mount St. Helens and is frequently used by horseback riders. Its trail, thick and mucky along the river, climbs steeply to meet very deep and sandy singletrack. Although it is not a long loop, the ride is quite fulfilling. The trail heads into the woods and around McBride Lake through prime Sasquatch-viewing territory, so keep your eyes peeled for big, hairy men (not to be confused with your riding partner).

Ride Specs

Start: Kalama Horse Camp
Other Starting Locations: Red Rock Pass
Length: 12 miles
Approximate Riding Time: 1 hour
Nearest Town: Cougar
Rating: Easy to moderate due to sandy single-track and mild grade climbs on forest road
Terrain: Forest Road and sandy singletrack
Other Trail Users: Hikers and horseback riders

Getting There

From Vancouver: Take I-5 North to Woodland. Take State Route 503 (Lewis River Road) east. After 34 miles , turn left on to Forest Road 83 to Ape Cave and Mount St. Helens viewpoint. Pass Forest Road 8303 to Ape Cave, taking Forest Road 81 to Climbers Bivouac, Marble Mount, and June Lake. Follow Forest Road 81 all the way to Red Rock Pass and Forest Road 8123. Turn left onto Forest Road 8123, and follow it approximately 2.5 miles to the Kalama Horse Camp.

Mother Nature. Would you think to call her Helen? Whether blowing her top or providing incredible landscapes to explore, Mount St. Helens certainly knows how to put on a show. You can't beat the adventures to be had at this historic site.

This first ride starts off in the trees surrounding a trail that has become very sandy. So sandy in fact, you may think you're at the beach—except the seagulls are now bald eagles. You'll be heading up and away from the river in a bit, but for the early section of the ride you'll feel the cool and somewhat clammy dankness of the river drainage. The climb out of the drainage is tough. You'll probably need to push your bike up.

At the top, the air clears and the tree cover opens. Occasionally along the trail you'll run across horse treats; be careful. If it's at all warm, these "treats" draw flies to the trail—though you can usually depend on a pleasant breeze to keep them away. Once on top, you may think you're still climbing because of the sandy trail conditions. If you stay on the upper sides of the trail, it'll be easier. The horses have made the path soft, so try to spin through as best you can. We thought this might actually make a nice downhill ride.

As you meander through these forests, be attentive; you're in perfect Sasquatch-spotting territory. Better known to Americans, at least since the 1950s, as Bigfoot, Sasquatch is believed by some to be the so-called "missing link," a possible relation of the believed-to-be-extinct race of Neanderthals. This is an even more curious theory when we look at how long humans have been spotting these creatures. The Kwakiutl Indians of British Columbia

carved the ferocious human-like face of "Bukwas" (Wild Man of the Woods) into their popular masks. And Sasquatch, the giant cannibal, is spoken of frequently in the tales of the
Salish Indians.

The Indians relayed their stories to some of the areas earliest Anglo-explorers, many of
whom were skeptical, but nonetheless curious. In 1792 explorer Jose Mariano Mozino wrote:

> "I do not know what to say about the matlox [Sasquatch], inhabitant of the mountainous
> districts, of whom all have an unbelievable fear. They imagine his body as very monstrous,
> all covered with stiff black bristles; a head similar to a human one but with much greater,
> sharper, and stronger fangs than those of the bear; extremely long arms; and toes and fingers
> armed with long curved claws. His shouts alone (they say) force those who hear them to the
> ground, and any unfortunate body he slaps is broken into a thousand pieces."

145

In 1811, while crossing the Rockies near the Athabasca River in British Columbia, David Thompson reported finding unusually large animal tracks that would not fit the characteristics of a bear. His men insisted they were the tracks of the "young Mammoth" the Indians had spoken of, but Thompson held that the tracks were simply left by an abnormally large bear who's claws had worn away from age. He admitted, though, that he had no explanation for the balls of the feet.

Some other notable accounts of brushes with Sasquatch include a report in 1884 by a British Columbian newspaper about a four-foot, hairy, ape-man creature they called "Jacko"—maybe a teenage Bigfoot. In the early 1900s, Fraser River in British Columbia seemed to be the place for spotting Sasquatch. The Seattle Times ran a story on July 16, 1918, about a band of Sasquatch that attacked a man in Kelso, Washington, while he searched for gold. People had a tough time believing the story, even though the man provided "eye-witnesses."

One of the most famous stories about Sasquatch involves a retired lumberman, Albert Ostman. In 1924, Ostman was on Vancouver Island searching for gold. On the second night of his trip, he was awakened by someone (or something) dragging his sleeping bag (with him in it) from his camp. He lay still in the bag for some 25 miles before slipping out. His escape attempt failed. In no time he found himself surrounded by a Sasquatch family. Ostman said he was not harmed by the animals, and thought the family of four was actually intrigued by him. It was a full six days before Ostman escaped. It was another 33 years, however, before he was willing to tell anyone his story, which he swore to before a justice of the peace at Fort Langley, British Columbia.

Whether fact or fiction, hundreds of Sasquatch sightings have been reported between northern California and British Columbia. It's worth noting, though, that there have been no known sightings in this area for over 20 years. But you never know when Sasquatch might reappear. In the interest of preparedness, if you happen to spot an eight-foot tall, hairy creature who looks half-human/half-ape, our expert advice is: take a picture and ride like hell!

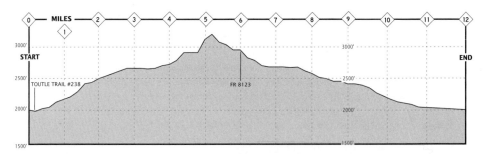

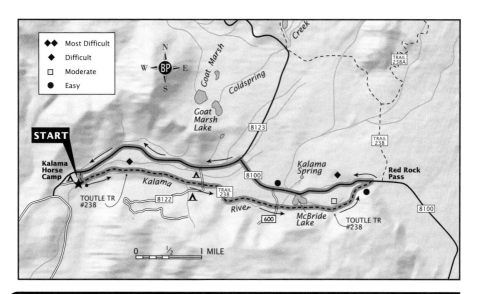

MilesDirections

0.0 START by taking the Toutle Trail #238 at Kalama Horse Camp up along the Kalama River.
0.4 Intersect with the Kalama Ski Trail. Keep to the Toutle Trail.
2.9 Cross Forest Road 8122 at the campground and continue on the Toutle Trail #238.
4.2 Pass Forest Road 600. Follow the river one-and-three-quarter miles toward Red Rock Pass.
4.6 Climb above McBride Lake.
5.0 Climb tops out. Descend to Red Rock Pass.

6.0 Arrive at the junction of Forest Road 8100. Turn left and follow it down for about three miles.
9.0 At Forest Road 8123 turn left and ride back to the Kalama Horse Camp.
12.0 Arrive at the Kalama Horse Camp

Note: For a smoother climb, a more interesting descent, and an easier ride overall, try this route in reverse.

Ride Information

Trail Maintenance Hotlines:
• *Mount Saint Helen's National Volcanic Monument, Amboy, WA*
  (360) 247-3900

Schedule:
Seasonal; cross-country skiing in winter

Costs:
New National Park fees: $8 for 3 day pass or $5 per day; rates subject to change; camp ground fees

Local Bike Shops:
• *Jack's Restaurant and Sporting Goods, Ariel, WA; (360) 231-4276—limited bike supplies, mostly back-packing gear*

• *Chelatchie Store, Amboy, WA*
  (360) 247-5529

Suggested Reading:
• *Hunter, Don and Rene Dahindenk. Sasquatch/Bigfoot The Search for North America's Incredible Creature*
• *Landau, Elaine. Sasquatch: Wild Man of the Woods*

Maps:
• *Maptech CD-ROM: Goat Mountain, WA; Mount Saint Helens, WA*
• *DeLorme's Washington Atlas & Gazetteer—Page 33 C6*

Mount St. Helens
Blue Lake Ride

Ride Summary

The route along Blue Lake showcases some of Washington's most vivid landscapes. Traveling along the still-forested sections of Mount St. Helens, this non-technical ride keeps to the trees, making a trail that cyclists of any skill level will enjoy—until the descent into Sheep Canyon. For those new to the sport, take caution entering the canyon. You might have to push your way back up. Pay close attention to the posted signs, as some of the trails are unfortunately not open to mountain bikes.

Ride Specs

Start: Redrock Pass Trailhead

Other Starting Locations: Kalama Horse Camp

Length: Out & Back, 12.8 miles; Loop, 12 miles

Approximate Riding Time: 2-3 hours

Nearest Town: Cougar

Rating: Easy to Moderate, except for one steep climb on non-technical singletrack

Terrain: Sand and gravel singletrack, and dirt road

Other Trail Users: Hikers and horseback riders

Getting There

From Vancouver: Take I-5 North to Woodland. Take State Route 503 (Lewis River Road) east. After 34 miles, turn left on to Forest Road 83. Then, turn north on Forest Road 81 to Redrock Pass. The road turns to gravel after a few miles and the trailhead is on the right next to Mount St. Helens.

A thick evergreen canopy covers the trails along Mount St. Helen's southwestern flank. From here, one might not realize that Mount St. Helens ever erupted. But on May 18, 1980, this serene mountain, which had been quiet for over a century, did, in fact, "wake up." The blast from Mount St. Helens scorched everything in its northeastern path, stripping trees of their branches, bark, and needles, and flattening them to create thousands of acres of giant toppled toothpicks. Lakes moved or disappeared as others were created by the accelerated melt of Mount St. Helen's glaciers. Even though their homes were decimated, deer and elk were seen wandering within the destruction zone just days after the event—they soon left for greener pastures. Within a year, plant-life began to spring from the scorched earth, and today, almost 20 years later, many animal species have returned to their homes. Though the toothpicks remain, the hillsides become greener every year, and trees have begun to grow once again. In 1982, 110,000 acres of land on and around Mount St. Helens received its official national monument designation and is now known as the Mount St. Helens National Volcanic Monument.

The Blue Lake Trail is located on Mount St. Helen's southwest side, shielded by the mass that was not lost in the eruption. This is a moderately challenging trail, due mostly to the ravine that leaves you gasping for breath at the top. It's a popular route, too, because it displays a different side to the mighty mountain, one that is still green and tree covered, reminiscent of the way it used to be all the way around.

The ride begins out in the open at first, in a field of huge, black boulders at Red Rock Pass, which are quite impressive. There may be a little pushing involved, but not much; and soon afterward, the trail begins to roll into the woods. Skirting the edge of the mountain, past a couple of intersections, the trail then leads to Blue Lake and beyond. The lake is actually more of a swamp by late summer and adds thick moisture to the air inside the forest. The trail climbs gently for about six miles until it drops like a rock into Sheep Canyon. At this point, there are a couple of options for the return trip.

The easiest ride back involves only the retracing of your tracks back to Red Rock Pass. A longer, more difficult option is to continue on down into the canyon and following the Loowit Trail back to Redrock Pass. Since the mountain's eruption, trail development has been growing steadily. Depending on the progress made on the Loowit Trail (which was under construction at the time of this writing), you may have no choice but to turn around.

The Loowit Trail, when completed, will encircle the mountain, but much of the trail will be open only to hikers. Since the area is still under development, it is difficult to accurately predict which trails you can use. Please check at the trailhead or at one of the four visitor information areas to make sure the Loowit Trail is open to mountain bikers if you plan to ride the loop option.

Ride Information

Trail Maintenance Hotlines:
Mount Saint Helen's National Volcanic Monument, Amboy, WA; (360) 247-3900

Schedule:
No winter riding; cross-country skiing in winter

Costs:
New National Park Fees: $8 for 3 day pass or $5 per day; rates subject to change; camp ground fees

Local Information:
Visitor Centers around Mount St. Helens from State Route 504 are:
- The Mount Saint Helens Visitor Center: (360) 274-2100
- The Cowlitz County Hoffstadt Bluffs Rest Area and Visitor Center at milepost 27 (360) 274-7750

- The Forest Learning Center, May through October only; (360) 414-3439
- The Coldwater Ridge Visitor Center (360) 274-2114
- The Johnston Ridge Observatory, five miles from the crater; (360) 274-2143

Local Bike Shops:
- Jack's Restaurant and Sporting Goods, Ariel, WA; (360) 231-4276—limited bike supplies, mostly backpacking gear
- Chelatchie Store, Amboy, WA (360) 247-5529

Maps:
- Maptech CD-ROM: Goat Mountain, WA; Mount Saint Helens, WA
- DeLorme's Washington Atlas & Gazetteer—Page C6

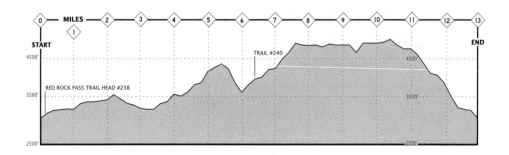

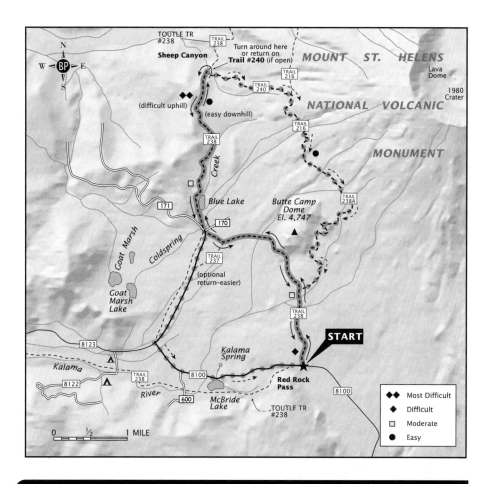

MilesDirections

0.0 START at the Red Rock Pass Trailhead #238 and head into the huge boulder field.

1.5 Pass Butte Camp Dome, behind and on the right.

3.1 Intersect with Blue Horse Trail #237. Continue straight.

3.4 Arrive at Forest Road 170 and the parking area for the Blue Lake Trailhead. Follow the trail over the wooden bridge and up alongside Coldspring Creek.

3.8 Arrive at Blue Lake. Take the trail up away from the lake.

4.0 The trail traverses and climbs into the forest.

6.4 Trail #240 is on the right and goes across the bridge over the creek. Loowit Trail #216 picks up

in 1.5 miles. This is the trail loop option that travels around the entire mountain. To the left is the Toutle Trail #238 continuing on. **For the Out and Back,** turn around here, and retrace your tracks back to Red Rock Pass for a 12.8-mile trip. **For the Loop Option,** (if the signs indicate that bikes are permitted), follow Trail #240 to the right and up the mountain side. At Loowit Trail #216, turn right and follow it along the northeast side of Butte Camp Dome. At Trail #238A, turn right and take major switchbacks to Trail #238 and back to Red Rock Pass. This loop is approximately 12 miles.

Mount St. Helens— Plains of Abraham

Ride Summary

Riding straight for the blast zone, the trail to the Plains of Abraham warms you up with a good climb into the trees. Passing above Ape Canyon, the Plains starkly contrast with the surrounding forest that somehow escaped 1980s scorching eruption. Traveling along a rocky, rolling moonscape, the Plains of Abraham trail will offer a challenge to mountain bikers of intermediate and lower skill levels, but the views are one in a million.

Ride Specs

Start: Ape Canyon Trail #234
Length: 13.6 miles short route/22.5 long route
Approximate Riding Time: 2-3 hours
Nearest Town: Cougar
Rating: Moderate climb and semi-technical singletrack
Terrain: Singletrack
Other Trail Users: Hikers

Getting There

From Vancouver: Take I-5 North to Woodland. Take State Route 503 (Lewis River Road) east. After 34 miles, turn left on to Forest Road 83 toward Ape Cave and Mount St. Helens viewpoint. Pass Spur 8303 to Ape Cave, Forest Road 81 to Climbers Bivouac, Marble Mount, and June Lake. Turn left at Ape Canyon Trailhead—44 miles from Woodland.

On May 18, 1980 Mount St. Helens, the smallest of Washington's volcanoes, changed the way she would appear to the world forever. Standing at 9,677 feet prior to the 1980 eruption, Mount St. Helens lost 1,300 feet in just nine hours. The eruption began as steam—enough steam to cast a fiendish 400-degree wind more than 650 miles per hour from the northeastern face of the mountain killing everything in its path for 150 square miles, including wildlife, plant life, and even human life. She also blew volcanic ash more than 15 miles into the air. Winds carried the ash, consisting of pulverized prehistoric rock and solidified lava, eastward across the country, falling most heavily on eastern Washington, but travelling as far away as western Montana.

Molten lava wasn't a problem with the Mount St. Helens eruption in 1980—not like it was two thousand years ago. Mount St. Helens did erupt with lava at one time. The proof can be seen today eight miles south of the Lewis River at Ape Cave. Smooth-flowing lava called "pahoehoe" basalt flowed down the sides of Mount St. Helens for weeks. When the lava began to cool, it formed a crust on the surface, but lava continued to flow beneath it. By the time the lava stopped flowing, a long tunnel had been formed, leaving behind what is called a lava tube.

Ape Cave is almost two-and-a half miles long (12,810 feet), making it the longest intact lava tube in the United States, and the second longest in the world. Ape Cave was named in honor of a local youth group called the Mount St. Helens Apes who hiked and explored the mountain and discovered the tube in the 1950s. It is definitely worth a visit. With the help of a bright lantern and jacket, there are two routes to explore. The Information Station at Ape Cave has additional details.

Ape Canyon.

Within the boundaries of the Mount St. Helens National Volcanic Monument there are over 500 miles of trail to discover. We've charted only three in this book, but the territory is so inviting you may want to explore on your own. The Plains of Abraham ride takes you through fertile forest and mudflow washouts and incredible views of the mountains. The Plains are like a moonscape: dry, crusted remnants of what used to be inside the mountain. This will be a rather warm ride in the heat of summer, yet stunning in the presence of three other active volcanoes: Rainier, Adams, and Hood.

Begin the ride at the trailhead into the forest on steady, mellow grade singletrack. In the fall, the colors are spectacular. Rounding the first bend, Mount St. Helens comes into view for a breathtaking first appearance. Along a narrow ridge, Ape Canyon can be seen below to the right until finally, breaking away from the trees, the trail enters the area of deadfall from the 1980 blast. The trail is well marked as it winds its way up the hillsides. The Plains of Abraham trail is dusty and rolling and intersects with trails heading up to the crater that are not open to mountain bikes. We've marked a turn-around point within the directions, but the trail goes as far as Forest Road 99 before connecting with the Loowit Trail and traveling along the perimeter of the mountain.

Ride Information

Trail Maintenance Hotlines:
- Mount Saint Helen's National Volcanic Monument, Amboy, WA (360) 247-3900

Schedule:
All year weather permitting; cross-country skiing in winter

Costs:
New National Park fees: $8 for 3-day pass or $5 per day; rates subject to change; camp ground fees

Local Bike Shops:
- Jack's Restaurant and Sporting Goods, Ariel, WA; (360) 231-4276— limited bike supplies, mostly backpacking gear
- Chelatchie Store, Amboy, WA (360) 247-5529

Maps:
- Maptech CD-ROM: Mount Saint Helens, WA; Smith Creek Butte, WA
- DeLorme's Washington Atlas & Gazetteer—Page 33 C8

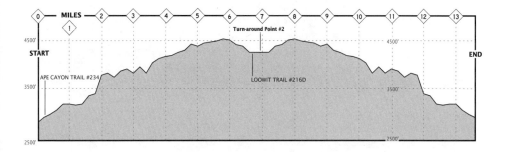

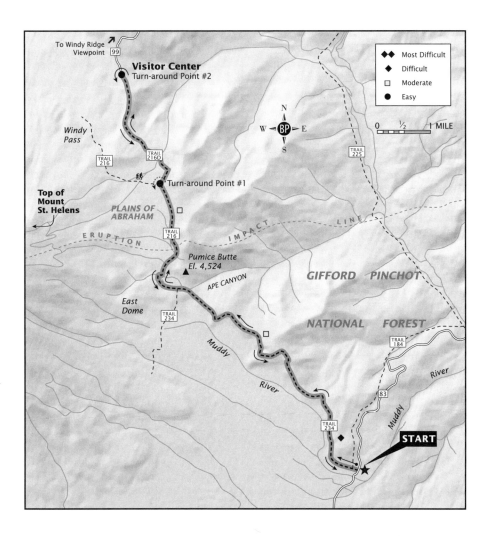

MilesDirections

0.0 START on the Ape Canyon Trail #234 from the parking lot at the base of Mount St. Helens. The sign also says: "Loowit trail #216, 5.5 miles, and Windy Ridge Road 99, 11.25 miles."

2.1 Switchback view of Mount St. Helens.

4.5 Viewpoint of the peak and washouts.

5.5 Intersection of Loowit Trail #216. Follow to the right to the Plains of Abraham, heading toward the south/southeast side of Mount St. Helens. Up ahead the next sign says: "Loowit Trail #216, Planes of Abraham Trail #216D, 1.75 miles, Windy Pass 2 miles, Windy Ridge Road 99, 5.75 miles."

6.5 Follow the rock cairns and see the depths of Ape Canyon and the heights of Rainier, Adams, and even Hood at times.

6.8 Pass the Loowit Trail #216 on the left. Stay straight on trail #216D toward Windy Ridge Road 99. This is the turn-around point. Just head back the way you came.

For a longer ride: Continue on #216D for 4.5 miles to Forest Road 99. At 11.25 miles, turn around and retrace your tracks back to the start for a 22.5-mile trip.

Service Trail/ Surprise Lakes

Ride Summary

A great way to start your day at Mount Adams, the Service Trail near Surprise Lakes offers a wonderful singletrack trip in a relatively short amount of time. There is a mellow road climb along fragrant berry-fields, and a winding trail around a couple of lakes before the singletrack races down into the woods on a very dusty trail frequently shared with motorcyclists. This trail doesn't gain much elevation, but climbs in and out of creek drainages, which is almost more tiring because there are few sections of straight-away. It's a quick trip, though, and it makes an invigorating prelude to your day at Mount Adams.

Ride Specs

Start: Cultus Creek Campground

Length: 12.9 miles (with option for nine additional miles)

Approximate Riding Time: 2-3 hours

Rating: Easy road climb and intermediate singletrack

Terrain: Singletrack and Forest Service road

Other Trail Users: Hikers, horseback riders, and motorcyclists

Getting There

From White Salmon: Travel north on State Route 141 . After about 28 miles, turn right onto Forest Road 24. Travel nine miles to the Cultus Campground.

Mount Adams.

The Mount Adams Recreational Area offers some of the most scenic trails and views in the state. With the combination of terrain and weather conditions, southern Washington couldn't be more ideal for summer mountain biking adventures and overnight camping. Though the tourism industry hasn't yet littered the base of the mountain with corporate lodges and bus terminals (thankfully), these lands around Mount Adams are still well known to locals and to Native American tribes.

One mile north of Red Mountain Road is a straightaway across an open meadow called the Indian Racetrack. Local tribes once held foot races and dried huckleberries here during the summer harvest. The area is now preserved and managed by the National Forest Service within the Indian Heaven Wilderness area. No longer a field for spectator sports, hikers and equestrians come through the Racetrack just to visit and to share in its beauty.

Even though they don't use the Racetrack anymore, Native Americans still frequent the hillsides of Mount Adams to harvest huckleberries. This ride passes by the Sawtooth Berryfields, well known for their sweet, juicy fruit. Certain portions of these fields are open only to Native American tribes. Other fields are open to the public by permit only. The Forest Service has maps and permits for designated public huckleberry fields. If you are just interested in eating but not picking berries, just check out any of the local diners; huckleberry shakes and pies are sure to be on the menu.

The Indian Heaven Wilderness covers 20,690 acres within the Gifford Pinchot National Forest—land that used to be inhabited by the Klickitat and Yakima tribes. This area includes three rather impressive peaks, though somewhat dwarfed by Mount Adams: Sawtooth (5,873 feet), Bird (5,706 feet), and Berry (5,050 feet). The Forest Service in Trout Lake has all sorts of information about the Indian Heaven Wilderness and neighboring Mount Adams Recreational areas. From the best trails to hike to recommendations on where to fish, the forest rangers know how to help you. They can tell you where to find the most picturesque waterfalls to photograph or even where to find choice singletrack. In fact, the Service Trail was one of their recommendations.

This trail runs around a few of the Surprise Lakes in a challenging and dusty singletrack adventure. A few erosion problems, combined with sharply banked turns, make for a thrilling downhill experience. It's a fairly fast ride and can easily be done in a couple of hours.

There are several creek crossings that churn the dust under your wheels into thick, pasty mud, which can make snapping into your clipless pedals difficult, and getting out of them even harder. Mountain bikers with toe clips will enjoy worry-free mud pedaling—just make sure you don't ever stop and put your feet down.

There are a couple of forest roads to be crossed along the route, and it seems like every one has a steeper out-take than the crossing before it. It gets tougher and tougher to ride away from the roads, and the embankments seem to get steeper and steeper. Only when you crest the climb and the trail gives you a switchback does your breath catch up with your heart rate. After completing the singletrack, the ride takes you back to camp on the well-graded Forest Road.

MilesDirections

0.0 START from Cultus Creek Campground. Turn right onto Forest Road 24, heading north.

2.1 Cross a bridge over the Middle Fork of Meadow Creek.

2.3 See a sign about the historic handshake agreement of 1932 giving Native Americans the sole right to pick huckleberries on the east side of the road.

2.8 Pass Forest Road 210 on the right, which goes to other camping areas.

3.4 Pass a dirt road on the right. See one of the Surprise Lakes on your right.

3.7 Pass Forest Road 221 on the left. At the Middle Trail #26, turn right, following a sandy doubletrack into Deadhorse Meadows. Keep to the right-hand trails as you encounter intersections.

4.1 At the "T" intersection, turn right onto the Service Trail (also called the Middle Trail #26, as indicated on the sign here). Sign also says that this is a "most difficult" trail. We disagree.

4.2 Pass another of the Surprise Lakes, keeping right at the intersection.

4.7 Another sign says you'll come to two road crossings in the next five miles—these are not on the Forest Service map.

6.1 Well into a white-knuckle descent, cross a couple of creeks and head into the forest.

6.4 Cross a wooden bridge and another creek.

6.6 Cross Forest Road 100. Continue climbing.

7.4 Cross Cultus Creek.

7.9 Trail empties onto a road (also not on the Forest Service map). Turn left and catch the trail on the left at the bend in the road. See the diamond marker on the tree. The trail crosses the road again and continues on through the woods.

8.4 Cross a fork of Little Goose Creek.

9.0 Cross the other fork of Little Goose Creek on a wooden bridge.

9.4 Cross another creek.

10.3 Reach a "Y" intersection with Trail #35 and #26. To add to your loop you can go left into the clear-cut and come out farther down the road. For this loop, stay to the right.

10.6 Turn right on Forest Road 24, heading back to Cultus Creek Campground.

10.7 Pass Little Goose Campground.

11.9 Pass Hidden Lakes Trail #106.

12.9 Arrive at Cultus Creek Campground.

Ride Information

Trail Maintenance Hotline:
(See Ride Information for Chapter 25)

Schedule:
This trail is best during summer months before and after snowfall.

Costs:
(See Ride Information for Chapter 25)

Local Attractions:
(See Ride Information for Chapter 25)

Local Bike Shops:
(See Ride Information for Chapter 25)

Maps:
• Maptech CD-ROM: Mount Adams West, WA
• DeLorme's Washington Atlas & Gazetteer—Page 34 D2

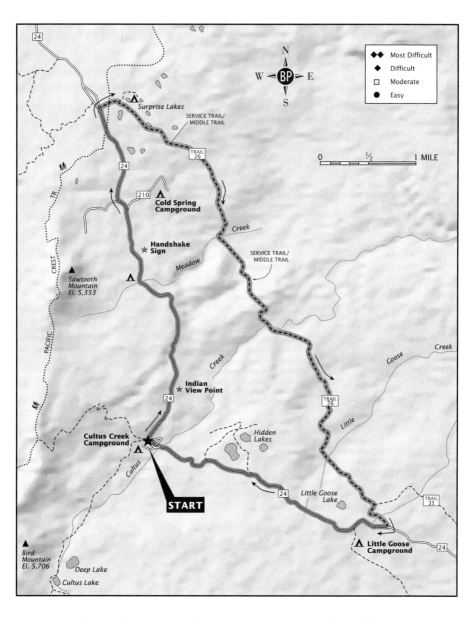

Legend:
- ◆◆ Most Difficult
- ◆ Difficult
- ☐ Moderate
- ● Easy

Surprise Lakes

SERVICE TRAIL/
MIDDLE TRAIL

TRAIL 26

Cold Spring
Campground

Handshake
Sign

Meadow

Creek

SERVICE TRAIL/
MIDDLE TRAIL

Sawtooth
Mountain
El. 5,353

PACIFIC CREST TRAIL

Creek

Goose Creek

Indian
View Point

TRAIL 26

Little

Cultus Creek
Campground

Hidden
Lakes

Cultus

START

Little Goose
Lake

TRAIL 35

Little Goose
Campground

Bird
Mountain
El. 5,706

Deep Lake

Cultus Lake

0   ½   1 MILE

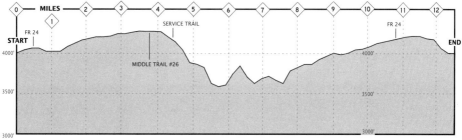

MILES

START

FR 24

MIDDLE TRAIL #26

SERVICE TRAIL

4000'

3500'

3000'

FR 24

END

Gotchen Creek

Ride Summary

Another intermediate ride with a memorable road climb, the route up to Gotchen Creek and down Mount Adams is neither too long, nor too technical. Hiking and biking trails fill the peaceful forest, and the singletrack down the mountain is sandy, steep, and as fast as you care to make it. Zipping around the creek toward the bottom, the trail completes its loop with some high whooptee-doos and brings you back around to the start before you know it.

Ride Specs

Start: Wicky Creek Horse Shelter
Length: 15.7 miles
Approximate Riding Time: 4 hours
Nearest Town: Trout Lake
Rating: Moderate to Difficult with steep, sandy descending singletrack
Terrain: Forest Service roads and singletrack
Other Trail Users: Hikers and horseback riders

The ride back to Wicky Creek.

Getting There

From White Salmon: Take State Route 141 north to Trout Lake. At the road split, follow the Mount Adams Recreational Area Road (Forest Road 80). At the "Y" intersection, stay straight. Follow Forest Road 80 toward South Climb Trail #183. You'll see signs for the county and forest boundary lines. Pass Buck Creek Trail #154. Follow the right fork onto a gravel road heading straight for Mount Adams. Pass two dirt spurs, following ahead as the road turns sharply right. Wicky Creek Horse Shelter is on the left.

The Gotchen Creek ride is a National Forest Service ranger's recommendation. Strung along the slopes of Mount Adams, the trail's name may throw you a bit since the ride doesn't exactly hit Gotchen Creek until the very end. But that aside, this is only one of the many exciting trails on and around Mount Adams—whatever they're named for. There are also some super cool geologic sites to witness on Mount Adams. To experience "super cool" quite literally, you must visit the Ice Cave, 10 miles west of Trout Lake off of State Route 141. Discovered more than 100 years ago, the Ice Cave is filled with icy stalactites, stalagmites, and huge ice blocks. In the pioneer days, settlers from Hood River and The Dalles, Oregon, harvested ice from this cave. The ice cave is actually an ancient lava tube that retains heavy, cold air from the winter. Because there is no real air circulation, the cave remains frozen year-round. Small amounts of snowmelt in the summer, followed by winter re-freezing, create the intricate ice formations that grow along the floor and ceiling. To check it out, you'll want a lantern or a good flashlight, boots, and warm clothing. A helmet wouldn't hurt. The Forest Service Ranger Station in Trout Lake has information on the Ice Cave. Be sure to pick it up and learn

Inside the Ice Cave.

what "pahoehoe" is and what is meant by "natural bridge."

After breathing the frosty air from the depths of the Ice Cave, resurface to ingest the sweet perfumed air of Mount Adams' forests. This ride begins at the Wicky Creek Horse Camp, on the south side of the mountain, with a gradual climb up a shaded forest road. The tree-filled hillsides of Mount Adams have an ethereal feel, especially along the road the higher you climb—it's as if you've entered an enchanted place. The forest has an openness to it, far different from the rain forests of the Olympic Peninsula. The trees come in every size, but it's the way shafts of afternoon summer sun filter through them that gives the forest a warm, cozy feeling. When the gravel road finally gives way to packed dirt, the climb becomes easier, but because you're riding up the interior of this special place, you hardly feel as if

Coming down the Cold Springs Trail.

you're climbing. Then of course, Mount Adams can be seen through the trees, watching silently as you traverse its sides in the name of that sacred word—FUN.

After seven miles of climbing, you may be greeted by climbers, skiers, and snow boarders coming and going from the peaks above. Judging by the size of the parking area and the number of portable toilets, there's a lot of traffic headed for the base of the snowline. Catch the trail at the end of the parking lot, and your descent begins quickly. As with other rides in the area, if there hasn't been a lot of rain, the trails will be dusty. You'll fly down the Cold Creek Trail and intersect with the Gotchen Creek Trail, which then launches you through the woods. The singletrack ends near a horse corral area, for a rolling ride back, complete with whooptee-doos and a short climb along low-use forest roads to Wicky Creek Horse Shelter.

Big Tree...

Only 15% of the Pacific Northwest's old-growth forests remain—only 5% throughout the U.S. Visit a rare site, the **Big Tree**. It is one of the largest known ponderosa pines in the Gifford Pinchot National Forest. (Follow Forest Road 820 up one-half of a mile on the right.)

Diameter: 84 inches.
Height: 202 feet.
Age: Probably 420 years or more.

MilesDirections

0.0 START from the Wicky Creek Horse shelter heading left, up Forest Road 80/8040.
1.3 Pass Spur Road 782 on the right.
2.1 Pass Spur Road 792.
3.1 Climbing the road, run into Gotchen Creek Trail #40 on the right. Stay on Forest Road 80/8040, continuing up.
3.7 Pass the Crofton Ridge Trail #73 trailhead on the left at Morrison Creek. This heads into Indian Heaven Wilderness (open to hikers and equestrians only). Parking and camping are available. Continue straight.
3.9 Pass Short Horn Trail #16 on the left. Forest Road 80/8040 turns into Spur Road 500. Continue.
6.7 The climb ends at the South Climb Trail #183 Trailhead parking lot.
6.8 Follow the road through the parking area to Cold Springs Trail #72. The trail starts out as doubletrack, climbing slightly until it levels out and becomes singletrack.

7.0 Follow the Cold Springs Trail #72.
8.2 Arrive at a small clearing. Catch the trail on the other side. Be prepared for a short, extremely difficult section to ride. Your descent averages 500 feet per mile.
10.3 Travel over a small, exposed arm of a lava bed—somewhat technical.
10.7 Intersect with Gotchen Creek Trail #40. Forest Road 80/8040 is two miles to the right and Forest Road 8020 is to the left. Turn left.
11.7 Arrive at the trailhead for the Gotchen Creek Trail. Go about 50 feet past the trailhead, beyond a fenced area, and turn right onto Forest Road 8020.
12.0 Turn right onto Spur Road 020.
12.6 Pass Spur 125. Switchback right and left.
13.6 Pass Spur 31 on the right.
14.2 Pass the last spur on the right, coming up to Forest Road 80/8040.
14.5 Arrive at Forest Road 80/8040. Turn right and head to Wicky Creek Horse Shelter.
15.7 Arrive at the horse shelter.

Ride Information

Trail Maintenance Hotlines:
• Gifford Pinchot National Forest Headquarters, Vancouver, WA (360) 891-5000
• Gifford Pinchot National Forest, Randle Ranger District (360) 497-1100
• Mount Adams Ranger District, Trout Lake, WA; (509) 395-2501
• Weather Radio: AM 1340

Schedule:
Open when free of snow. Best between Memorial Day and mid-October.

Cost:
$3 per day per car or $25 for an annual pass; appropriate camping fees for overnight camping

Local Events/Attractions:
• Arts Festival & Volkssport Walk in July, Trout Lake, WA (509) 395-2294
• Community Fair and Dairy Show in August, Trout Lake, WA (509) 395-2241
• Huckleberry picking in August all over the Mount Adams area. Map and permits are available at the Trout Lake Ranger Station.

Local Bike Shops:
• Dick's Bicycle Center, Vancouver, WA (360) 696-9234
• Excel Fitness, Vancouver, WA (360) 834-8506
• Discovery Bicycles, Hood River, OR (541) 386-4820
• Mountain View Cycles & Fitness, Hood River, OR; (541) 386-2888

Maps:
• Maptech CD-ROM: Mount Adams East & Mount Adams West, WA
• DeLorme's Washington Atlas & Gazetteer—Page 34 C4
• Mt. Adams Ranger District Map (Pacific Northwest Region)

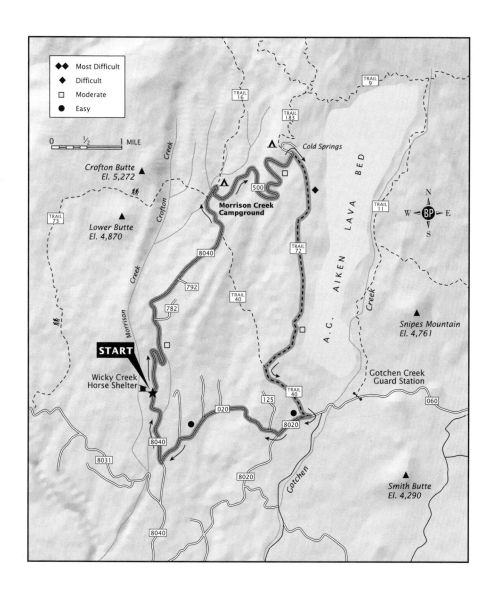

Most Difficult
Difficult
□ Moderate
● Easy

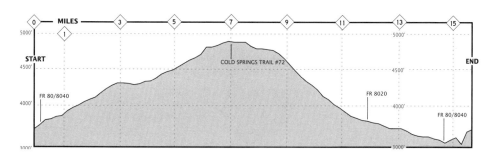

Siouxon Creek
Out & Back

Ride Summary

If you like smooth singletrack, lush forests, and little elevation gain, this ride will easily become one of your favorites. In fact, the ride begins downhill, so the only gain is in climbing back up from the trail along Siouxon Creek. Ride as fast as you want or slow down to enjoy the view. This trail is enjoyable to all.

Ride Specs

Start: Trailhead on Forest Road 5701
Length: 14 miles
Approximate Riding Time: 2-3 hours
Nearest Town: Chelatchie
Rating: Easy, though long
Terrain: Singletrack, beautifully maintained with some technical sections
Other Trail Users: Hikers and horseback riders

Getting There

From Woodland: Take State Route 503 east (toward Cougar). Turn right at the traffic light following the signs for LaCenter/Amboy, heading onto County Road 16, also called Hayes Road. At the "Y" intersection turn right up the hill onto Northeast Cedar Road. Follow for about 17 miles. Just north of Amboy, stay straight at the "Y" intersection. Travel two miles to Chelatchie. Pass the Ranger station on the left. Turn right onto Northeast Healy Road. Follow for seven miles over a one-lane bridge. At the "Y" intersection turn right following the paved road. Enter the Gifford Pinchot National Forest. Veer left at the "Y" intersection on Forest Road 57. Turn left at the "T" intersection on Forest Road 5701. Follow to the sharp bend in the road and look for the trailhead marker on the left-hand side. If you can't find it, drive two miles to the end of the road and park. Pick up the trail there.

This southern Washington ride is located a little over an hour north of the Oregon border in the Gifford Pinchot National Forest, making it an easy trip to and from the cities of Vancouver and Portland. If you're not coming from these cities, they're definitely worth visiting. Situated opposite one another, with the Columbia River and state line running between, both towns, despite their nearness, have histories distinctly their own.

Occupying the Columbia's north bank is Vancouver, named for British explorer Capt. George Vancouver who's team, in 1792, landed on what is today Vancouver soil. Now one of Washington's fastest growing cities, Vancouver began as the British-owned Hudson's Bay Company's Northwest outpost, Fort Vancouver. In less than two years, it was a fully functioning town, with 40 buildings, a sawmill, and 700 grazing cattle. At the center of British and American dispute for years, the fort was eventually abandoned by the Hudson's Bay Company in the 1840s when America and Britain finally settled on a boundary along the 49th parallel.

Soon after the Hudson's Bay Company left, the United States took over the fort, using it as a military post. Such notable military leaders as Phillip Sheridan and Ulysses S. Grant were stationed here briefly. In short order, a townsite was plotted. Still on the fringe, the town became a thriving settlement. By the late 1800s to early 1900s shipbuilding was the big industry. During both World Wars, the city churned out hundreds of ships for the war effort. Woodie Guthrie, the famed folksinger and political activist, contributed to this effort as a laborer for the Kaiser Shipyards. In the years to follow, shipbuilding waned. Today Vancouver's economy depends more heavily on wood products, electronics, and food processing—as well as on the economy of neighboring Portland.

Vancouver has plenty of historic sites to visit. Six of Fort Vancouver's original 27 buildings have been reconstructed and are

A crossing of West Creek.

now managed by the National Park Service. Daily tours are available year-round. Actors in period dress portray what life was like during the Hudson's Bay Company's trading post days. If you'd like to see a real piece of history, stop off at the Old Apple Tree Park along the river, east of I-5. In 1826 John McLoughlin, the chief factor of Fort Vancouver, planted the park's centerpiece with seeds he received from London. Many contend that this apple tree, which still produces tiny green apples, is the oldest apple tree in the Northwest.

From Vancouver, the Siouxon Creek ride is about an hour northeast. Starting at the trailhead on Forest Road 5701, you head immediately down into the woods. This trail is incredibly smooth. Rip-roaring into some great downhill, your tires hardly make a sound as they whirl across the needle-covered forest floor in fast pursuit of the river below. Reaching Siouxon Creek, the trail then chases alongside it until you decide to turn around and head back. The gurgling, bubbling water of Siouxon Creek can be heard occasionally over your own breath, urging you to hurry. Cooling waterholes are inviting on hot days, but there is a good portion of the trail that is fairly high above the water.

This huge washout was repaired in August 1997.

There are a couple of trail intersections along this ride. Adventurous trails to Siouxon and Huffman peaks make a great loop that will take all day to complete—probably 25 to 30 miles round-trip. The one trail you must be sure to avoid is the Horseshoe Ridge Trail. Totally overgrown, the Horseshoe Ridge Trail is ridiculously steep and mountain bikers will find themselves carrying their bikes over 75 percent of the trail. There has been little maintenance here, and many fallen trees block the way—perfect hideouts for communities of bees (a painfully realized fact).

The Siouxon Creek Trail follows the river for a long way though, all the way to Forest Road 58 if one is inclined to ride that far—about seven to eight miles. This ride turns around a bit earlier than that. And when you're done, you can camp out at the trailhead and ride it again the next day.

Ride Information

Trail Maintenance Hotlines:
- Gifford Pinchot National Forest, Amboy, WA; (360) 247-3900
- Gifford Pinchot National Forest Headquarters, Vancouver, WA (360) 891-5000

Schedule:
This ride is open year-round depending on snow levels.

Costs:
$3 per day per car or $25 for an annual pass.

Local Information:
- Vancouver/Clark County Visitors Center: (360) 694-2588 or 1-800-377-7084
- Historic Fort Vancouver, Vancouver, WA (360) 696-7655 or 1-800-832-3599
- Outdoor Recreational Information (206) 470-4060

Local Events/Attractions:
- Vancouver Festival in mid-June, Vancouver, WA; (360) 693-1313
- Vancouver Days, 4th of July weekend, Vancouver, WA; (360) 693-1313
- Heritage Weekend in May, Vancouver, WA; (360) 693-1313
- Victorian Gaming Days and Marshall House Tours in July, Vancouver, WA (360) 693-1313

Local Bike Shops:
- Dick's Bicycle Center, Vancouver, WA (360) 696-9234
- Excel Fitness, Vancouver, WA (360) 834-8506
- Discovery Bicycles, Hood River, OR (541) 386-4820
- Mountain View Cycles & Fitness, Hood River, OR; (541) 386-2888

Maps:
- Maptech CD-ROM: Siouxon Peak, WA and Bare Mountain, WA
- Green Trails: Lookout Mountain No. 396
- Washington Atlas & Gazetteer— Page 23 A7

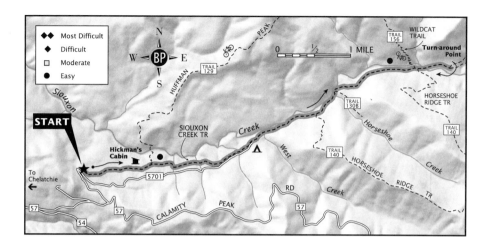

MilesDirections

0.0 START at the 4"x4" post trailhead marker on the north side of Forest Road 5701.

1.2 Intersect with Huffman Peak Trail #129, which leads down to and across Siouxon Creek, then up to Huffman Peak. Continue straight for the river trail.

3.2 At the "T" intersection turn left toward the river. The right turns take you up to the camping areas at the end of Forest Road 5701. Traverse down the ridge.

3.5 Cross a bridge over West Creek. Follow the main trail to Siouxon Creek.

4.4 Intersect with Horseshoe Ridge Trail #140. (Avoid this trail.) Keep straight.

4.9 This wooden bridge makes a good lunch spot over Horseshoe Creek.

5.0 Intersect with Trail #130B, a spur to Horseshoe Creek Falls. Keep to the Siouxon Creek Trail.

5.3 Arrive at a bench with a beautiful view of the waterfall on Siouxon Creek.

7.0 Come to the other end of the Horseshoe Trail #140, having passed signs for the Siouxon Peak Trail #156A, Wildcat #156, and Wildcat Falls. Chinook Trail #130A is coming up. This is the turn-around point. The Siouxon Creek Trail can also be continued on as far up the drainage as you want.

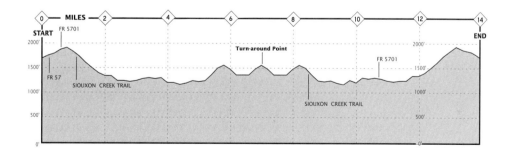

Falls Creek Shuttle

Ride Summary

With falls, sponge cake-like trail, and lava caves, this route has all the ingredients for a great mountain biking trail. It's a 16-mile moderate shuttle ride that can be made into a loop by riding back to the sno-park at Oldman Pass (elevation 2,788 feet) from the bottom of Falls Creek on a paved forest road. Riding this route in reverse from the river to the pass is quite difficult, and not much fun either.

Ride Specs

Start: Oldman Pass Sno-Park

Other Starting Locations: Falls Creek Trailhead

Length: 15.8 miles

Approximate Riding Time: 2-3 hours

Nearest Town: Carson

Rating: Moderate to difficult for technical descents

Terrain: Singletrack, forest road, and paved road without a shuttle

Other Trail Users: Hikers, horseback riders, and cross-country skiers

Getting There

From Woodland: Take State Route 503 (The Lewis River Road) east past Cougar. State Route 503 becomes Forest Road 90 at the Swift Creek Reservoir. Follow Forest Road 90 east toward Carson. Turn right on Curly Creek Road. Turn right on Wind River Road. Follow to Oldman Pass Sno-Park area. Park at Oldman Pass for the ride. To shuttle, take one car down Wind River Road (National Forest Road 30) 10 miles to the sharp left up Forest Road 3063. Park here or farther north at the Falls Creek Trailhead.

Mount St. Helens and Mount Rainier in the distance.

The Falls Creek Shuttle is located in the heart of the Wind River Ranger District within Gifford Pinchot National Forest. Whether you access this ride from the northwest or southwest, the route will be very scenic. From the northwest, you'll travel below the edge of the Mount St. Helens National Volcanic Monument. Even from the road, the views are outstanding. Coming from the southwest, follow the Columbia River along State Route 14 and see what caught the attention of early explorers Lewis and Clark. Rising 848 feet above the river is a solid basalt landmark. Beacon Rock is the largest feature of its kind in North America, second only in the world to the Rock of Gibraltar. Just take State Route 14 (the Lewis and Clark Highway) north of the town of Bonneville—you can't miss it. Beacon Rock is now the center attraction of its own state park; a gift from the family of Henry Biddle who, in 1915, saved it from becoming a rock quarry. Lewis and Clark are reputedly the first white men to have seen it as they journeyed west to the Pacific in 1805. The rock was later seen by a fur trader named Alexander Ross, who, in 1811, called it "Inshoach Castle," which may explain why the rock was referred to as "Castle Rock" until 1916—the year the U.S. Board of Geographic Names officially proclaimed it Beacon Rock.

Continuing east on State Road 14, you'll come to the Columbia River Gorge Interpretive Center, a mile west of Stevenson. After peering through the museum's 40-foot tall picture window at the Columbia River, you can tour their amazing exhibits (like an interior basalt cliff, a waterfall, a 37-foot fishwheel, etc.—not to mention the world's largest collection of Rosary beads). To round out your educational experience, stop off at the Skamania

County Historical Museum in Stevenson. If you enjoy history, especially about Washington and the Columbia River, you'll love their collection.

The town of Carson is the end of the line before stepping off into the Gifford Pinchot National Forest (which, incidentally, is named after the founder of the U.S. Forest Service, Gifford Pinchot). Depending on how you feel after the ride, you may opt to return to this quaint little town, complete with old-fashioned false storefronts. This quiet destination is slow-paced and relaxed. Should you need to sooth your mountain bike aches and pains, the historic Carson Hot Springs Resort has some 126-degree mineral baths that might do the trick. Discovered in 1876, these springs have long been considered the cure for whatever ails you.

If you need more than one night of pampering, you can stay at the St. Martin Hotel, built in 1897. This bathhouse resort was the vision of Isadore St. Martin. The three-story hotel quickly became a well-known stop for visitors seeking the healing waters of the hot

Taking a rest at the Falls Creek Falls.

springs. Patrons arrived mostly by steamboat, up the Columbia River. But you can get there via Wind River Road from State Route 14, or follow Hot Springs Road toward Carson. You might also try the Government Mineral Springs, 15 miles north of Carson on Wind River Road.

After you've completed your brief site-seeing tour, travel to Oldman Pass, just south of Mount St. Helens and Mount Adams. The terrain is similar to high desert—dry and warm with low relative humidity. The forest is thick but the ground below its canopy is hardly lush. Ferns and saplings push through long, brown, spiny needles on the forest's floor. The air is crisp, making your skin feel dry and your body thirsty. This is the type of climate where even after a heavy workout, your clothes will feel instantly dry.

The trail starts near a sno-park along the paved road. It's used by cross-country skiers in the winter and is well marked as it meanders through meadows and singletrack. There are lava caves about halfway down, which you'll want to check out if you have time. Eventually, the trail leads a winding descent along Falls Creek to Falls Creek Falls. Below the falls, the singletrack is as smooth as silk and as fast as lightning. About two miles from the end, the trail becomes steep and has surprising, sharp turns. Cross the beautiful, sturdy wooden bridge over Falls Creek. The trail stops at the trailhead parking area where welcoming picnic tables and cool river pools await.

After the ride, especially if you've traveled a ways, you'll want a quiet place to camp— that is, unless you head back to the Carson Hot Springs Resort. You'll find a couple of pay-to-camp places between Oldman Pass and the trailhead where the ride ends: Paradise Camp, Little Soda Springs, and Beaver Camp—along Meadow Creek Road. There are always pull-offs from the main road, if you prefer. These sites, usually logging roads, are often more quiet than designated campsites. But, they may not always be legal, so make sure you read any postings on trees or telephone poles to make sure you're not trespassing.

MilesDirections

0.0 START from the Oldman Pass Sno-Park. Follow the trail running next to Wind River Road to the right. Turn right on Trail #150.

1.2 Look for the blue diamond cross-country ski markers on the trees. Cross a small wooden bridge.

1.8 Turn right on Forest Road #3053.

2.0 Pass a clear-cut on the right.

3.0 Pass Snowfoot Trail #151 on the right. Continue on the road.

3.2 Intersect with Trail #159. Take Trail #157 toward Forest Road 65.

3.3 The road turns into McClellan Meadows Trail #157.

4.0 Cross a wooden bridge over a creek into Pete's Gulch.

4.5 Cross a dry drainage on a bridge.

5.0 The trail crosses Forest Road 6701. Continue straight.

6.5 Intersect with Forest Road 65. Turn right down the hill on a gravel road.

6.6 Enter Falls Creek Horse Camp at the apex of the hill. Find the trail on the right. Take trail #157 heading to the Lava Caves.

8.0 The trail opens to a great view of Mount Hood.

8.3 Cross Forest Road 6701. Continue down.

9.4 The singletrack turns into doubletrack.

9.7 The trail enters a picnic area. Follow Forest Road 6701.

10.0 The doubletrack becomes improved dirt road and the trail is directly across. Follow the trail.

11.0 The trail enters a junction with Forest Roads 67 and 6701. Follow the sign for Falls Creek Trail, continuing straight.

12.0 Turn left as the singletrack turns onto a gravel road, #6053.

13.1 When the doubletrack ends, take the trail to the left.

13.3 Follow the singletrack to the right as the trail widens.

14.8 Arrive at a campsite clearing. Check out Falls Creek Falls on the left.

15.0 Arrive at a "Y" in the trail. The left is to an overlook. Take the trail to the right.

15.8 Turn left to cross a wooden bridge and right after crossing to the parking lot of the Falls Creek Trailhead.

From here, pick up your shuttle or pedal back to Oldman Pass Sno-Park on Meadow Creek Road –Route 30 (8.5 miles).

Ride Information

Trail Maintenance Hotlines:
- *Gifford Pinchot National Forest's Wind River Ranger Station, Carson, WA (509) 427-5645*
- *Gifford Pinchot National Forest Headquarters, Vancouver, WA (360) 891-5000*

Schedule:
This trail is open year-round depending on seasonal snow levels.

Costs:
$3 per car per day or $25 for an annual pass

Local Information:
Stevenson Chamber of Commerce and Visitor Information Center (509) 427-8911

Local Events/Attractions:
- *Beacon Rock State Park: (509) 427-8265*

- *Columbia Gorge Interpretive Center, Stevenson, WA; (509) 427-8211*
- *Skamania County Historical Museum, Stevenson, WA; (509) 427-9435*
- *Columbia Gorge Bluegrass Festival, Stevenson, WA; (509) 427-8928*
- *Carson Hot Springs Resort, Carson, WA (509) 427-8292 or 1-800-607-3678*

Local Bike Shops:
- *Discovery Bicycles, Hood River, OR (541) 386-4820*
- *Mountain View Cycles & Fitness, Hood River, OR; (541) 386-2888*

Maps:
- *Maptech CD-ROM: Termination Point, WA*
- *Green Trails: Lookout No. 396 and Wind River No. 397*
- *DeLorme's Washington Atlas & Gazetteer—Page 24 A2*
- *Gifford Pinchot NF–Windriver Ranger District Map*

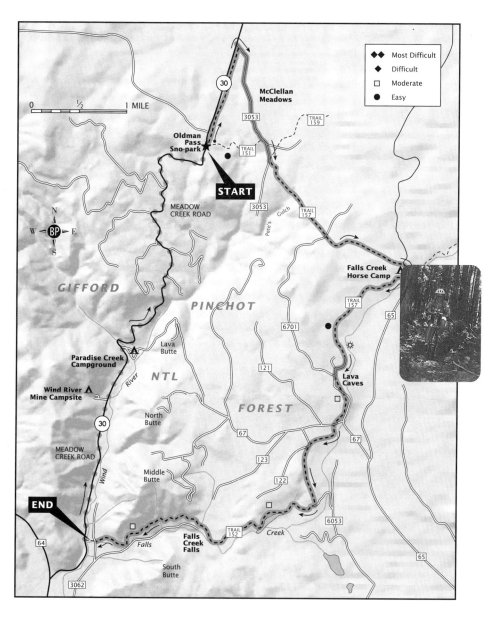

Most Difficult ◆◆
Difficult ◆
Moderate □
Easy ●

30

McClellan
Meadows

3053

TRAIL
159

Oldman
Pass
Sno-park

TRAIL
151

START

MEADOW
CREEK ROAD

3053

Pete's Gulch

TRAIL
157

Falls Creek
Horse Camp

TRAIL
157

65

N
W — BP — E
S

GIFFORD

PINCHOT

6701

Lava
Butte

121

NTL

Lava
Caves

Paradise Creek
Campground

River

FOREST

Wind River
Mine Campsite

30

North
Butte

67

67

MEADOW
CREEK ROAD

123

Middle
Butte

122

6053

Wind

END

TRAIL
152

Creek

65

64

Falls

Falls
Creek
Falls

South
Butte

3062

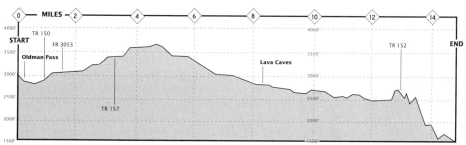

MILES
0 · 2 · 4 · 6 · 8 · 10 · 12 · 14
4000'
START
TR 150
FR 3053
END
3500'
Oldman Pass
3000'
Lava Caves
TR 152
2500'
TR 157
2000'
1500'

171

33

Yacolt's Larch Mountain

Ride Summary

This trail is a favorite among local mountain bikers. In an area that is hot and dry in the summer, the cool shade of the initial singletrack climb along Cold Creek is inviting, though it can get a bit humid. It's not an easy climb along the river. There are roots and rocks and slippery surfaces. But, once it moves up and away from the water, the trail conditions improve all the way to the top, where the terrain, more like a rock quarry than a mountain biking trail, is challenging to ride but spectacular for its views.

Ride Specs

Start: Rock Creek Campground
Other Starting Locations: Cold Creek Campground
Length: 13.4 miles
Approximate Riding Time: 3-4 hours
Rating: Moderate with steep climbing and technical trails
Terrain: Singletrack, muddy in some places and extremely rooty and rocky in others; and Forest Road
Other Trail Users: Hikers and horseback riders

Getting There

From Woodland: Take State Route 503 east to Cougar. Turn right at the traffic light toward LaCenter/Amboy, following County Road 16 (also called Hayes Road). At the "Y," turn right onto NE Cedar Road. Travel 17 miles (from Cougar) to a stop sign. Follow the signs to the right for Amboy on County Road 16. Travel through Amboy to Moulton Falls County Park. Continue 1.5 miles to Dole Valley Road. After approximately four miles, the pavement turns to gravel and the road becomes Forest Road L-1000. Rock Creek Campground is within one mile on the left. Cold Creek Campground is another half-mile ahead on L-1000. The Trail starts from either place.

L arch Mountain is located within the Yacolt Burn State Forest, bordering the Gifford Pinchot National Forest. There are several mountain biking trails within this Department of Natural Resources operated tract, some connecting with national forest trails. One such trail is an oasis within this fire-torn forest called the Rock Creek/Larch Mountain Trail.

Sheltered from the burning rays of the sun, the Rock Creek/Larch Mountain Trail offers a thick wooded climb along Cold Creek. Riding to the peak of Larch Mountain is a great way to get a lot of exercise in a rather short amount of time; but there are longer loop options as well. Considerably more comfortable (and more interesting) than riding under the open-sky of a road climb, the singletrack up this trail offers a moderate-to-technical ascent and a powerful return descent. Pedaling by forest ferns and families of mushroom garlands, the climb grows steeper as the trail pulls away from the creek. Narrow sections of exposed roots and rocks offer a challenge to advanced riders. Less advanced riders might be inclined to walk through these more difficult places. The climb tops out just past an exposed boulder field at a picnic area. At this point, you can do an about-face and head back or take the trail farther up to a radio tower on the peak.

The ride begins at Rock Creek Campground, a first-come/first-serve DNR regulated facility. The camp host/ grounds-keeper is a lovely fellow who lives right at the campground

and has maps if you need them and advice on which trails are best to ride. The trail described here is one of his recommendations.

Depending on trail conditions, you could begin at the Rock Creek Campground up the Tarbell Trail, but it's often muddy and chopped up from horses' hooves. Especially after a rain, the trail can have thick, tire-sucking muck. To avoid the muck, ride the L-1000 Road about a mile up to the Rock Creek/Larch Mountain Trailhead, crossing at Cold Creek. There are a few sticky sections in the beginning of this trail, down by the river, but conditions improve quickly as you climb.

Toward the top, after a climb that never seems to end, the trail crosses a cluster of huge boulders imbedded in the forest floor. The surface of the trail is rounded like lumpy, air-hardened Play-Doh. Moss grows in the shady crevices, which can make the surface treacherously slick. Trees grow next to, on top of, and in-between the boulders, making it a curious site—and a highly technical place to ride.

Closer to the top of Larch Mountain, after passing through the "em-bouldered forest," the trail crosses over a field of talus. Huge chunks of sharp, black-gray granite are piled on top of each other. As the rock peaks weaken from lack of forest cover, large sections simply break off and fall to level ground, leaving a sloped pile of debris—what geologists call "talus." A picnic table has been set up in the center of the talus field. A sign alongside reads: "The Flintstone Picnic Area." The technically skilled rider may be able to negotiate wheels-over-rock through here. Anyone else will recognize his or her limits in short order. The trail, at this point, is nothing more than a faint dusty line made by the dirty bottoms of hikers' boots and a few dirty knobbies.

The top of the mountain is a short ride from a crossroad of trails. This is the turn-around point. From here you can take the trail back the way you came—which takes about half the time it did to climb up, or you could continue a little less than one mile further along steep doubletrack to a radio tower and an open field. The views from here are not as rewarding as you'd expect. In fact, they're pretty uninspiring. The trees and the tower tend to obstruct a good view. The talus field actually offers the best views.

There are a few other options to get to the top of Larch Mountain. For a road climb, take

Table Mountain. Photo Courtesy of DNR.

The 1902 Yacolt Burn

On September 12, 1902, sparks from a cut-over being cleared for farmland ignited the nearby forest. On the wings of the fierce autumn winds, the fire blossomed into an inferno and went on to kill thirty-eight people and destroy 238,000 acres of forest before it was through. So big and destructive was the fire that it earned a name: the Yacolt Burn. It lasted only 36 hours but managed to travel 30 miles, between the towns of Carson and Yacolt. It was something that no one at the time was prepared to handle.

The fire was so hot, people say, that paint blistered on houses in the small town of Yacolt. And the skies were so blackened that chickens went to roost at midday. It's estimated that enough wood burned to build every third Washington resident a three-bedroom home—that's 12 billion board feet of lumber, valued in 1902 at $30 million. An informational sign in the area says that it took 20 years for loggers to "clean up" the forests and salvage what they could of the burned timber.

In this arid part of the state, fire is fed easily and can spread quickly when fanned by gusty winds. Although fire is Mother Nature's way of rejuvenating a forest, the lack of forest fire prevention methods are blamed for the 1902 Yacolt fire burning out of control for so long. Despite the state's efforts to reforest the Yacolt area, warm summer winds continue to blow and have fed several fires over the years since 1902. Where fire usually activates new growth in a forest, the fires in the Yacolt have left the soil badly damaged and unable to sustain much plant life.

In recent years, modern methods of reforestation have been employed to bring the forests back. Combined with advanced fire control action, these new methods have allowed a new, green look to come to the Yacolt Burn State Forest. Barren areas are once again beginning to see life return. In the years to come, maybe historians will have to think hard about why this forest has such a name.

Photo courtesy of DNR.

the L-1200 road up the Grouse Creek drainage to the Grouse Creek Vista. At the vista, turn right on the Tarbell Trail and ride two miles to the top of Larch Mountain. From the top, ride down the Rock Creek/Larch Mountain Trail. The total mileage will be about the same as if riding the singletrack up and back. Keep in mind that the road is very gravelly and steep and fully exposed. In the heat of summer, this can be a very hot way to climb.

Another option is to follow the trail as explained in the directions to the top of Larch Mountain. From there, take the Tarbell Trail left for two miles to Grouse Vista. Just past the L-1200 Road, the trail forks. Stay left for the Tarbell Trail, (the right heads onto National Forest Service Trail #172 to Silver Star Mountain). Follow the Tarbell Trail through some amazing switchbacks, around Sturgeon Rock, past some falls, and around Squaw Butte for a total of nine miles to the Tarbell Campground. Continue on the Tarbell Trail three miles to complete the loop at Rock Creek Campground. This loop can, of course, be ridden in reverse order, making it about a 21-mile ride.

MilesDirections

0.0 START from the Rock Creek Campground. Turn left onto Road L-1000.

0.4 Stay right at the "Y" on Road L-1000.

1.0 Pass the entrance for Cold Creek Campground to the right (day use only.) Stay on L-1000.

1.4 As the road crosses Cold Creek, see the trailhead on the south side to the left. The sign says: "5.5 miles—Larch Mountain/Grouse Mountain Vista Junction; Larch Mountain 6 miles; Grouse Creek 7.25 miles; Grouse Vista 8.5 miles." This ride follows the Rock Creek/Larch Mountain Trail (also called the Tarbell Trail).

1.8 Cross a wooden bridge over the creek.

2.0 Cross another wooden bridge over a marshy area.

2.9 Pass a trail turnout that dead-ends.

3.2 Cross a wooden bridge and begin some serious climbing to the summit of Larch Mountain (3,496 ft.).

3.8 Cross another bridge over Cold Creek.

3.9 Encounter more switchbacks, still heading up.

4.2 At the five-way intersection, take the trail heading up—the third trail if you count left to right.

5.6 Reach the boulder field for views of Mount Rainier and Mount St. Helens. Enjoy a moment at the Flintstone Picnic Area.

6.2 Arrive at the intersection with Tarbell Trail. Continue straight to Larch Mountain and the radio tower, a half-mile ahead.

[To ride to Grouse Vista, follow the Tarbell Trail up and left for 2.5 miles. This also leads to Road L-1200 for an optional road descent.]

6.7 Reach the top. Turn around and head back the way you came.

Ride Information

Trail Maintenance Hotlines:
Department of Natural Resources Southwest Region; (509) 925-6131, 1-800-527-3305

Schedule:
This trail is open year-round depending on snow levels.

Local Information:
• Vancouver/Clark County Visitors Services; (360) 694-2588 or 1-800-377-7084
• Historic Fort Vancouver, Vancouver, WA (360) 696-7655 or 1-800-832-3599
• Gifford Pinchot National Forest, Amboy, WA; (360) 247-3900

Local Events/Attractions:
• Yacolt Herb Festival in May, Yacolt, WA (360) 686-3537
• Vancouver Festival in mid-June, Vancouver, WA; (360) 693-1313

• Vancouver Days, 4th of July weekend, Vancouver, WA; (360) 693-1313
• Heritage Weekend in May, Vancouver, WA; (360) 693-1313
• Victorian Gaming Days and Marshall House Tours in July, Vancouver, WA (360) 693-1313

Local Bike Shops:
• Dick's Bicycle Center, Vancouver, WA (360) 696-9234
• Excel Fitness, Vancouver, WA (360) 834-8506

Maps:
• Maptech CD-ROM: Dole, WA; Larch Mountain, WA
• DeLorme's Washington Atlas & Gazetteer Page 23 C6
• Tarbell & Jones Creek Trail Systems/DNR

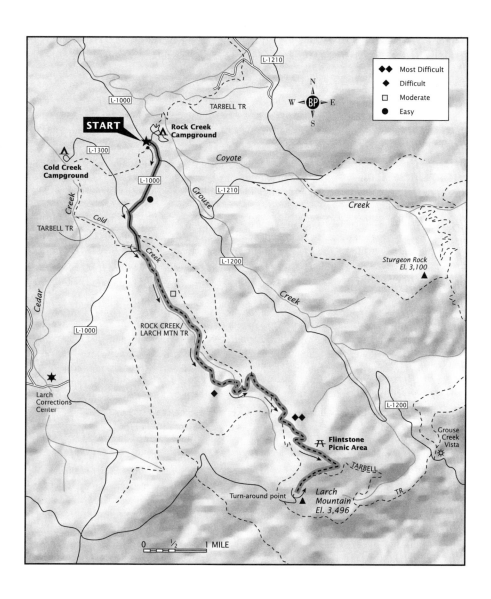

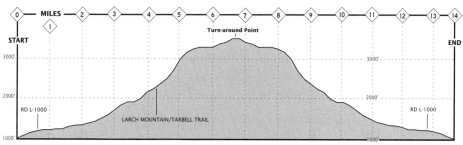

Honorable Mentions

Southwest Washington

Compiled here is an index of great rides in the Southwest region that didn't make the A-list this time around but deserve recognition. Check them out and let us know what you think. You may decide that one or more of these rides deserves higher status in future editions or, perhaps, you may have a ride of your own that merits some attention.

(K) Iron Horse Trail

A great ride for beginning mountain bikers, this scenic path is just east of Snoqualmie Pass and has great views of Lake Keechelus.

From Seattle, take I-90 to exit 54 at Snoqualmie Pass to the Keechelus Trailhead. Riding east on the trail, you'll eventually run into Easton. Ride west on the trail to bike through the Snoqualmie Tunnel, the longest hiking/biking tunnel in the U.S. Go as far as North Bend if you have the legs for it. For more information, call the Snoqualmie Pass Visitors Center at (360) 677-2414. See *DeLorme's Washington Atlas & Gazetteer: Page 65, A&B-5&6*.

(L) Taneum Creek Loop

This is a great ride on a super-hot day, but be prepared in case Mother Nature gives you a surprise. The first time we rode this trail, in early August, it was hot, and crossing the rivers was wonderfully refreshing. The second time we visited—the very next weekend— it snowed on us at the summit! The route's elevation gains and technical trails make this a difficult ride. The loop begins climbing from creekside at Forest Road 3300 up Forest Road 135, paralleling the South Fork of Taneum Creek. Toward the top, roads interchange as Forest Road 135 ends and becomes Forest Road 3300 on the left. Pass the Taneum Ridge Trail (also a good route) and turn right on Fishhook Flats Trail #1378. The descent screams past meadows for almost three miles, racing back to the road. Arrive at Forest Road 3300 again and head down to the North Fork of Taneum Creek. After 3.5 miles, turn right onto North Fork Taneum Creek Trail #1377 where the real fun begins. On hot summer days, you'll relish the number of creek crossings on this trail as the course runs through thick forest. Ride past a spur back to Forest Road 3300 and the Fishhook Flats Trail. Cross Forest Road 133. When the path ends, turn right downhill. In half a mile, turn right again onto a trail that leads to Forest Road 33 and back to the creekside parking area at Forest Road 3300.

Take I-90 to Exit 93 east of Cle Elum. Cross the highway and turn right at the "T" intersection driving east alongside I-90. Cross back over the next overpass and turn left on Taneum Creek Road. Travel 10 miles to a three-way intersection, turning left onto Forest Road 3300. Park on the other side of Taneum Creek. For more information call the Cle Elum Ranger District at (509) 674-4411. *See DeLorme's Washington Atlas & Gazetteer: Page 66, D1*.

(M) Oak Creek Trail

A feeding station for elk just outside of Naches, this desert ride is also a popular place for rattlesnakes. The 10 miles out and back are well maintained and begin moderately but become more advanced. Start from the bridge and pass through the elk gate. After that, the directions are simple: follow the trail west about five miles to the canal and turn around. The canal route continues for a couple of miles with many side trails to explore.

Take U.S. Route 12 north from Yakima. Shortly after Naches the road splits. Stay to the left on U.S. Route 12 (State Route 410 goes right). Continue to the Oak Creek Elk

Feeding Station. Park immediately before the bridge. For more information, contact the Naches Ranger Station at (509) 653-2205. See *DeLorme's Washington Atlas & Gazetteer: Page 50, C2.*

N Cowiche Canyon Conservancy Trails

Ideal for all mountain bikers, this ride is situated just outside of Yakima's city limits in a locally-maintained conservancy area. Cowiche Canyon's main trail is an old railroad grade. Follow the well-kept gravel course over nine bridges along the Cowiche Creek east to the Scenic Trail. It's possible to take the Overlook Trail between bridges eight and nine and climb from the canyon floor to the uplands area for a gorgeous view. There is a trailhead and parking on the plateau, also offering great mountain biking trails. Explore the area's miles of rideable trails and create various loops. But do this with care. The Cowiche Canyon Conservancy is a designated shrub-steppe ecosystem. It's very fragile and home to many rare plants. Stay on existing trails and avoid heading in and out of the canyon when the trails are wet to prevent further problems with erosion. Park at the main trailhead at the west end of Summitview at Weikel Road.

From Yakima, head west on Summitview. Pass 96th Avenue. Turn right at Weikel Road (at the log-built veterinary clinic). Travel a quarter of a mile to a green marker sign for the Cowiche Canyon Trail and turn right into the parking lot. Contact the Cowiche Canyon Conservancy in Yakima at (509) 577-9585. See *DeLorme's Washington Atlas & Gazetteer: Page 50, C3.*

O Juniper Ridge Loop

One of the state's most beautiful yet demanding rides, the Juniper Ridge Loop covers 18 miles of pavement and approximately 17 miles of singletrack. Not far from Randle, this course encounters about 4,000 feet of elevation change through a variety of mountain and lowland zones. However, there are several alternate routes along this ridge, allowing cyclists to tailor the ride to their own fitness level.

Ride over the Cispus River, then turn right onto Forest Road 23 and again at the North Fork Campground, following Forest Road 23. Climb Forest Road 23 past several spur roads. Turn right on Trail #263 toward Dark Mountain and Jumbo Peak. Turn right at the "T" intersection onto Trail #261 heading into some steep switchbacks. Follow the trail around Jumbo, Sunrise, and Juniper peaks, which becomes Trail #294—the Tongue Mountain Trail. Continue down to Forest Road 2801.

Turn left on Forest Road 2801 to get back to your car.

From I-5 south of Chehalis, exit onto State Route 12 east. Follow 12 to Randle. Turn right onto Woods Creek Road. Turn right onto Cispus Road, following it to the Cispus River. Park along Forest Road 2801.For more information, contact the Randle Ranger District at (360) 497-1100. See *DeLorme's Washington Atlas & Gazetteer: Page 50, D3&4*.

Ⓟ Lewis River

A fast and furious loop along the Lewis River in the southern part of the state, this moderate trail is just about as good as a trail can get. Start at the southern end of the Lewis River Trail #31 from Forest Road 9039. Follow the trail for almost 10 miles, passing Trail #24 on the left, until it reaches Forest Road 90. Turn right on Forest Road 90 and ride back to Forest Road 9039 to your car. You can also arrange for a shuttle at both ends of the trail to make the ride easier.

From I-5 north, take the Woodland exit heading toward Cougar and Forest Road 90. Or, from I-5 south, take State Route 503 east to Forest Road 90. Follow Forest Road 90 to Forest Road 9039. Turn left on 9039, and the trailhead is just over the Lewis River after the bridge. For more information, contact Mount Saint Helens Ranger Station at (360) 247-3900. See *DeLorme's Washington Atlas & Gazetteer: Page 34, D1*.

Ⓠ Siouxon Peak/Huffman Peak Loop

The Siouxon Peak/Huffman Peak Loop has 25 to 30 miles of advanced singletrack. Toward the top of each mountain, the trail encounters forest roads. Riding in early spring or late autumn months may mean pushing through snow at the highest elevations. Follow the Siouxon Creek Trail Ride about seven or eight miles to the Chinook Trail #130A, the entrance for this ride. Follow the path up and around Siouxon Peak and then over to Huffman Peak before descending the Huffman Peak Trail #129 down to the Siouxon Creek Trailhead.

From Interstate 5, take exit 21. Follow State Route 503 east toward Cougar. Turn right on County Road 16 (also called Hayes Road), toward La Center/Amboy. Turn right up the hill onto Northeast Cedar Road. Follow for about 19 miles to Chelatchie. Pass the Ranger Station on the left. Turn right onto Northwest Healy Road. Follow it to a one-lane bridge. Keep right at the "Y" intersection. Pass the Gifford Pinchot National Forest boundary. Come to a "Y" in the road and veer left onto Forest Road 57. Turn left at the "T" intersection onto Forest Road 5701. Follow to the sharp bend in the road and look for the trailhead marker on

the left-hand side about 50 yards past the bend. For more information, contact the Ranger District in Amboy at (360) 247-3900. See *DeLorme's Washington Atlas & Gazetteer: Page 23, A1.*

(R) Buck Creek Trail System

Located between Mount Hood and Mount Adams in the southern end of the Gifford Pinchot National Forest, the Buck Creek Trail System is open to all non-motorized recreational users and offers two picturesque rides. Whistling Ridge Trail's 26-mile loop traverses thick forest up to Oklahoma Campground and back. The entire route is well marked. The other option, the Buck Creek Falls Loop Trail, is only two-and-a-half miles and runs along a creekside route to a view of the waterfall. Both trails can be accessed from the same trailhead.

From State Route 14, turn north on State Route 141 through White Salmon. Turn left on Northwestern Lake (B-1000) Road. Turn left on N-1000 Road. The trailhead is two miles ahead. For more information, contact the Department of Natural Resources at (360) 577-2025 or 1-800-527-3305. See *DeLorme's Washington Atlas & Gazetteer: Page 24, B4.*

Eastern Washington

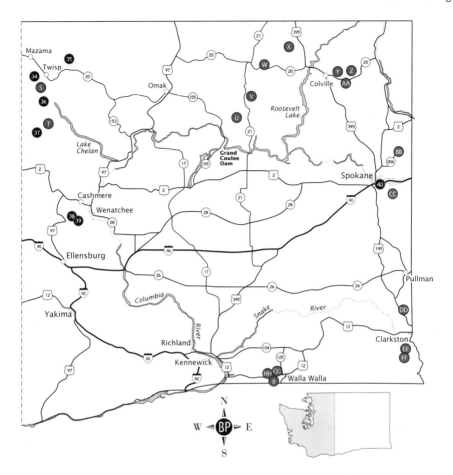

I n the land well known for its apples and wine, the territory east of the Cascade Range offers an alternative to mountain bikers for weather and terrain conditions. From the foothills to the plains, Eastern Washington has miles of uncharted and charted trails to experience and explore.

Protected from Pacific Ocean tradewinds are the landscapes of the Wenatchee Valley, the highlands of Lake Chelan, the Selkirk Mountains, and the Columbia River Valley. Arid, with elevations less extreme than the western face of the Cascades, Eastern Washington is ideal for mountain biking in the spring, summer, and fall.

Out here the town of Wenatchee, positioned dead-center in the state, is a central location for both foothill and desert-like trails. Roll through the Apple Capital of the country, the Wenatchee Mountains, or along the Columbia River.

Trails in the upper northwest quadrant wander through the striking forests of Okanogan and Colville bordering our international neighbor British Columbia. Picturesque groves of ponderosa and fir offer enchanting company for some fabulous mountain biking.

Eastern Washington's largest city, Spokane, is a recreational hub on the Idaho border. From the popular in-city Riverside State Park to the heights of Mount Spokane, mountain bikers from this far-east destination often wander farther east to "pick their line" on Idaho soil.

Filled with both hills and valleys, landscapes splashed in hues of brown, beige, and green, even to the regions toward our southeast corner from Yakima to Pullman, there are acres of trail throughout DNR, BLM, and state park lands anxiously awaiting the attention of mountain bikers, rounding out the experience that is considered prime Eastern Washington mountain biking.

Mount Spokane

Rising to 5,883 feet out of the Selkirk mountain range, Mount Spokane dominates the region for miles around and offers up 360-degree views of the surrounding mountains, encompassing glimpses of Spokane, Idaho, and as far away as Montana and British Columbia. The mountain serves as the main attraction to the 13,643-acre Mount Spokane State Park. Only 30 miles northeast of the island metropolis of Spokane (a mere 40-minute drive up U.S. Route 2 and State Route 206), Mount Spokane, along with its brother-peak Mount Kit Carson, provides the perfect weekend getaway for the pavement-bound city-dwellers of Spokane. It was soon after Francis Cook completed his narrow, winding road to the summit of the mountain in 1912 that Spokanites began flocking here by the busloads. The state began acquiring land as early as 1927, chiefly through private donations. The park grew, one parcel at a time, until 1977 when it reached its current size. In total the state only had to spend $6,156 for the more than 13,000 acres of parkland. By the 1950s, the mountain was already well known as a ski area. Today, the mountain and the park provide year-round recreation, from camping, hiking, horseback riding, and mountain biking in the summer to skiing, sledding, and snowmobiling in the winter.

Mt Spokane
El. 5,883

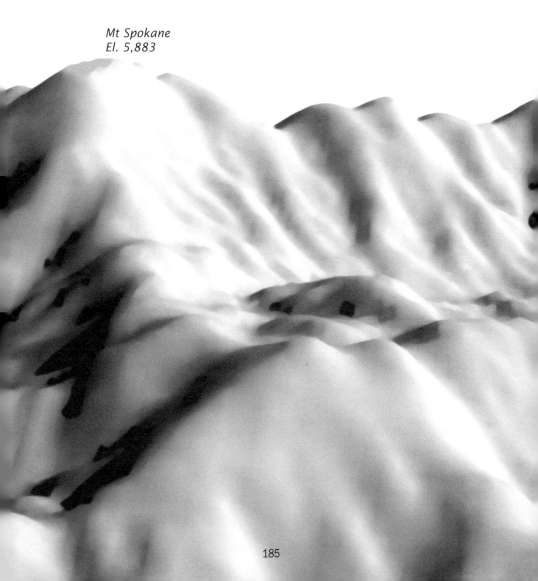

Sun Mountain

Ride Summary

The cross-country skiing trails on Sun Mountain make incredible mountain biking routes for every skill level. Ride the lower trails to warm up, then ride to the upper trails for a good work-out and some fast descents. You'll likely be sharing the mountain with a few others out here, especially in the summer, so come with your best face on.

Ride Specs

Start: Chickadee Trailhead
Length: 12.5 miles
Approximate Riding Time: 2 hours
Nearest Town: Winthrop
Rating: Moderate due to climb
Terrain: Singletrack and dirt road
Other Trail Users: Hikers, horseback riders, and cross-country skiers

Getting There

From Winthrop: Head west on Twin Lakes Road just south of the Methow River bridge. This turns into Patterson Lake Road at the intersection of Wolf Ridge Road. Follow the signs for Patterson Lake Road and Sun Mountain Lodge. Patterson Road turns right—follow the signs for the lodge. Continue around the east side of Patterson Lake. Turn left at the Chickadee Trailhead.

A Sun Mountain Meadow.

Riding along the eastern edges of the Cascades, it's easy to get swept away in the beauty of it all and forget that fire is a real threat to this region. Much drier than the western portion of the Cascades, in the summer this area can get quite hot and dusty, making it susceptible to Mother Nature's forest rejuvenation plan (i.e. forest fires). About five miles east of Winthrop is the North Cascades SmokeJumpers Base. Established in the 1930s, the base has served the U.S. Forest Service as the center for developing the technique of smoke-jumping.

Sending fire fighters by regular roads into a forest deluged with fire can take time; maybe too much time, especially if the wind is cranking. So, first attacks on fires usually involve hotshot helicopter crews who drop smoke-jumpers to set up fire breaks which keep the fire from spreading, allowing it to burn out naturally. Parachuting men into fires may seem a little crazy—and it is incredibly dangerous—but it is a quick means of getting firefighters on the scene.

Since nothing was known in the 1930s about parachuting into hot coals, the Forest Service had to design and test the necessary equipment. They constructed suits made of heavy cotton canvas for the firefighters to wear. Long pockets were sewn into the pants to hold ropes that could be used in climbing out of trees, should the chute become ensnared in branches. These early smoke-jumpers also wore retrofitted football helmets with wire masks to protect their heads. After a test with a stunt dummy and 60 successful live jumps, the smoke-jumping method became common practice for fighting forest fires. Today, it is still the standard for advanced suppression of wildfires in the West.

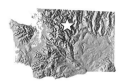

There is one thing forest fires share with mountain bikers, and that's a love of the forest. And the Methow Valley caters to both. When you arrive in Winthrop with a mountain bike on your car, the first place most people will recommend is the Sun Mountain Lodge. Because this is a cross-country ski resort, the trails are incredibly smooth, and they're great for the first or the last ride of a long, fat-tire weekend. There are several loops to be made here and the trails are very well marked, making it difficult to get lost.

Moderate climbs and good descents begin with the Thompson Ridge Road. This road takes you to the top of Sun Mountain's property and leads you to some rip-roaring single-track descents. One beautiful reason for climbing the Thompson Ridge Road (as if you needed another) is Patterson Lake. Its cobalt-blue water stands out in sharp contrast to the dusty hues of the landscape surrounding its banks.

The lower trails around Beaver Pond are wonderful warm-up or beginner trails. Smooth and wide, there's room to ride side-by-side. There are even welcoming benches along the way for weary legs to rest. And when the day's riding is done, Sun Mountain Lodge is close by with food and facilities. You can even get a room for the night.

The Methow Valley from Sun Mountain

MilesDirections

With Sun Mountain Lodge's detailed map, you can see that the network of ski trails offers multiple riding opportunities. Every trail can be ridden at least once in a full day. We recommend you test out the warm-up loops on the lower trails and then advance to the upper trails for some elevation work and fast descents.

A good Warm-up Loop (approximately 6 miles)
Riding from the Chickadee Trailhead, cross the Thompson Ridge Road to the Beaver Pond Trail. At the Hough Homestead, follow any of the other trails, like the Fox Loop Trail to the Aqualoop, which circles back to the Hough Homestead. There is also the Rodeo Trail just past the Beaver Pond Trail, that heads back to the Chickadee Trailhead.

0.0 START from the Chickadee Trailhead climbing up the Thompson Ridge Road.

5.5 Pass Pete's Dragon Trail.

6.1 Reach the Goshawk Trail. Turn left and follow the Goshawk to the Meadowlark Trail.

6.5 Take the Meadowlark Trail and fly down the mountain.

7.9 Arrive at the Lower Inside Passage on the right, and follow it to the Rader Creek Trail.

8.5 Turn right on the Rader Creek Trail, continuing down toward Patterson Lake.

10.0 Arrive at the intersection for Elbow Coulee and Patterson Lake—turn left for Patterson Lake. Ride along the narrow, cliff-like Patterson Lake Trail, carefully.

11.8 At the intersection, continue straight for the Chickadee Trailhead. The right heads to the Patterson Lake Cabins.

12.5 Arrive back at the trailhead.

Ride Information

Trail Maintenance Hotlines:
- Sun Mountain Lodge: (509) 996-2211 or 1-800-572-0493
- U.S. Forest Service: (509) 996-4000 **www.fs.fed.us**
- Okanogan Nation Forest: (509) 826-3275
- Methow Valley Ranger District: (509) 997-2131

Schedule:
Open April until it snows (about November)

Local Information:
- Winthrop Chamber of Commerce Information Station: (509) 996-2125 or 1-888-463-8469
- Methow Valley Visitors Center: (509) 996-4000

Local Events/Attractions:
- The Bone Shaker Mountain Bike Bash (a NORBA sanctioned race), in May, Winthrop, WA; (509) 535-4757
- Winthrop Rodeo Days in May and Labor Day Weekend, Winthrop, WA (509) 996-2125

- Mountain Triathlon 2nd Sunday in September, Winthrop, WA (509) 996-3287
- Methow Valley Mountain Bike Festival in early October, Winthrop, WA (509) 996-3287
- "October-West" 2nd weekend in October, Winthrop, WA (509) 996-2125
- MVSTA Ski & Sports Swap November, Winthrop, WA; (509) 996-3287
- North Cascades Smokejumper Base, between Winthrop and Twisp along State Hwy. 20, WA; (509) 997-2031
- Sun Mountain Lodge, Winthrop, WA (509) 996-2211 or 1-800-572-0493

Local Bike Shops:
Winthrop Mountain Sports, Winthrop, WA (509) 996-2886

Maps:
- Maptech CD-ROM: Thompson Ridge, WA; Winthrop, WA
- DeLorme's Washington Atlas & Gazetteer—Page 99 A7

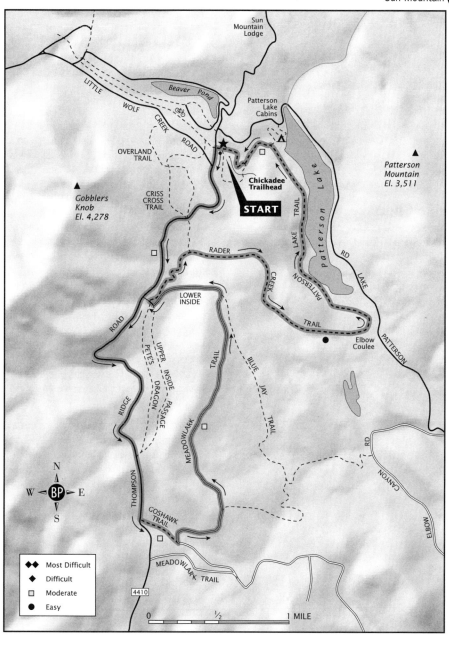

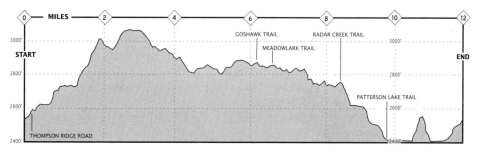

Lightning Creek to Starvation Mountain

Ride Summary

Following the trail along the banks of beautiful Lightning Creek is simultaneously heart thumping and peaceful. This is one of the more popular routes in the Winthrop/Twisp area, we've even encountered gun-toting hunters on mountain bikes. The road ride that leads to the top of Starvation Mountain offers river and mountain views, and the steep climb makes for a screaming descent. The singletrack back along Lightning Creek takes about half the time it did to ride up, allowing for an exhilarating finish.

Ride Specs

Start: Beaver Creek Campground
Other Starting Locations: Along Forest Road 4230
Length: 21 miles
Approximate Riding Time: 3-4 hours
Nearest Town: Winthrop
Rating: Moderate due to the elevation gain
Terrain: Singletrack and forest road
Other Trail Users: Horseback riders, hikers, and hunters (in the fall)

Getting There

From Winthrop: Drive east on State Route 20, following the signs for the airport, keeping to the north side of the Methow River (do not cross the bridge). After six miles turn left on Bakke Hill Road (Road 1600). Follow it to Beaver Creek Road (Road 1637). Turn left on Beaver Creek Road and continue three miles to the Beaver Creek Campground. Continue beyond the campground two-tenths mile. Pass Forest Road 4225 (the Loup Loup Summit Road) and into the Okanogan National Forest shortly thereafter. Park inside the campground or at the end of the road by the gate.

Interest in mountain biking and hiking has made the quaint northwestern town of Winthrop a mecca, of sorts, for adventurers. The North Cascades Highway (State Route 20), which opened in 1972, allows more tourists quicker access to the valley than ever before. Winthrop has responded over the years by building new hotels and stores, while somehow managing to maintain the quiet charm of a small, western town. The number of bed and breakfasts, inns, lodges, and hotels is rising as quickly as is the number of recreational trails in the Methow Valley. One of the most comfortable inns in Winthrop is the Chewuch Inn. Or should we say the "resuscitated" Chewuch Inn.

In 1994, Dan and Sally Kuperberg arrived in Winthrop, this time not as tourists. They came not to escape the hustle of everyday life in the big city but rather to escape their city lives all-together. And so they made Winthrop their new home and bought an inn. The Chewuch Inn.

The Chewuch Inn once stood alone by the river, just an old abandoned fish hatchery, until a local man, Hank Dammann, decided to renovate it. He hoped to one day turn it into a hotel. But first he wanted to move it to a better location. Along the way though, the building fell from its trailer and landed sort of askew on the side of Twin Lakes Road, within walking distance of downtown Winthrop.

Leaving the building where it landed, Mr. Dammann decided to begin renovations there. But renovations were slow, and he grew older. It was clear that he wasn't going to be able to

complete the task. That's when the Kuperbergs arrived. Buying it and putting their heart and soul into it, Dan and Sally created something special out of that old fish hatchery. Mountain bikers especially will appreciate the Chewuch Inn for its warm cozy beds, large windows with captivating views, and hearty home-cooked breakfasts. For a more private setting, the Kuperbergs have a few small one-room cabins in the woods a few yards away from the inn. With cathedral ceilings, these cabins combine creature comforts with a slightly rustic touch—a perfect place to crash after a hard mountain bike ride. For information and reservations, call The Chewuch Inn at 1-800-747-3107 or email Dan and Sally at chewuch@methow.com.

The word chewuch (pronounced "chee-WUK", meaning "creek") is a word from the Methow (pronounced MET-how) Indian tribe, who are now affiliated with the Colville Confederation. For 9,000 years Native Americans have lived along the banks of this and the other Methow Valley rivers. The government established the Colville Reservation nearby in the 1800s and many tribes continue to live in the Methow Valley.

During the same time period (1800s), trappers came to this area and found gold—the lure of the wild west began to shine. Three of the white settlers who came searching for their fortunes were James Ramsey, Ben Pearygin, and Guy Waring. Waring is considered the founding father of Winthrop, even though the town is named after Theodore Winthrop, an author and graduate of Yale, who was well-known for his adventurous spirit.

In 1893 a great fire consumed the town of Winthrop, which at the time was built solely of wood. Waring's original Duck Brand Saloon, built in 1891, survived the fire and is now Winthrop's Town Hall. The novel *The Virginian*, credited with being the first Western novel, is said to have been penned in Winthrop by Owen Wister, Waring's roommate from Harvard.

Located about a half-hour away from Winthrop is the Lightning Creek Trail, above the Methow Valley to the north. The starting point at Beaver Creek Campground is filled with tall ponderosa pines and larch trees. Singletrack leads the way up alongside Lightning Creek where intersections are well marked. After the first mile of level riding, the trail crosses Lightning Creek and begins ascending away, gradually becoming steeper. Although there are a few small technical areas, the trail is very fun to ride.

Clear-cut areas, burned forest, sandy trail, and hard-packed earth are all represented along this ride. The forest road to the top of Starvation

Mountain may seem like a long five miles after climbing the single-track. Consider a loop option by riding up the forest road from the campground to the top instead, and descend the singletrack on the way back. The forest road is steep in some sections and becomes a bit of a grind. On cooler days, if you're not properly dressed, the heights of Starvation Mountain can be windy and cold, but the views are great from the top.

MilesDirections

0.0 START from Road 200, following the sign for the Lightning Creek Trail #425. Follow the road through the campground and look for the trail leading into the woods toward the river. At the cattle guard, the sign reads: "Lightning Creek 5.5 miles, Blue Buck Creek Trail 1 mile, Beaver Meadows 11 miles."

0.3 Cross Lightning Creek over a wooden bridge.

1.1 Come to a "T" intersection with Blue Buck Creek Trail and Buck Creek Meadows. Stay right following Lightning Creek.

1.6 Cross Lightning Creek again and begin a steep climb up and away from the river.

3.1 The trail turns into an old doubletrack road cut.

3.8 Enter a clearcut area.

4.0 Intersect with Spur Road 4230. Follow the trail to the right down the road just a hundred feet or so. Take the trail on the left side of the road, Trail #100, the continuation of The Lightning Creek Trail.

5.1 Singletrack continues again, climbing steeply. Cross a creek. Head up over the ridge, keeping the creek to your right.

6.0 The Lightning Creek Trail intersects with Spur Road 200 to the left, and Road 4235 just beyond that, running north/south. Follow Road 4235 left up to Starvation Mountain.

6.2 Pass turnout on the right at mile marker #7.

6.7 Pass another turnout.

6.8 Pass Spur Road 255 on the right.

7.2 Pass mile marker #8.

8.1 Passing a burned area about one quarter mile long.

8.2 Pass mile marker #9.

8.9 Cross a wide-open area on the right.

9.3 Pass mile marker #10.

10.5 Check out the summit and then head down for a fast descent.

21.0 Reach the bottom at the campground and the trailhead.

Ride Information

Trail Maintenance Hotlines:
- U.S. Forest Service (509) 996-4000 or **www.fs.fed.us**
- Okanogan National Forest (509) 826-3275 or **www.gorp.com**
- Methow Valley Ranger District (509) 997-2131

Local Information:
(See Chapter 34 Ride Information)

Local Events/Attractions:
- The Chewuck Inn, Winthrop, WA; 1-800-747-3107
(See Chapter 34 Ride Information)

Local Bike Shops:
(See Chapter 34 Ride Information)

Organizations:
Methow Valley Sport Trails Association, Winthrop, WA; (509) 996-3287, 1-800-682-5787 **www.methow.com/~mvsta/ welcome.html**

Maps:
- Maptech CD-ROM: Loup Loup Summit, Old Baldy, WA
- DeLorme's Washington Atlas & Gazetteer—Page 100 A1

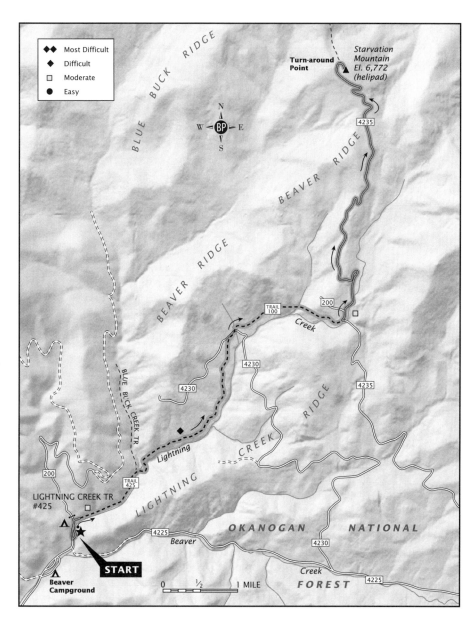

Most Difficult
Difficult
Moderate
Easy

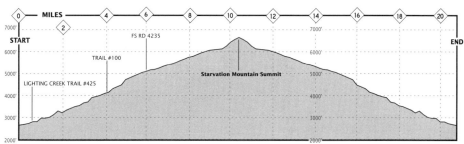

In Addition:**The Cascade Loop**

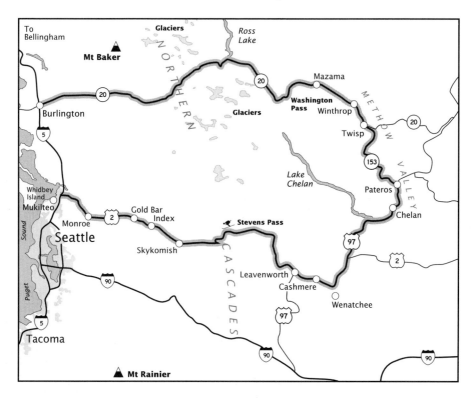

The Cascade Loop is considered one of the hallmark driving trips in Washington. Practically speaking, it's the quickest way to get across the Cascades. What it actually amounts to is a series of connected highways. All told, the loop travels for some 400 miles past snow-covered peaks, pristine mountain views, and small, friendly, western towns.

Technically, the loop begins (or ends) with a ferry ride between Mukilteo and Whidbey Island. State Route 525 picks up at the ferry landing and runs half the length of Whidbey Island (which, incidentally, is the longest island in the continental U.S.) before joining with State Route 20. Traveling east, State Route 20 crosses the Northern Cascades and safely deposits you in the Methow Valley. The towns of Winthrop and Twisp are the first real pit stops. The interesting name "twisp" comes from a slightly modified form of the Native American term "twips," which means "yellow jackets." Apparently this area was once loaded with them.

Continuing east, leaving the mountains behind, State Route 20 merges with State Route 153 and U.S. Route 97, along the mighty Columbia River and into the Wenatchee Valley, the Apple Capital of the world. Here, the sun seems to shine a little brighter than it does on the western side of the Cascades. It's as if by crossing the mountains you've stepped into another world—a world of perpetual sunshine. The mountains form a physical barricade to the moisture that collects along the coast, making the eastern regions of the state ideal for growing all kinds of produce, especially crunchy, mouth-watering apples.

Turning back into the sunset, the Cascade Loop heads west leading directly through the towns of Cashmere and Leavenworth along U.S. Route 97 to U.S. Route 2. Leavenworth is a Bavarian village with Old World charm. It's also a gateway to the curvaceous Tumwater Canyon. Rapids and waterfalls adorn this spectacular section of highway. Be sure to use the pull-offs to get a good look at the raging Wenatchee River below.

After a most scenic drive, you'll arrive at the 4,061-foot high Stevens Pass—named after John F. Stevens, the builder of the Panama Canal. You're now in the heart of the Cascade Mountains and at the top of a great winter ski resort, Stevens Pass Ski Area. Not much biking is done at the resort itself, but Nordic trails just to the east of the pass are open to mountain bikers in the summer. To complete the Cascade Loop, U.S. Route 2 heads into the Everett area north of Seattle. Traveling north on I-5 will lead back up to State Route 20, beginning the loop again.

Along the Cascade Loop we've mapped a series of rides between Wenatchee and the Puget Sound that give a great sampling of what's available to mountain bikers. One of the most distinctive places to ride off the Loop is along State Route 20 about 20 miles east of Washington Pass, outside of Winthrop, back in the Methow Valley. There are tons of great rides in this area: Cedar Creek, Lightning Creek—just to name a couple from this book. But there's also Buck Mountain, Goat Wall, and many others that are waiting to be discovered.

Foggy Dew Creek/ Merchants Basin

Ride Summary

This hoofer is not for the weak of heart. Consistently steep, the mega-climb begins around 3,600 feet and doesn't quit until it hits almost 8,000 feet—all within only five miles! It's a slightly technical ride as well, as the trail travels over loose rocks from time to time. This is one of the more challenging trails in the state and will take all day to ride, giving real meaning to the word epic.

Ride Specs

Start: Foggy Dew Trailhead
Length: 16.5 miles
Approximate Riding Time: 4-6 hours
Nearest Town: Carlton
Rating: Difficult due to steep climbs and technical singletrack descents
Terrain: Technical singletrack and hike-a-bike
Other Trail Users: Hikers, horseback riders, and motorcyclists

Getting There

From Pateros: Head north on State Route 153 toward Twisp. At mile marker 16.8, turn left heading west onto Gold Creek Road, which is Forest Service Road 4340. Follow for almost one mile. Turn left at the "T" intersection toward the Foggy Dew Guard Station and Crater Creek Camp. After one mile, continue straight through the intersection for the Foggy Dew Campground. After four miles, turn left and cross a bridge onto Forest Service Road 200. Drive past the Foggy Dew Campground on the left after the bridge. The pavement ends here. Continue three and a half miles to the trailhead parking lot.

Lake Chelan is a narrow, 55-mile long, natural lake of pure glacial melt. To quote an overzealous *Seattle Times* reporter: "It's deeper than the Grand Canyon!" Well, not quite. It's only 1,484 feet deep (versus the Grand Canyon's 5,816 feet), but you get the point: it's deep. A more accurate superlative would be to say that it's the third deepest lake in the United States (after Crater Lake in Oregon and Lake Tahoe in California). There are two main roads that will take you to the lake, State Route 151 or U.S. Route 97. Otherwise, there are just forest roads, which are few and far between. There are a couple of towns of decent size on the lake as well: Chelan, at the southeastern tip; Manson a few miles north up the eastern side; Lucerne to the northwest; and Stehekin, to the far north, a completely isolated community accessible only by boat from Chelan. Float-plane is another alternative to getting around the lake, and of course there is your mountain bike.

There are several designated campsites around the lake, the largest is at the Chelan State Park. Located on the southeastern end of the lake, the park covers 127 acres, with 6,545 feet of waterfront. The park has 127 campsites, a bathhouse, 300 linear feet of beach, a boat launch and a dock, water ski floats, a homestead cabin, and a contact station. Everything a traveler could need!

"Chelan" (pronounced "sha-LAN") is the name of an Indian tribe that used to winter at the site where the town now stands. In 1880, Chelan became a military post with civilians arriving a few years later. The town was incorporated in 1902 with mining as the chief means of income. People arrived by steam ship up the Columbia River to stake their min-

The south side of Cooney Lake.

ing claims, until 1914 when the railroad finally came to Chelan. Today there are about 3,500 people living in Chelan year-round. It has become quite the resort spot. Many of the large Victorian homes from the early days are used today as bed and breakfasts.

Stehekin, to the far north of Lake Chelan, is a quiet, isolated village,. There are no cars, no phones, and no televisions in Stehekin—only pristine wilderness, wildlife, and trails to keep you entertained. Mountain bikers can take their choice of summertime boats to get there. By taking the Lady II up and the Lady of the Lake back, there will be about three hours in between to explore Stehekin. In the summer of 1998, the newest addition to the ferry fleet will be running. It will cut the travel time down to under two hours from Chelan, allowing for longer visits. There are a few places to rent bikes in Chelan and Stehekin, but it's only a $13 round-trip to take your own bike. If you'd like to spend the night in Stehekin, there are lodges, like the North Cascades Stehekin Lodge and the Stehekin Valley Ranch. Or you can simply camp under the stars.

The climate around Lake Chelan is ideal for mountain biking. With an average of only 24 days a year of sub-32 degree temperatures and 33 days above 90 degrees, you can't go wrong. On average, it rains less than nine days a year, and so you can plan on about 300 per-

Sunrise Lake from near the top of Merchants Basin.

fectly sunny days. And though this area gets its share of snow, the lake never freezes.

For a sun-filled, truly rugged mountain biking experience, try the Foggy Dew Trail, situated inside the Okanogan National Forest, east of the long and slender Lake Chelan. This trail is consistently steep. It begins at roughly 3,600 feet and takes you up to about 8,000 feet in the first five miles. It's moderately technical with a few loose rocky places here and there. Local motorcycle groups maintain the trails, and consequetly they stay in fairly good shape. The trails that are closed to motorcycles are typically steep and tough to ride.

After the first six miles of climbing, the trail is transformed into some incredibly steep switchbacks. The hardest part of the climb is toward the top of Merchants Basin. Passing Cooney Lake and heading down, the elevation loss will give you a head rush. Some sections are daringly steep, so don't be embarrassed to walk your bike down. The final downhill back along the Foggy Dew Trail is a sweet reward after the tough climb.

Ride Information

Trail Maintenance Hotlines:
- Okanogan National Forest (509) 826-3275 or **www.gorp.com**
- Twisp Ranger District; (509) 997-2131
- Wenatchee National Forest: Chelan Ranger District; (509) 682-2576
- U.S. Forest Service Information Office: (206) 442-0170

Schedule:
Best between May and October

Local Information:
- Lake Chelan Chamber of Commerce: (509) 682-3503 or 1-800-424-3526
- Lady of the Lake, and Lady II ferries from Chelan and Stehekin: (509) 682-4584

Local Events/Attractions:
- Earth Day in April, Chelan, WA 1-800-424-3526

- Beachin' Hang Gliding Tournament in May, Chelan, WA; 1-800-424-3526
- Cross-Country Hang Gliding Classic in July, Chelan, WA; 1-800-424-3526
- North Cascades Stehekin Lodge, Stehekin, WA; (509) 682-4494
- Stehekin Valley Ranch, Stehekin, WA (509) 682-4677

Local Bike Shops:
- Der Sportsmann, Leavenworth, WA (509) 548-5623
- Winthrop Mountain Sports, Winthrop, WA; (509) 996-2886

Maps:
- Maptech CD-ROM: Martin Peak, WA; Hungry Mountain, WA
- Green Trails, Prince Creek, WA No. 115
- DeLorme's Washington Atlas & Gazetteer—Page 99 C7

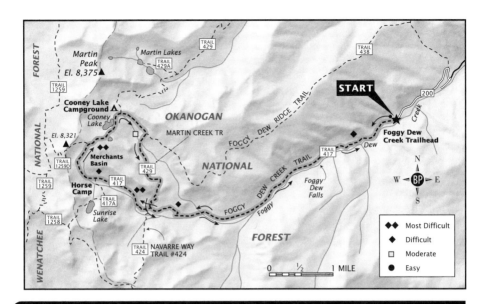

MilesDirections

0.0 START riding up the Foggy Dew Creek Trail #417.

1.7 Pass a small waterfall on the left.

3.0 Pass Foggy Dew Falls on the left.

5.2 Reach the trail junction with the Martin Creek Trail #429 on the right. This is where you'll connect on the way down. Continue straight for now up the trail, following signs to Merchants Basin, Sunrise Lake, and Sawtooth Ridge.

5.3 Reach the junction with the Navarre Way Trail #424. Continue to the right on Trail #417. This is the worst part of the climb.

6.4 Pass the trail junction 417A to Sunrise Lake on the left at the Horse Camp. Continue up the trail to Merchants Basin.

7.6 Reach the top of Merchants Basin and the trail junction with the Angels Staircase Trail #1259D (which heads west to the top of the

Sawtooth Ridge). For a great view, ride or hike up Trail #1259D for 0.4 miles) to the top of the ridge, and then to the north, to the top of the 8,321-foot peak. It's worth it. Once back at the saddle, head down the other side of the pass toward Cooney Lake.

8.5 Arrive at the Cooney Lake Campsite. Continue along the trail and cross the north fork of Foggy Dew Creek.

8.6 Come to a junction with the Martin Creek Trail #429. Turn right and enjoy the ride.

9.7 Cross a bridge, again over the north fork of Foggy Dew Creek.

11.4 Arrive at the junction with the Foggy Dew Creek Trail #417. Turn left. Follow Trail #417 back down to the trailhead.

16.5 Arrive back at the Foggy Dew Creek Trailhead parking area.

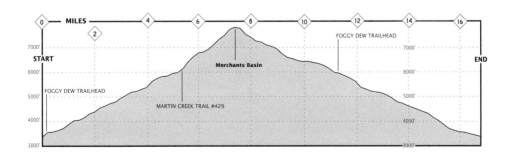

37

Pot Peak

Ride Summary

This ride gains 4,300 feet of elevation—it isn't easy. Steady along a ridge top, this singletrack comes with long, painstaking climbs and fast, furious descents. Motorcyclists use this trail too, and contrary to popular stereotypes, the trails are in excellent condition (they are actually maintained by local ORV groups). Mountain bikers rocket down the ridge on banked and occasionally rocky turns. It's a good thing there's a campground at the bottom because, while this ride is exhilarating, it's also totally exhausting.

Ride Specs

Start: Ramona Park Campground
Other Starting Locations: Sno-park at the intersection of Forest Service Road 5900 (Shady Pass Road) and Forest Service Road 8410 (to Ramona Park Campground).
Length: 28.7 miles
Approximate Riding Time: 7-9 hours
Nearest Town: Chelan
Rating: Difficult with long, steep climbs and technical singletrack descents
Terrain: Singletrack and short gravel road sections
Other Trail Users: Hikers, horseback riders, hunters, motorcyclists, and cross-country skiers

Getting There

From Wenatchee: Head north on U.S. Route 97 (which is on the west side of the Columbia River, not the east). At marker 223, turn left onto State Route 971, the Navarre Coulee Road. Travel 30 miles to a "T" intersection at the shore of Lake Chelan. Turn left onto South Lakeshore Drive. Follow to just past the Twentyfive Mile Creek State Park. Turn left onto Shady Pass Road, which is Forest Service Road 5900. Travel three miles to a "Y" at a sno-park. Park here, or turn left onto Forest Road 8410 and park (or camp) at the Ramona Park Campground. There is a trailhead at the campground where the ride will end. There is no parking at the trailhead where you start.

The Pot Peak ride is one serious cardiovascular workout. From the North Fork of the Twentyfive Mile Creek to the top of the ridge, it's a steady, non-technical grinder the entire way up. There are the occasional short, steep sections that you might have to hike, but for the most part, this trail just goes up, up, and up. Starting out at 2,400 feet, don't be alarmed that the high point is 6,881 feet. The good part is that this is a loop, so you're in for some amazingly fast downhill, dropping to 1,900 feet at the finish. How about that! Almost 5,000 feet of elevation work. Are you up to it? Better grab an extra energy bar.

The motorcross group in the area is responsible for the marvelous upkeep of these trails. Please do your part to keep the trails in good condition. There are quite a few cinderblock-banked turns that really help with traction, especially when taking tight switchbacks at high speed—they also minimize trail erosion. You can thank the motocross crowd for that, too. In general, the trails are really well maintained and, for the most part, they're pretty smooth . When it's time to head down, just point

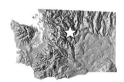

Looking back at the talus slope, Sawtooth Ridge and Angle Peak .

your bike in the direction you wish to go, and hang on. An optional trip might be to Stormy Mountain and back. It looks fun, but there'll be a road climb on the return.

Just south of Pot Peak is the raging Columbia River, first explored by Anglos in May of 1792. Captain Robert Gray, a fur trader from Boston, decided to name the river he'd found after his ship, the Columbia Rediviva—"redivivus" means to be reborn or restored to life and is also the name of Montana's state flower. The United States government used Gray's exploration as a basis for their claim on the Oregon and Washington territories, which were constantly being disputed by Britain.

A lot has changed along the river. As for the river itself, the Columbia now has 14 dams, 300 miles of main canals, and 2,000 miles of secondary canals that irrigate land stretching as far as 100 miles away from the river's banks. Within 30 years, the Columbia Basin Project of the early 1950s turned a half-million acres of dry, arid land into lush green farmland.

The primary force behind the irrigational restructuring of the west is the Grand Coulee Dam. On December 3, 1933, the pouring of concrete began for the dam. Where most other large dams are filled with soil, the Grand Coulee is solid concrete—the largest all-concrete structure on earth, measuring almost one mile long. That's enough concrete to build a six-foot sidewalk around the Earth's equator. And to further emphasize the dam's enormity, more wood was used in building the Grand Coulee Dam than in any other structure on the planet. And, only two other dams, the Guri Dam in Venezuela and the Itaipu Dam of Brazil, generate more power than the Grand Coulee. It's only logical, then, that the lake behind the Grand Coulee would be large as well. And so it is. Roosevelt Lake is the second largest man-made lake in the world.

The engineers of the 1930s knew surprisingly little about building a dam. Some of the clever quick fixes they came up with as they went along are quite funny. When sliding mud was a problem, they'd freeze it with a refrigeration unit. When the coffer dam sprang a leak, they'd mix together whatever they could with bentonite clay and stuff it into the holes to stop it from leaking—including mattresses and Christmas trees.

The Grand Coulee was finally completed in 1941, three months before the U.S. entered World War II. The power it generated helped with manufacturing aluminum for the war effort. Over half of the country's aluminum was made in Northwest plants which drew their energy from the dam. If you'd like to visit the 12 million cubic yards of concrete and steel that comprise the Grand Coulee Dam, just stop by the Visitor Center on State Route 155. They offer tours daily.

Ride Information

Trail Maintenance Hotlines:
- Twentyfive Mile Creek State Park: (509) 687-3610
- Wenatchee National Forest: Chelan Ranger District: (509) 682-2576
- Entiat Ranger District: (509) 784-1511

Schedule:
Best between May and October

Local Information:
- Grand Coulee Visitor Arrival Center: (509) 633-9265
- Lake Chelan Chamber of Commerce: (509) 682-3503 or 1-800-424-3526

Local Events/Attractions:
- Earth Day in April, Chelan, WA 1-800-424-3526
- Beachin' Hang Gliding Tournament in early May, Chelan, WA 1-800-424-3526
- Cross-Country Hang Gliding Classic in July, Chelan, WA; 1-800-424-3526

Local Bike Shops:
Der Sportsmann, Leavenworth, WA (509) 548-5623

Maps:
- Maptech CD-ROM: Stormy Mountain, WA
- Green Trails, Brief, WA; - No. 147
- DeLorme's Washington Atlas & Gazetteer—Page 83 A6

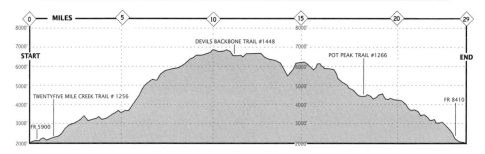

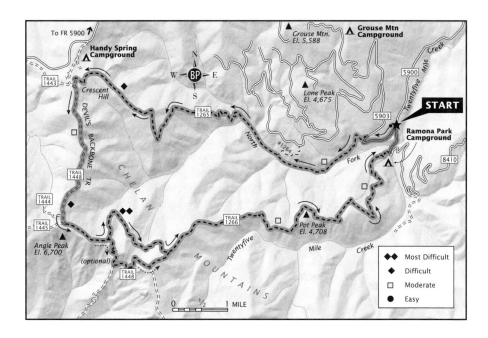

MilesDirections

0.0 START from the sno-park up Forest Road 5900 (it may be marked 5903).

1.0 Arrive at the North Fork of the Twentyfive Mile Creek Trail #1265. Take this trail, which also leads to the Lone Peak Trail and the Devils Backbone Trail.

3.7 Arrive at a junction with the Lone Peak Trail #1264. Continue left up Trail #1265.

4.4 Cross a fork of the Twentyfive Mile Creek and head up the ridge.

5.8 Reach the ridge top.

7.2 Hit the ridge-line and ride across it.

7.5 Reach the first false summit on the ridge-line. Continue across for typical ridge top ascents and descents.

11.4 Arrive at the trail junction for the Devil's Backbone Trail #1448. This is the top of the main ridge. Follow the Devil's Backbone Trail #1448 left, now heading south to the junction at Angle Peak (6,700 feet). (To bail out, follow the trail to the right to a spur road of Forest Service Road 5900. Follow it back to the campground.)

NOTE: For the next three miles (until Angle Peak) this area has been bulldozed as a firebreak. Some sections of the singletrack no longer exist.

14.4 Pass a trail junction with Trail 1444 on the right. Continue straight to the next intersection, up the ridge to Angle Peak.

14.5 Reach a trail junction with the Four Mile Ridge Trail #1445. Turn left following the Devil's Backbone Trail #1448. You're close to the top of Angle Peak at this point.

16.0 Pass a right-hand offshoot trail to a viewpoint overlooking Devil's Backbone. Follow the Devil's Backbone Trail #1448 to the left, down a very steep, rocky, and technical downhill with tight turns and steep drop-offs.

17.2 Reach the bottom of the downhill. Put your bike on your shoulder and follow the switchbacks up the talus slope.

17.8 Back to the ridge top.

18.3 Arrive at a junction with the Pot Peak Trail #1266. Follow the Pot Peak Trail left. (The trail straight leads to Stormy Mountain on the Devil's Backbone Trail.)

23.4 Reach Pot Peak. Follow the trail around the base of the summit.

28.1 Reach the bottom of the trail at Ramona Park Trailhead. Turn left up Forest Road 8410.

28.7 Arrive back at the "Y" and the sno-park.

Mission Ridge

Ride Summary

This is a true ridge ride: located out in the open, exposed to the views and the sun. The 14-mile ascent is gradual with the occasional steep section. It hooks up with some exceptional ridge-top singletrack that leads to false summits and around tight switchbacks. There is a little bit of everything here. It will be a challenge to intermediate riders, but for the advanced mountain biker it's a true delight.

Ride Specs

Start: Mission Ridge Trailhead
Length: 26.4 miles
Approximate Riding Time: 3-5 hours
Nearest Town: Cashmere
Rating: Moderate to Difficult
Terrain: Gravel road and singletrack
Other Trail Users: Hikers, horseback riders, and motorcyclists

Getting There

From Cashmere: Exit onto Division Street from U.S. Route 2. Follow Division Street around the Vale School—Division becomes Pioneer Street. Take the immediate left onto Mission Creek Road, following it to Binder Road. Turn right on Binder Road; Mission Creek Road picks up again immediately on the left. Turn left on Mission Creek Road. Follow for 10.4 miles to a fork in the road. Turn left onto Forest Road 7100 for two-and-a-half miles to the Mission Ridge and Devils Gulch trailheads.

During the summer-time, Mission Ridge provides an exceptional opportunity for soaking up the sun along the Wenatchee Mountains. Not far from Mission Ridge is the town of Wenatchee, a moderately-sized city nestled between the Wenatchee and Columbia rivers, due-south of Cashmere. Houses almost 3,000 years old were discovered in an orchard here, and ancient buffalo-spearheads and other stone tools have been discovered in and around Wenatchee dating back 11,000 years. Though it's unclear exactly how long people have resided here, we know that "Wenatchee" has only been around since the late 1800s.

It was in those first few years of settlement that the Great Northern Railroad, who owned a considerable chunk of land not far from Wenatchee, convinced Wenatchee's citizens to move their town closer to the railroad's proposed train depot site. No sweat; the railroad was footing the bill. When trains began running through town in 1892, Wenatchee blossomed like a fertilized field of sun-fed apple trees.

One person responsible for the growth of the orchard business in eastern Wenatchee was Jacob Shotwell. He built an irrigation ditch to bring water from the Wenatchee River to the

dry benchlands of Wenatchee. His irrigation channel caused such a boom that land plots which had been going for $25-an-acre, jumped to $400-an-acre. In 1908, Bridge Street was constructed over the Columbia River to carry the water pipelines from the channels to the benchlands. The bridge also allowed wagons, and later cars, to cross the river. In 1951 the bridge closed to all vehicles and is now open only to bicycle and foot traffic. Shotwell's irrigation channels brought to the Wenatchee Valley the most crucial element to successful fruit growing. Fruit growing continues, but the channels have since been replaced by underground and drip-method irrigation systems.

If Washington is famous for anything, it's apples. Even though thousands of apple varieties are grown in Washington, Red and Golden Delicious apples are by far the most popular varieties. Hot, dry summer days cooled by crisp, clear nights provide ideal growing conditions for juicy, delicious apples. Apple growing is a year-round process. Pruning trees begins in January. Bees are brought in to assist pollination in the spring. And finally in September and October the apples are harvested. The Washington State Apple Commission offers a brief video presentation on the apple industry development. Their facility is located south of Wenatchee.

After you've completed your tour of the orchards and learned all you can about Washington's apple growing industry, gather your apple-stuffed fanny-pack and your mountain bike, and get ready to roll. The Mission Ridge ride begins with a 13.8-mile ascent up Forest Road 7100. It has moderate-to-steep grades, but is easily ridden. Don't be surprised if you are passed along the way by cars shuttling mountain bikers to the top—just remember, you're earning your descent.

The Mission Ridge ride begins on Forest Road 9712, just below Mission Peak. The three-mile climb between the Devils Gulch Trail and the Mission Ridge Trail is the steepest climb of the ride. The singletrack of the Mission Ridge Trail begins in the open woods on the ridge-top.

Mission Creek.

Mom's Apple Pie

3 cups of peeled apples, cored and sliced (Recommended varieties include: Macintosh, for good pie texture; Granny Smith, tart and sweet; or Golden Delicious, simply sweet.)

$\frac{3}{4}$ Cup sugar (+ or - depending on tartness of apples used)

$\frac{1}{2}$ Tablespoon lemon juice

2 Tablespoons flour

$\frac{1}{4}$ – $\frac{1}{2}$ teaspoon cinnamon

1 Tablespoon cold butter cubed small

Mix all ingredients, except the butter. Add optional $\frac{1}{4}$ – $\frac{1}{2}$ Cup oatmeal to thicken. Let the apple mixture sit for $\frac{1}{2}$ hour. Pour into pie or pastry shell. Dot butter on top. Secure the top pastry and add decorative slices or cut slits in the top crust and crimp edges. Bake for one hour at 400 degrees. Hint: Pre-cooking the bottom shell for 5-7 minutes at 400 degrees will help dry the crust so it doesn't get mushy after baking.

These are fast running trails that alternate with steep downhills and tight switchbacks. Follow the singletrack for about four miles until arriving at a four-way intersection with the Devils Gulch Trail. Continue straight through the intersection—then the good stuff begins. There is a steep nine-tenths-mile climb here, but, just to warn you, there are plenty of false summits on the way down as well. Take in the great views from the ridge-tops and enjoy the ride all the way down. This is as true a ridge-ride as you can get.

The icing to this epic ride is the downhill. A good amount of it is steep—so steep, in fact, that you'll be riding with your belly on the back of your saddle. Some drop-offs here and there may surprise you, and fast-riding sections quickly fall into switchbacks, so stay alert. The Mission Ridge ride offers a great trip with a little bit of everything.

Ride Information

Trail Maintenance Hotlines:
- Wenatchee National Forest, Leavenworth Ranger District (509) 782-1413
- Lake Wenatchee Ranger District: (509) 763-3103 or 1-800-452-5687

Schedule:
This trail is open year-round but is best between April and November, when there's less snow.

Costs:
$3 per car per day or $25 for an annual pass.

Local Information:
- Leavenworth Chamber of Commerce Visitor Center; (509) 548-5807
- Wenatchee Chamber of Commerce (509) 662-2116

Local Events/Attractions:
- Washington State Apple Blossom Festival in April, Wenatchee, WA; (509) 662-3616
- Apple Industry Tour in October, Wenatchee, WA; (509) 663-9600
- Founder's Day in June, Cashmere, WA (509) 782-7404
- Apple Days in October, Cashmere, WA (509) 782-7404
(Also see Ride Information for Chapter 11)

Local Bike Shops:
- Arlberg Sports, Wenatchee, WA (509) 663-7401
- Asplund's Outdoor Recreation 1, Wenatchee, WA; (509) 662-6539
(Also see Ride Information for Chapter 11)

Maps:
- Maptech CD-ROM: Monitor, WA
- DeLorme's Washington Atlas & Gazetteer—Page 67 B5

MilesDirections

0.0 START from the Mission Ridge/Devils Gulch Trailhead parking area. Ride up Forest Road 7100.

2.5 At the "T" intersection with #7101, turn right continuing on Forest Road 7100.

9.2 Arrive at the intersection with Forest Road 9712. Turn right on the well traveled Road 9712.

9.7 Pass a spur road. Continue straight up Forest Road 9712.

10.4 Pass another spur on the right-hand side.

11.7 Pass the Devils Gulch Trailhead on the right. The Pipeline Trail on the left takes you to the Mission Ridge Ski Area.

13.8 Pass the Squilchuck Trail which goes to the Mission Ridge Ski Area. Arrive at the Mission

Ridge Trailhead on the right. Take the trail. This is the official beginning of the singletrack.

17.7 Arrive at another junction of the Devils Gulch Trail. Go straight through the four-way intersection and climb. For the next nine miles there are many false summit climbs.

26.2 Arrive at a "T" intersection with the Devils Gulch Trail. Turn right. Follow the Devils Gulch Trail from here on out.

26.3 The Red Hill Spur Trail intersects with the Devils Gulch Trail from the left. Stay on the Devils Gulch Trail.

26.4 Arrive back at the Mission Ridge/Devils Gulch Trailhead parking area.

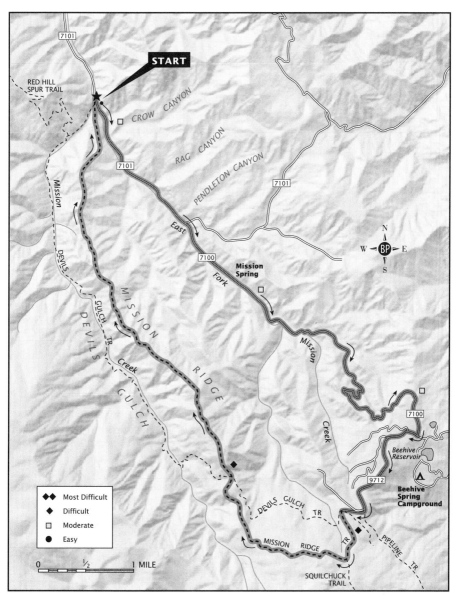

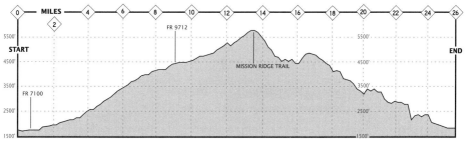

Devils Gulch

Ride Summary

Reputedly the best mountain bike ride in the state, the Devils Gulch Trail is a great place to escape the damp weather farther west. In the heart of the eastern Cascade foothills, this trail begins with a forest road climb before cutting into the woods and riding along Mission Creek below Mission Ridge. Not too tough, not too technical, this ride is just right for strong climbing legs and the desire for fast singletrack.

Ride Specs

Start: Devils Gulch Trailhead
Other Starting Locations: Along Forest Road 7100
Length: 24.4 miles
Approximate Riding Time: 2-4 hours
Nearest Town: Cashmere
Rating: Moderate to Difficult with a steep trail climb
Terrain: Singletrack and steep forest roads
Other Trail Users: Hikers, horseback riders, and motorcyclists

Getting There

From Cashmere: Exit onto Division Street from U.S. Route 2. Follow Division Street right around the Vale School—Division turns into Pioneer Street. Take the immediate left onto Mission Creek Road, following it to Binder Road. Turn right. Mission Creek Road picks up again immediately on the left. Turn left on Mission Creek Road. Follow for 10.4 miles to a fork in the road. Turn left on Road 7100 for 2.6 miles to the Mission Ridge and Devils Gulch trailheads.

The Devils Gulch ride is nestled in the hills east of the Cascade mountain range, an area well regarded for its tasty apples, but also known for its award winning wines. Just southeast of Yakima, all the way to the Columbia River, and as far north as Spokane, juicy grapes of all varieties grow. Similar to the climes of northern France, the weather in this eastern Washington region is ideal for growing fine wine fruit. Long sunny summer days that aren't too hot produce the best fruit, which in turn make the best wine. Some of the better years for wine in this area were 1985, 1988, 1989 and 1992—all were exceptionally good weather years. But grapes wouldn't survive here without water. The water issue changed dramatically with the damming of the Columbia River, which turned the once desert-like territory of eastern Washington into fertile farmland. Other crops thrive here now as well (fruits, vegetables, herbs, hops, etc.), making this area the leading source of Washington's produce.

Award winning grapes can be found in western Washington, too. Bainbridge Island and Whidbey Island within Puget Sound boast several local wineries. The Olympic Peninsula and a few places scattered along Washington's southern border also produce fine wine grapes. The southeast portion of the state grows juicy grapes, too. But out of the 85 wineries in the state that grow some 11,000 acres of wine-destined grapes, the best region for wine is clearly within the Columbia Valley.

Grapes aren't the only fruit used to make wine. Berries of all varieties populate the state, and it's not uncommon to find wines made of raspberries, blackberries, loganberries, straw-

berries, or gooseberries. But, if you'd rather munch on berries than sip them, head out into the sunshine on your bike and gather all the wild varieties you like—being careful to identify them first, of course.

A popular, sun-filled ride is the trail through Devils Gulch. Many Washington mountain bikers agree that Devils Gulch is one of the best rides in the state. It has everything a mountain biker could want: a long climb, ultra-smooth singletrack, more downhill than uphill, beautiful scenery, the soothing sounds of Mission Creek, great views of Mount Stewart, views of Wenatchee, banked turns, creek crossings, wild flowers, open meadows, sneaky switchbacks, and lots of hot sunshine (usually). And during the weekends an increasing number of cars shuttle riders to the trailhead to ride the downhill without working for it. With us as your ride guides, however, you'll be earning your descent.

Actually, this ride isn't too horrible on ascents. The first 11.5 miles take you up a not-too-steep gain in elevation. After the initial two-to-three miles of riding on gravel, the road turns into smooth, hard-packed dirt. The climb is surprisingly easy from then on. It winds up through the canyon and crosses Mission Creek several times along the way. As easy as this climb is, it's surprising how many riders still opt for the two-car shuttle.

After six miles, the road crosses into the National Forest boundary. Eventually the views turn toward Wenatchee where you are able to make out the town and the mighty Columbia River. As the road climbs, Glacier Peak and Mission Ridge come into view. When you hit the trail on the back side of Mission Ridge, the real fun begins. It's all fast, silky-smooth, downhill singletrack. You can't beat it. At first the trail is rolling, then it takes on a different attitude. Sharp

switchbacks will surprise you—controlled speed will be more fun than flying over the edge because you missed a turn. And when you arrive at the bottom, you'll be ready to do it all over again, maybe this time on the Mission Ridge Trail.

Ride Information

Trail Maintenance Hotlines:
- Wenatchee National Forest, Leavenworth Ranger District: (509) 548-6977
- Lake Wenatchee Ranger District; (509) 763-3103 or 1-800-452-5687

Costs:
$3 per car per day or $25 annual trail pass

Local Information:
- Leavenworth Chamber of Commerce Visitor Center; (509) 548-5807
- Wenatchee Chamber of Commerce: (509) 662-2116

Local Events/Attractions:
(See information in Chapter 38)

Local Bike Shops:
- Der Sportsmann, Leavenworth, WA (509) 548-5623
- Leavenworth Ski & Sports, Leavenworth, WA; (509) 548-7864
- Leavenworth Outfitters, Leavenworth, WA; 1-800-347-7934 or **www.thrillmakers.com**
- Arlberg Sports, Wenatchee, WA (509) 663-7401
- Asplund's Outdoor Recreation 1, Wenatchee, WA; (509) 662-6539

Maps:
- Maptech CD-ROM: Blewett Pass and Mission Peak, WA
- DeLorme's Washington Atlas & Gazetteer—Page 67 B5

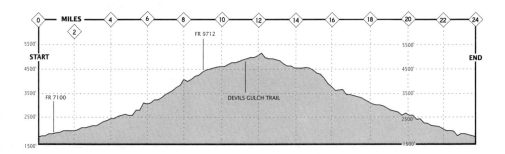

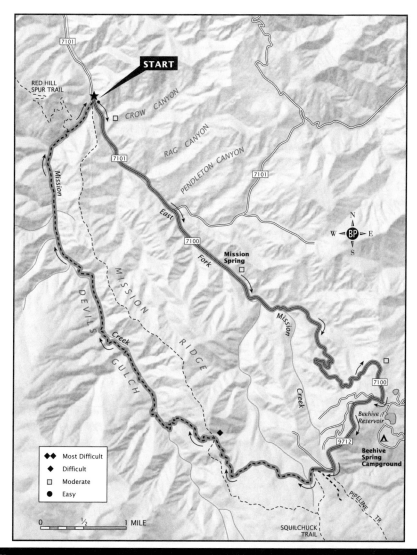

MilesDirections

0.0 START from the Devils Gulch/Mission Ridge Trailhead, riding up Forest Road 7100.

2.3 Stay right on Forest Road 7100, following along the East Fork of Mission Creek. This is where the climbing begins. Forest Road 7100 is on the left.

5.5 The gravel road turns to hard packed dirt.

6.0 Enter the National Forest boundary.

9.2 At the intersection, turn right on Forest Road 9712.

9.5 Enter the Beehive Soil and Management Area.

9.7 Pass a spur road. Stay straight on Forest Road 9712.

10.4 Pass a road on the right.

11.5 Turn right on to the Devils Gulch Trail.

14.0 The trail, once rolling, now flattens and straightens somewhat. The trees are open, offering an unobstructed view. This trail is porcelain smooth.

15.8 Encounter some sneaky switchbacks. Prepare to cross Mission Creek and feeder creeks a dozen times or so.

18.0 Continue rolling on the trail as it drops down and across the creek several times.

24.4 Arrive at the Devils Gulch/Mission Ridge Trailheads.

Centennial Trail— Riverside State Park

Ride Summary

The city of Spokane is very bicycle-friendly. The Centennial Trail that begins in Idaho, runs all the way through the city, smack into Riverside State Park. The Centennial Trail itself is obviously very popular for more than just mountain biking, but the singletrack within the park, well, that's where the mountain bikers leave the others behind. There are miles of trail, double and singletrack, to explore within the park. Take an hour or take a full day. You won't be able to ride them all in one visit.

Ride Specs

Start: *Riverside State Park:* Parking lot at Seven Mile Road and Aubrey White Parkway. *Centennial Trail:* Visitors Center at the Idaho border.

Length: *Riverside State Park:* Varies depending on routes chosen. *Centennial Trail:* 37 miles one-way.

Rating: Easy paved path. Trails range from Easy to Difficult depending on elevations.

Terrain: Centennial Trail is paved. Riverside State Park trails are singletrack, doubletrack, fire roads, washboard, and sand.

Other Trail Users: Paved path: pedestrians, runners, and in-line skaters. Trails: hikers, horseback riders, and cross-country runners.

Getting There

To the Paved Centennial Path. From Interstate 90: Take the Maple Street exit heading north. Follow it over the City Bike Path to Nora Avenue—turn left. Turn right on Pettet Drive and look for the signs for Riverside Park parking.

To the Riverside State Park Trails. From Interstate 90: Take the Maple Street exit heading north. Follow Maple to Northwest Boulevard—turn left. Follow for a mile or two until it turns into Assembly Road and then Nine Mile Road. Continue on Nine Mile Road about one mile to Seven Mile Road. Follow Seven Mile Road over the bridge. Turn left immediately after the bridge onto Aubrey White Parkway (also called Riverside Park Drive). Follow this to the parking lot.

The city of Spokane is built alongside the Spokane River—both of which are named after the Native American tribe of this region. The first Anglo pioneer to be drawn to the roar of Spokane's falls was James N. Glover, who in 1872 began the task of building a township. Glover expected big things from this new town that he called "Spokane Falls." He waited anxiously for the railroad to arrive, realizing that this would determine the success or failure of his venture. In 1878, Spokane Falls became "official," and its population grew to 100 within a year. The railroad finally came in 1881. By 1883, a Dutch mortgage company began financing the construction of the town, envisioning the potential for waterpower along the mighty river, which meant industry development and future capital.

In 1889, Spokane Falls succumbed to a fate that befell many pioneer towns of the West in those rugged days of isolation. Cause unknown, a devastating fire destroyed 32 blocks of the town's financial district. The townspeople quickly gathered their resources and within a year rebuilt—this time in brick and granite. From the ashes the city of Spokane emerged, dropping "Falls" from its name. The city developed quickly—500 buildings were erected the first year. Due to inflated wages that came with the insistence on quick recovery, workmen flocked to Spokane, and the population escalated to 25,000 in two years' time.

Spokane was probably a relatively easy place to build a town in the 1800s. The weather is sunny and dry most months of the year—which explanes the Indian word "spokan" meaning "Sun People." The climate is markedly different from its sister cities to the west. Spokane is protected by the Cascade range to the west—which keeps precipitation on average below 20 inches a year—and the Rocky Mountains to the east—which keep winters rather mild. This combination of low rainfall and mild winters gives Spokane a longer mountain biking season as well. There are many places to mountain bike on the outskirts of town and within the city limits. Travel to the top of Mount Spokane to ride the singletrack that the National Off-Road Bicycle Association (NORBA) has used for mountain bike races, or stay close to town and follow a self-guided tour along The Centennial Trail.

The Centennial Trail is a 37-mile paved pathway that begins at the Washington/Idaho state line (connecting to the Idaho Centennial Trail) and ends, presently, at the Nine Mile Dam where the Spokane and Little Spokane rivers converge. Some of the most scenic sections of trail run through Riverside State Park—where approximately 10.5 miles of dirt singletrack and doubletrack trail can be found for in-city mountain biking. The trails are accessed easily from several places along The Centennial Trail. Riverside State Park has at least seven parking lots of its own. The most direct access to the singletrack is from the Seven Mile Road parking area, mid-center of the park. There you'll find an entrance to an area jam-packed with singletrack. While our map attempts to provide a general rendering of the trail system, it should in no way be considered complete. The trail network continues to grow all the time. Its pathways are nonetheless fun to explore even without the most complete map and getting lost shouldn't be of great concern. (Riverside State Park administrators are currently working on creating such a map, but at present there is no specific date when it will be available.)

The route along the Centennial Trail is open to everyone: strollers, skaters, bicycle riders, and hikers. If you want to ride the entire Washington portion of the trail, begin at the Washington State Visitor Information Center at the Idaho border. From there, the trail continues west past small parks and river rapids. A dozen or so miles into the trail, you'll pass Boulder Beach and Minnehaha Rocks (a great place to rock climb). Moving into the city, still following the Spokane River, the Centennial Trail passes the Spokane Community College and Gonzaga University (Bing Crosby's alma mater) before meandering through town a little and heading into Riverside State Park's 7,655 acres. From there you can ride to the current end-point at Nine Mile Dam. Riding the Centennial Trail out and back, you can cover almost 80 miles!

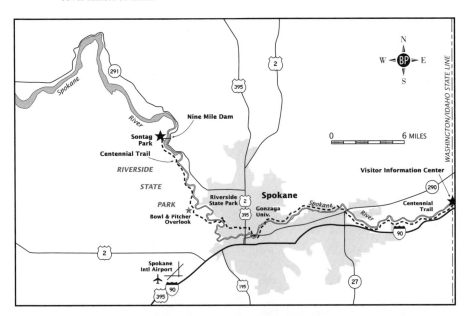

Ride Information

Trail Maintenance Hotlines:
Riverside State Park; (509) 456-3964

Schedule:
Open dawn to dusk

Local Information:
- Spokane Regional Convention and Visitors Bureau, Spokane, WA; (509) 747-3230 or 1-800-248-3230
- Friends of the Centennial Trail, Spokane, WA; (509) 624-7188
- Spokane Outdoors web site: **www.spokaneoutdoors.com**

Local Events/Attractions:
- Spokane House Interpretive Center, 12 miles NW of Spokane on SR 291 (509) 466-4747

Local Bike Shops:
There are a number of quality bike stores and outdoor stores in Spokane, around almost every corner. Check out the local phone book for the one nearest your point of departure.

Maps:
- Maptech CD-ROM: Nine Mile Falls, WA; Airway Heights, WA
- DeLorme's Washington Atlas & Gazetteer—Page 88–89 C4–C5

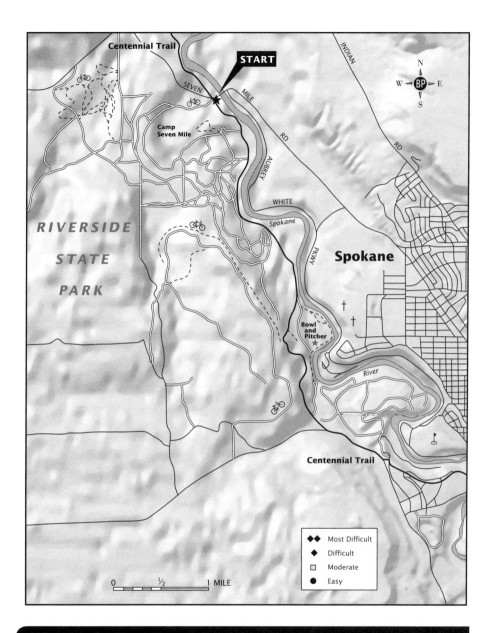

MilesDirections

Centennial Trail: START from the Washington/Idaho state line at the Washington State Visitor Information Center. Travel west through downtown Spokane for 37 miles to the trails end at Nine Mile Dam.

Riverside State Park: START from the parking lot at Seven Mile Road and Aubrey White Parkway near Camp Seven Mile to access the park's vast network of off-road bicycling trails. Make up your own rides within the park and have a blast!

Honorable Mentions

Eastern Washington

Compiled here is an index of great rides in the Southwest region that didn't make the A-list this time around but deserve recognition. Check them out and let us know what you think. You may decide that one or more of these rides deserves higher status in future editions or, perhaps, you may have a ride of your own that merits some attention.

(S) Sawtooth Backcountry

This region has 28 miles of singletrack and connects to the Foggy Dew area (see chapter 36) for epic mountain biking possibilities. Every trail in the area is open to mountain biking except the Summer Blossom Trail and Trails #420, #1254, and #1259 which are in Wilderness Area. From the 4.5-mile Foggy Dew Trail at the Foggy Dew Campground, head north to Cooney Lake, Martha Lakes, and down to the Crater Creek Trailhead for a 12.5-mile shuttle ride. Or, begin at the Crater Creek Trail and take the northwest Trail #431 to Horsehead Pass and Boiling Lake for a 20-mile out-and-back. From State Route 97 north to Pateros: Head north on State Route 153 toward Twisp. At mile marker 16.8, turn left heading west onto Gold Creek Road, which is Forest Service Road 4340. Follow for almost one mile. Turn left at the "T" intersection toward the Foggy Dew Guard Station and Crater Creek Camp. After one mile, continue straight through the intersection for the Foggy Dew Campground. After four miles, turn left and cross a bridge onto Forest Service Road 200. Drive past the Foggy Dew Campground on the left after the bridge. The pavement ends here. Continue three-and-a-half miles to the trailhead parking lot.

From Pateros: Head north on State Route 153 toward Twisp. At mile marker 16.8, turn left heading west onto Gold Creek Road, which is Forest Service Road 4340. Follow for almost one mile. Turn left at the "T" intersection toward the Foggy Dew Guard Station and Crater Creek Camp. After one mile, continue straight through the intersection for the Foggy Dew Campground. After four miles, turn left and cross a bridge onto Forest Service Road 200. Drive past the Foggy Dew Campground on the left after the bridge. The pavement ends here. Continue three and a half miles to the trailhead parking lot. For more information, call the Chelan Ranger District at (509) 682- 2576. See *DeLorme's Washington Atlas & Gazetteer, page 99 C-7.*

(T) Echo Valley

North of Chelan on Cooper Mountain Road, this snow park area has great trails for mountain biking. At least 30 kilometers of trail run through this valley, making this a great area to explore while hanging out at Lake Chelan.

From U.S. Route 2, head north on U.S. Route 97 to Lake Chelan. Follow State Route 150 up the east side of the lake. Turn right on Boyd Road and left on Copper Mountain Road. For more information, call the Chelan Visitors Information at 1-800-424-3526. See *DeLorme's Washington Atlas & Gazetteer, page 83 B-8.*

(U) Steamboat Rock State Park

Sitting out in the middle of Banks Lake, there are 25 miles of paths and trails on, around and over Steamboat Rock — a massive basalt bluff. The 3,500-acre park is well maintained and has lots of camping available. This area is also a popular water sport destination.

From U.S. Route 2 east, travel on State Route 155 north toward Grand Coulee, following the signs for the park to the west. For more information, call the State Park at 1-800-233-0321. See *DeLorme's Washington Atlas & Gazetteer, page 85 B-7.*

(V) Down River Trail

Follow the Columbia River downstream for about seven miles from the Grand Coulee Dam and turn around. A great family trail, just pick up the path at the Mason City Park.

From U.S. Route 2 and Coulee City, head north on State Route 155, or State Route 174 farther east, to Grand Coulee. Follow State Route 155 to the dam. For more information, call the Grand Coulee Visitor Center at (509) 633-9265. See *DeLorme's Washington Atlas & Gazetteer, page 86 A-1.*

(W) 13-Mile ORV Area

This trail system lies within the peaks of Cougar, Granite, Fire, and Seventeenmile Mountains. Alternate trails to the peaks of Fire Mountain (5,890 feet) and Thirteen Mile Mountain (4,885 feet) make great side trips. Lower trails weave around the rock cliffs of the Sanpoil River Canyon. Check out the eagles here in late April and early May.

From the town of Republic, head south on State Route 21. Take Hall Creek Road #99 south to the trailhead for Trail #23, or take State Route 21 south 13 miles to the Thirteen Mile Trailhead. For more information, call the Colville National Forest Republic Ranger District at (509) 775-3305. See *DeLorme's Washington Atlas & Gazetteer, page 116 D-3.*

(X) Taylor Ridge Trail #74

This trail begins at the Taylor Ridge Trailhead and ends at the Indian Creek Road #430. Almost 10 miles long one-way, this trail is steep and moderately difficult. It can be ridden as a shuttle or as an out-and-back. Located within an area that has over 20 miles of mountain bike and ORV trails, this system offers incredible views of the Kettle Range. Climbing from the valley floor, this trail crosses several creeks before topping-out after a 3,550 foot climb between the two trailheads.

From Spokane, travel north on I-395, 22 miles past Kettle Falls to the Boulder-Deer Creek Road #6100. Head west on Boulder-Deer Creek Road #6100 to South Boulder Road #6110, turning left. The trailhead is two miles ahead. For more information, call the Colville National Forest Republic Ranger District at (509) 775-3305. See *DeLorme's Washington Atlas & Gazetteer, page 117 B-7.*

(Y) Narcisse Block of the Pend Oreille Area

This is a large area consisting of 68 miles of multi-purpose trails, great views of Thomas and Green Mountain, as well as fields full of huckleberries in late summer. Access the system from either of three places. Although there are several loops to make, consider making one big 30-mile shuttle trip between Frater Lake and Clark Creek Trailhead. This trail is west of State Route 20, so park at both ends and ride the Radar Dome Trail in between. On the east side of State Route 20 is the 6.5 mile Tacoma Divide Trail that leads to Lake Sherry or to the 8.3-mile Rufus Trail and up to Frater Lake.

From Colville. A.) The Clark Creek Trailhead, 3.1 miles south of the Radar Dome Vista: Travel on State Route 20 twenty miles east of Colville to Forest Service Road 2389 continuing to the trailhead. B.) The Mill Creek Trailhead: Take State Route 20 26 miles east of Colville to County Road #4954 and the trailhead. And C.) The Frater Lake Trailhead: Follow State Route 20 29 miles east of Colville finding the trailhead adjacent to the highway.

For more information, call the Northeast Region of the Department of Natural Resources at (509) 684-7474 or the Colville Ranger District at (509) 684-7010. See *DeLorme's Washington Atlas & Gazetteer, page 118 D-3&4.*

(Z) Batey/Bould Trails

Just west of the Idaho border, along the Oreille River, are 38 miles of trail ranging from easy to most difficult. The Alpha and Lone Wolf trails are the easiest. The Arctic, Howter, and Scapegoat Trails are the toughest, ranging in elevation from 2,500 feet to 4,400 feet.

From Spokane, head north on U.S. Route 2 to State Route 211 to State Route 20 north. Turn west on to Kapps Lane. Head north on West Calispell (County Road 9205) to County Road 2341, following the signs to the trailhead. For more information, call the Colville Ranger District at (509) 684-7010. See *DeLorme's Washington Atlas & Gazetteer, page 105 A-6.*

(AA) 49-Degrees North Alpine Ski Area

Open for mountain biking during the year, this resort actually supports a World Cup dual slalom race in the snow on Valentine's Day every year. There is also an annual WIM (Washington, Idaho, Montana) Series race offering both cross-country and downhill divisions for novice to expert racers. Singletrack and logging roads are accessed either from the base area or a mile from the ski area opposite Crest Drive.

From Spokane, travel 42 miles north on I-395. Turn right at the light onto Flowery Trail Road, and continue 10 miles more to the resort. For more information, call the ski area at (509) 935-6649 or 458-9208. See *DeLorme's Washington Atlas & Gazetteer, page 104 B-4.*

(BB) Mount Spokane State Park

Mount Spokane State Park surrounds the highest peak around for miles: Mount Spokane, which stands at 5,883 feet. The cross-country ski trails weaving throughout the park make ideal mountain biking routes in the summer. There are several trails on the mountain to try, including the Spirit Lake Trail, Valley View Trail, and the Larch Trail. Just about every level of rider can find an appropriate route here. Park at the sno-park for most rides on Mount Spokane. Maps are available at the resort or on the outdoor board at the trailhead.

Take U.S. Route 2 to State Route 206. Follow State Route 206 for 15 miles to the State Park entrance, continuing on to the sno-park parking area. The trailhead has an outdoor board map. Call Mount Spokane State Park for more information at (509) 238-4258. See *DeLorme's Washington Atlas & Gazetteer, page 89 A-7&8.*

(CC) Liberty Lake Regional Park

Part of the Spokane County Parks and Recreation system, equi-distant from both Spokane and Coeur d'Alene, ID, this ORV area has miles of trail between its 3,000 acres, spanning into both Washington and Idaho soil.

From Spokane, take I-90 to Idaho Road heading south, just west of the Idaho border in Washington. For more information, call Spokane Country Parks and Recreation at (509) 456-4730. See *DeLorme's Washington Atlas & Gazetteer, page 89 C-8.*

(DD) The Bill Chipman Palouse Trail

Part of the Rails-to-Trails Program, this easy-grade, eight-mile paved trail opened in April of 1998, in a cooperative effort between active citizens and several government agencies. This trail was named in the memory of Bill Chipman, a local businessman, civic leader, family man, and friend, who was admired in Pullman and Moscow. Running between Washington State University in Pullman and the University of Idaho in Moscow, this all-purpose recreational trail crosses 12 old railroad tresses along scenic Paradise Creek. Access the path at Bishop Boulevard in Pullman near Bishop and State Route 270. For more information, contact Whitman County Parks at (509) 397-6238. See *DeLorme's Washington Atlas & Gazetteer, page 57 C-7.*

(EE) The Snake River Bikeway

Along the Snake River, which marks the boundary line between Washington and Idaho, there is a wonderful paved path running from Clarkston to Asotin, past several parks and scenic stops, including Swallow's Nest Rock, a one-million-year-old slab of basalt that hosts thousands of nesting swallows each spring.

The trail begins at Beachview Park in Clarkston at the corner of Beachview and Chestnut Streets. For more information, contact the Clarkston Chamber of Commerce at (509) 758-7712. See *DeLorme's Washington Atlas & Gazetteer, page 43 A-8.*

(FF) Asotin Creek Trail

The route along Asotin Creek is an easy-grade, scenic, and popular trail. Just follow the trail along the creek for about eight miles and then turn around. For a more moderate loop option, ride the trail eight miles, and instead of turning around, follow the trail up and away from Asotin Creek. The trail will loop around and end at the parking area, completing a 15-mile loop.

From Clarkston, head south on State Route 129 to Hells Canyon. Turn right onto Asotin Creek Road. Drive four miles to the split and the parking area. For more information, contact the Washington State Parks and Recreation Department at 1-800-233-0321. See *DeLorme's Washington Atlas & Gazetteer, page 43 B-8.*

(GG) North Fork Trail/Table Springs Loop

This advanced ride requires technical skill and endurance. At one point, a three-mile climb gains over 2,300 feet. Begin on the Forest Road 65. Follow a mile or so to U.S. 040 and turn right. Turn right onto the North Fork Trail. Follow the trail over Forest Road 6512 after half a mile. Out of the woods, a Jeep trail heads right; follow the trail left across the meadow. Ride over eight miles up and down to Cub Saddle at Bear Creek. Turn left on the Table Springs Trail. At the end of the trail turn left onto Forest Road 6512. Stay left at the junction with Forest Road 090, and to the right at the junctions of Forest Road 080 and 060. Follow Forest Road 6512 back to your car.

From Walla Walla, take Isaacs Avenue east to Mill Creek Road. Turn right on Mill Creek and continue 13 miles, turning right on Tiger Canyon Road. Park here to add to the climb, or drive up seven and a half miles to the top of the canyon. For more information, contact the U.S. Forest Service at (509) 522-6290. See *DeLorme's Washington Atlas & Gazetteer, page 41 D-7.*

(HH) South Fork Trail Out and Back

This 13-mile, easy-grade ride is by far the busiest trail in the area. There are a creek or two to cross and some rocky singletrack, but the climb is minimal, unless you decide to hoof it all the way up to the Burnt Cabin Bridge. From the BLM parking area, follow the South Fork Walla Walla Road up the river. Turn right in one mile, just before the third bridge, onto the South Fork Walla Walla Trail. Follow this singletrack/doubletrack trail up the north side of the river. Pass the Table Springs Trail after five miles and turn around when you get to the Burnt Cabin Bridge Trail, a mile or so farther.

From Walla Walla, head south on Park Street to Howard Street. Follow Howard south a mile-and-a-half where it becomes Cottonwood Road. Follow Cottonwood straight to Powerline Road, continuing straight. Cross the North Fork of the Walla Walla after almost nine miles. Turn left and climb the valley of the South Fork. Drive seven miles to Harris Park. The parking area is half a mile ahead. For more information, contact the U.S. Forest Service at (509) 522-6290, or the Bureau of Land Management in Baker City, OR, at (541) 523-1256. See DeLorme's Washington Atlas & Gazetteer, page 41 D-7.

Ⅱ Elbow Creek—Walla Walla

Heralded as one of the best rides in Walla Walla, this 26-mile loop features 3,000 feet of climbing, tight switchbacks, and rocky singletrack. The best part of the ride is the refueling stop at the half-way mark, offering a welcome opportunity to restock your water or food. Start at the BLM parking area, above Harris County Park. Follow the South Fork of the Walla Walla River on a dirt road for one mile. Branching left, cross a bridge and begin following Elbow Creek. Climb about 2,000 feet in six miles to Lincton Mountain Road. Bear right at the fork on top of the ridge toward Lincton Mountain Road. Turn left onto the road. The Tollgate Mountain Chalet is just up the road. Turn left at the Chalet onto paved Oregon State Highway 204 and ride for 4.6 miles to the Tollgate store, past Langdon Lake. Turn left on Forest Road 64 following the sign for Jubilee Lake. Turn left onto Forest Road 6401 to Target Meadows and right into Target Meadows Campground. Find the Burnt Cabin Trail on the left fork just after the campground. Take this singletrack to the South Fork of the Walla Walla River. Crossing a bridge, turn left onto the South Fork Walla Walla Trail. Descend another five miles to South Fork Walla Walla Road and turn right. One mile down is the BLM parking area.

From Walla Walla, head south on Park Street to Howard Street. Follow Howard south a mile-and-a-half where it becomes Cottonwood Road. Follow Cottonwood straight to Powerline Road, continuing straight. Cross the North Fork of the Walla Walla after almost nine miles, turn left and climb the valley of the South Fork. Drive seven miles to Harris Park and the parking area half a mile ahead. For more information, contact the U.S. Forest Service at (509) 522-6290, or the Bureau of Land Management in Baker City, OR, at (541) 523-1256. See DeLorme's Washington Atlas & Gazetteer, page 41 D-7.

BONUS HONORABLE MENTIONS—Western Idaho

Canfield Mountain Trail System

A popular mountain biking area for Spokane bicyclists, the area along the Buttes is central to many activities and has 46 miles of old roads and trails open to mountain bikers.

From Spokane, take I-90 east into Idaho, then head north up Forest Road 268 to the Canfield Buttes and the Cannfield Mountain Trail System. The Coeur d'Alene National Forest has trail information at (208) 752-1221.

The Coeur d'Alene River Trail

Twenty-one miles long, this beautiful trail is easy to ride. You can access it from several locations, including Jordan Camp at Cathedral Peak on Forest Road 412.

From Spokane, head east on I-90 through Coeur d'Alene and Kellogg to Wallace. Turn left on Forest Road 465 to Bunn. Continue north on Forest Road 456. Turn right on Forest Road 208. Follow 208 past Forest Road 442, turning right on Forest Road 412. Stay on 412 all the way to the trailhead at Cathedral Peak. The Coeur d'Alene National Forest has trail information at (208) 752-1221.

Fourth of July Pass

This cross-country ski area has extensive forest roads and ski trail roads to explore. Have a map and a compass—it is easy to get turned around.

From Spokane, head east on I-90 through Coeur d'Alene, ID, to exit 28 north. The Coeur d'Alene National Forest has trail information at (208) 752-1221.

Silver Mountain Alpine Ski Area

Near the town of Kellogg, ID, this ski resort opens to mountain bikers only on weekends and holidays from the first weekend in July to Labor Day weekend. Take the gondola up (the world's longest!) and experience their 12-mile long runs for some super sweet descents.

From Spokane, head east on I-90 to exit 49. Head south on County Road 90 to Silver Mountain just west of Kellogg. For more information, call the resort at (208) 783-1111 or visit their web site, www.silvermt.com.

Farragut State Park

The park has 4,000 acres and is one of Idaho's largest and most popular parks on the shores of Lake Pend Oreille. There is a nine-mile designated mountain biking trail here and over 20 miles of hiker only paths.

From Spokane, head east on I-90 in to Coeur d'Alene to I- 95. Follow I-95 north to State Route 54 northeast to Lake Pend Oreille and the park. For more information, call Farragut State Park at (208) 683-2425.

Elsie Lake Trail #106

Within the Coeur d'Alene National Forest, follow this 1.7-mile trail from the lake into the Saint Joe Divide area. Connect with Trail #16, which heads east and west, for some fabulous mountain biking. Take the trail as far east as Montana or back into the Silver Mountain mountain biking trail system. There are several trail accesses to the St. Joe district: from the Dot Creek Trail, the Striped Peak Trail up to Moon Pass, or to the Silver Hills Trail on the way up to Lake Elsie along the Coeur d'Alene Divide. Give yourself a week and you may be able to explore a good portion of this trail system.

From Spokane, travel east on I-90. Turn south on Big Creek Road between Kellogg and Wallace, or south on Placer Creek Road from Wallace to Forest Road 389. For more information, call the Coeur d'Alene National Forest at (208) 765-7223.

Schweitzer Basin Ski Resort

Close to Sandpoint, ID, this ski resort is a great mountain biking destination. Hosting one of the National Off-Road Bicycle Association (NORBA) series races in August (1998), this ski resort is open for mountain biking July 1 to Labor Day weekend. The chair lift is open Fridays, Saturdays, and Sundays in the summer for easy access to the upper trails, but lower trails are great fun, too.

From Spokane, travel east on I-90 to Coeur d'Alene. Head north on U.S. Route 2/95 for 11 miles to Sandpoint and follow the signs for the resort. For more information, call the resort at 1-800-831-8810.

Clubs and Trail Groups

Backcountry Bicycle Trails Club

Their motto: Education, Recreation, and Advocacy on behalf of mountain bikers. Affiliated with IMBA (International Mountain Bicycling Association), the BBTC is nine years old, has 400 members, and is run completely by volunteers.
21288 P.O. Box
Seattle, WA 98111-3288
(206) 283-2995
bbtc@cycling.org
www.dirtnw.com/bbtc

B.I.K.E.S. of Everett

Established in 1979, this bicycle club promotes cycling for fun and exercise. Volunteer ride leaders sponsor rides every weekend all year. There are even regular weekday ride schedules.
P.O. Box 5242
Everett, WA 98206
(425) 339-ROLL or (206) 972-AWAY
www.virtualcafe.com/~cathy/
bikes/index.html

Capital Bicycling Club

For mountain bikers and road bike riders into racing, or group rides. This group has been active since 1978.
P.O. Box 642
Olympia, WA 98507
(360) 956-3321
www.olywa.net/cbc/

Cascade Bicycle Club

This is the largest cycling club in the U.S. with over 5,000 members. They strongly promote safe cycling, host many road bicycling events, and are very active in cycling advocacy and education.
P.O. Box 31299
Seattle, WA 98103-1299
(206) 522-BIKE
www.cascade.org/

Different Spokes

Seattle's gay and lesbian bicycling club. They offer many organized rides for all levels of interest and abilities.
P.O. Box 31542
Seattle, WA 98103
(206) 689-6811
Rtyrell@evansgroup.com

Emerald Tea & Cycling Society

Formerly sponsored by the Rainier Brewery, this group was formed just for fun. ("Tea" refers to the prohibition word for alcoholic beverages. The club name used to be "Team Green Death".) Meets monthly, rides for all abilities and interests.
6019 51 Ave. NE
Seattle, WA 98115-7077
(206) 522-3701

Green River Bicycle Club

A group that's been around since 1982. Rides are both on and off-road in the Green River Valley and beyond.
P.O. Box 1209
Auburn, WA 98071-1209
(360) 897-8026
simploe@TC-NET.com

Northwest Bicycling

Home of the Memorial Weekend Bicycling tour of Orcas Island, WA. Food and 3-day cabin stay, round-trip ferry ticket and the works included for under 100 bucks. Since 1974. Open to mountain bikers and road bike riders.
6629 113th Pl. SE
Bellevue, WA 98006
(425) 235-7774

Northwest Mountain Bikers

Spur of the moment fun. This loosely organized mountain biking group promotes races, rides, exploration and some advocacy.
6304 6th Ave.
Tacoma, WA 98406
(253) 565-9050

Now Bike

A non-profit advocacy group promoting "More People Bicycling More Often, Safely." They influence bicycle transportation, develop education programs for safe cycling, and encourage bicycle commuting.
Susie Stevens
P.O. Box 2904
Seattle, WA 98111
(206) 224-9252
nowbike@accessone.com
www.nwlink.com/mcw/nowbike/nowbike.html

Port Townsend Bicycle Association

Not a club, but an organization dedicated to promoting bicycling through educational, recreational, and sporting events. Host of The Roadie Tour in May, to explore and discover the rural roads of Jefferson County.
P.O. Box 649
Port Townsend, WA 98368
(360) 385-3912
jdmcc@olympus.net

Redmond Cycling Club

Road bike riders that ride together for inspiration, camaraderie, and fun. Offering rides that "cover the spectrum of cycling, from casual social jaunts to the most challenging ultramarathons to be found in the Northwest." Organizers of the Ride Around Mount Rainier in One Day (RAMROD); Don's End of the Year Century; many training rides; and the fully supported 2-day ride to Mazama through the North Cascades to the Methow Valley and back; as well as others.

P.O. Box 1841
Bothell, WA 98041-1841
(425) 739-8609
rcc@blarg.net
www.blarg.net/~rcc/

Single Track Minds

This club was originally formed with the thought that you never leave anyone behind. Primarily a recreational paced group, there are specific organized group rides for racers, too. They average 25 rides per month and organize five or six huge mountain biking camping trips per year in Washington and Oregon. The club began in 1994 and has 200 members, promoting cycling through stuardship and education.

6824 19th St. W #147
Tacoma, WA 98466
(253) 565-5124
members.aol.com/STMClub/stmclub/html

Skagit Bicycle Club

Organizers of weekly mountain biking and road biking rides for all ability levels.

1325 North 19th
Mount Vernon, WA 98273
(360) 428-9487

Spokane Bicycle Club

Ride the roads or the trails, this club has something going on all the time for everyone who wants to ride a bike and make new friends.

Gordon Savatsky
P.O. Box 62
Spokane, WA 99210
(509) 325-1171

Spokane Mountaineers

Established in 1920, there are now over 700 members to this group. Organized group mountain bike rides are held every Tuesday night and general membership meetings are held the third Thursday of every month. Other activities include backpacking, mountaineering, ski touring, hiking and paddle sports.

P.O. Box 1013
Spokane, WA 99210-1013
(509) 838-4974

Tacoma Wheelmen's Bicycle Club

This club has been around since 1888 and welcomes road bicycle riders of all skill levels. They promote safe bicycling for recreation, health, and alternate transportation, sponsoring two organized rides each year, the Daffodil Classic and the Peninsula Metric.

P.O. Box 112078
Tacoma, WA 98411
(253) 566-1822
Bikerbabe@sprynet.com
www.twbc.org/

The Greatful Tread Bicycling Club

Established in March 1994, this group has over 100 members. Their mission is to promote "the sport we love so much." Contact them for information on bike trips, where to ride, and upcoming events.

909 S. 34th Ave.
Yakima, WA
98902
(509) 697-9695
www.ewa.net/users/jdmtnbiker/tread1.htm

West Sound Cycling Club

Founded in 1985, this club now has about 100 members. Their main focus is promoting bicycling as a safe and healthy form of recreation and an environmental form of transportation. They get involved in some legislative issues and conduct several educational clinics. Their two main sponsored rides per year are the Countryside Classic in July and the Tour de Kitsap in September. Weekly social rides on Saturday and Sunday for all levels, and bimonthly Welcome Rides for new members. They meet the first Wednesday of every month.

P.O. Box 1579
Silverdale, WA 98383
(360) 698-3876

Whatcom Independent Mountain Pedalers (WIMPs)

A group of mountain bikers who welcome all skill levels to wander the back roads and trails in northwestern Washington.

Craig Stephens
1410 Girard St. Suite 9
Bellingham, WA 98225
(360) 671-4107

Washington Festivals

March

Coffee Fest and Swap Meet, Olympia, WA; (360) 753-8380 [Chapters 16, 17]

Skagit Valley Tulip Festival, Mount Vernon, WA; (360) 428-5959 www.tulipfestival.org [Chapter 8]

April

Art Walk, Olympia, WA; (360) 753-8380 [Chapters 16, 17]

Earth Day, Chelan, WA; 1-800-424-3526 [Chapters 36, 37]

Orcas Island Farmers Market, Saturdays, April to October, Eastsound, WA. [Chapter 1]

Washington State Apple Blossom Festival, Wenatchee, WA; (509) 662-3616 [Chapters 38, 39]

Wheelsport Bike Sale, Spokane Interstate Fairgrounds, Spokane, WA; (509) 326-3977 [Chapter 40]

May

Armed Forces Festival and Parade, Bremerton, WA; (360) 479-3579 [Chapter 6]

Beachin' Hang Gliding Tournament, Chelan, WA; 1-800-424-3526 [Chapters 36, 37]

Heritage Weekend, Vancouver, WA; (360) 693-1313 [Chapters 31, 32, 33]

Juan De Fuca Festival of the Arts, Port Angeles, WA; (360) 457-5411 [Chapters 3, 4, 5]

Maifest, Leavenworth, WA; (509) 548-5807 [Chapters 11, 12, 38, 39]

Northwest Folklife Festival, Seattle, WA; (206) 684-7300 [Chapter 18]

Seattle International Film Festival, Seattle, WA; (206) 324-9996 [Chapter 18]

Ski to Sea Race/Festival, Bellingham, WA; (360) 734-1330 [Chapter 2]

The Annual Bloomsday Race, Riverfront Park, Spokane, WA; (509) 838-1579 [Chapter 40]

The Lilac Festival, for 10 days in May, Spokane, WA; (509) 326-3339 [Chapter 40]

Tumwater Bluegrass Festival, Tumwater, WA; (360) 357-5153 [Chapters 16, 17]

University District Street Fair, Seattle, WA; (206) 547-4417 [Chapters 18]

Winthrop Rodeo Days, Winthrop, WA; (509) 996-2125 [Chapters 7, 34, 35]

Yacolt Herb Festival, Yacolt, WA; (360) 686-3537 [Chapters 32, 33]

June

All That Jazz in the Olympics, Sequim, WA; 1-800-737-8462 [Chapters 4, 5]

Classic Mariners Regatta, Port Townsend, WA; (360) 385-3628 [Chapters 4, 5]

Founder's Day, Cashmere, WA; (509) 782-7404 [Chapters 38, 39]

Leavenworth Craft Fair, Leavenworth, WA; (509) 548-5807 [Chapters 11, 12, 38, 39]

Rodeo City Round-Up, Ellensburg, WA; (509) 925-1488 [Chapters 13, 14, 15]

Vancouver Festival, Vancouver, WA; (360) 693-1313 [Chapters 31, 32, 33]

Wildflower Festival, Darrington, WA; (360) 436-1794 [Chapter 8]

July

Arts Festival & Volkssport Walk, Trout Lake, WA; (509) 395-2294 [Chapters 25, 29, 30]

Bite of Seattle, Seattle, WA; (206) 684-7200 [Chapter 18]

Bumbershoot, Seattle, WA; (206) 684-7200 [Chapter 18]

Capital Lakefair, Olympia, WA; (360) 943-7344 [Chapters 16, 17]

Columbia Gorge Bluegrass Festival, Stevenson, WA; (509) 427-8928 [Chapters 31, 32, 33]

Croatian Picnic, Roslyn, WA; (509) 649-2714 [Chapters 13, 14, 15]

Cross-Country Hang Gliding Classic, Chelan, WA; 1-800-424-3526 [Chapters 36, 37]

King County Fair, Enumclaw, WA; (360) 825-7666 [Chapters 19, 20, 21]

Pacific Northwest Highland Games, Enumclaw, WA; (360) 825-7666 [Chapters 19, 20, 21]

Pioneer Days, Roslyn, WA; (509) 674-5958 [Chapters 13, 14, 15]

Premiere Jazz Festival, Port Townsend, WA; 1-800-733-3608 [Chapters 4, 5]

Seafair, Seattle, WA; (206) 728-0123 [Chapter 18]

Sultan Summer Shindig Logging Show, Sultan, WA; (360) 793-2565 [Chapters 10, 9]

Sweet Pea Festival, Roslyn, WA; (509) 649-2758 [Chapters 13, 14, 15]

Vancouver Days, Vancouver, WA; (360) 693-1313 [Chapters 31, 32, 33]

Victorian Gaming Days and Marshall House Tours, Vancouver, WA; (360) 693-1313 [Chapters 31, 32, 33]

Whisky Dick Triathlon, Ellensburg, WA; (509) 925-3137 [Chapters 13, 14, 15]

August

Blackberry Festival, Bremerton, WA; (360) 377-3041 [Chapter 6]

Chalk Art Festival, Bellingham, WA; (360) 676-8548 [Chapter 2]

Community Fair and Dairy Show, Trout Lake, WA; (509) 395-2241 [Chapters 25, 29, 30]

Ellensburg Rodeo, Ellensburg, WA; (509) 962-7831 or 1-800-637-2444 [Chapters 13, 14, 15]

Fair Days, Monroe, WA; (360) 794-4344 [Chapter 10]

Harbor Days, Olympia, WA; (360) 352-4557 [Chapters 16, 17]

International Accordion Celebration, Leavenworth, WA; (509) 548-5807 [Chapters 11, 12, 38, 39]

Nudestock, Tiger Mountain, WA; (425) 392-NUDE (You'll just have to see this to believe it.) [Chapter 18]

Old Time Tractor Pull and Threshing Bee, Monroe, WA; (360) 659-1682 [Chapters 10, 9]

Roslyn Wing Ding, Roslyn, WA; (509) 649-2795 [Chapter 13, 14,15]

Salmon Bake, Sequim, WA; (360) 683-7988 [Chapters 4, 5]

September

Kingston Bluegrass Festival, Kingston, WA; (360) 297-7866 [Chapter 5]

Mountain Triathlon, Winthrop, WA; (509) 996-3287 [Chapters 7, 34, 35]

Washington State Autumn Leave Festival, Leavenworth, WA; (509) 548-5807 [Chapters 11, 12, 38, 39]

October

Apple Days, Cashmere, WA; (509) 782-7404 [Chapters 38, 39]

Apple Industry Tour, Wenatchee, WA; (509) 663-9600 [Chapters 38, 39]

Methow Valley Mountain Bike Festival, Winthrop, WA; (509) 996-3287 [Chapters 7, 34, 35]

"October-West", Winthrop, WA; (509) 996-2125 [Chapters 7, 34, 35]

November

MVSTA Ski & Sports Swap, Winthrop, WA; (509) 996-3287 [Chapters 7, 34, 35]

The Perfect Guidebook Companions

Tired of lugging your guidebook along on rides? Try CycoActive's BarMap or BarMap OTG. Simply photocopy the route map and ride cues, slip them into your BarMap, and leave that beautiful guidebook on the coffee table.

The BarMap™ mapcase is a simple, lightweight solution to an age-old problem. Its soft mapcase, sewn of Cordura™ and clear vinyl, velcros easily to the handlebar. Those days of digging maps out of your fanny pack, unfolding, refolding, and stuffing them back in, are forever in the past. $7.95

The BarMap OTG™ (Of The Gods) carrying case goes a step further, allowing you to view an entire 8.5"x11" map, while still folding down to a compact 5"x6", wallet-size case that fits right on the stem. On the outside is a 4"x5" clear pocket for route maps; inside you'll find a mesh pocket for keys or money, and another pocket for energy bars, tools, and stuff. $19.95

Call Now To Order:
1-888-232-2492

CycoActive Products are designed and manufactured in Seattle, WA

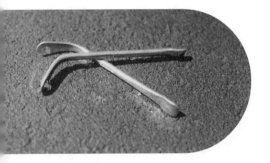

Appendix: Repair and Maintenance

FIXING A FLAT

TOOLS YOU WILL NEED

- Two tire irons
- Pump (either a floor pump or a frame pump)
- No screwdrivers!!! (This can puncture the tube)

REMOVING THE WHEEL

The front wheel is easy. Simply open the quick release mechanism or undo the bolts with the proper sized wrench, then remove the wheel from the bike.

The rear wheel is a little more tricky. Before you loosen the wheel from the frame, shift the chain into the smallest gear on the freewheel (the cluster of gears in the back). Once you've done this, removing and installing the wheel, like the front, is much easier.

REMOVING THE TIRE

Step one: Insert a tire iron under the bead of the tire and pry the tire over the lip of the rim. Be careful not to pinch the tube when you do this.

Step two: Hold the first tire iron in place. With the second tire iron, repeat step one, three or four inches down the rim. Alternate tire irons, pulling the bead of the tire over the rim, section by section, until one side of the tire bead is completely off the rim.

Step three: Remove the rest of the tire and tube from the rim. This can be done by hand. It's easiest to remove the valve stem last. Once the tire is off the rim, pull the tubeout of the tire.

CLEAN AND SAFETY CHECK

Step four: Using a rag, wipe the inside of the tire to clean out any dirt, sand, glass, thorns, etc. These may cause the tube to puncture. The inside of a tire should feel smooth. Any pricks or bumps could mean that you have found the culprit responsible for your flat tire.

Step five Wipe the rim clean, then check the rim strip, making sure it covers the spoke nipples properly on the inside of the rim. If a spoke is poking through the rim strip, it could cause a puncture.

Step six: At this point, you can do one of two things: replace the punctured tube with a new one, or patch the hole. It's easiest to just replace the tube with a new tube when you're out on the trails. Roll up the old tube and take it home to repair later that night in front of the TV. Directions on patching a tube are usually included with the patch kit itself.

INSTALLING THE TIRE AND TUBE
(This can be done entirely by hand)

Step seven: Inflate the new or repaired tube with enough air to give it shape, then tuck it back into the tire.

Step eight: To put the tire and tube back on the rim, begin by putting the valve in the valve hole. The valve must be straight. Then use your hands to push the beaded edge of the tire onto the rim all the way around so that one side of your tire is on the rim.

Step nine: Let most of the air out of the tube to allow room for the rest of the tire.

Step ten: Beginning opposite the valve, use your thumbs to push the other side of the tire onto the rim. Be careful not to pinch the tube in between the tire and the rim. The last few inches may be difficult, and you may need the tire iron to pry the tire onto the rim. If so, just be careful not to puncture the tube.

BEFORE INFLATING COMPLETELY

Step eleven: Check to make sure the tire is seated properly and that the tube is not caught between the tire and the rim. Do this by adding about 5 to 10 pounds of air, and watch closely that the tube does not bulge out of the tire.

Step twelve: Once you're sure the tire and tube are properly seated, put the wheel back on the bike, then fill the tire with air. It's easier squeezing the wheel through the brake shoes if the tire is still flat.

Step thirteen: Now fill the tire with the proper amount of air, and check constantly to make sure the tube doesn't bulge from the rim. If the tube does appear to bulge out, release all the air as quickly as possible, or you could be in for a big bang.

• When installing the rear wheel, place the chain back onto the smallest cog (furthest gear on the right), and pull the derailleur out of the way. Your wheel should slide right on.

LUBRICATION PREVENTS DETERIORATION

Lubrication is crucial to maintaining your bike. Dry spots will be eliminated. Creaks, squeaks, grinding, and binding will be gone. The chain will run quietly, and the gears will shift smoothly. The brakes will grip quicker, and your bike may last longer with fewer repairs. Need I say more? Well, yes. Without knowing where to put the lubrication, what good is it?

THINGS YOU WILL NEED

• One can of bicycle lubricant, found at any bike store.
• A clean rag (to wipe excess lubricant away).

WHAT GETS LUBRICATED

• Front derailleur
• Rear derailleur
• Shift levers
• Front brake
• Rear brake
• Both brake levers
• Chain

WHERE TO LUBRICATE

To make it easy, simply spray a little lubricant on all the pivot points of your bike. If you're using a squeeze bottle, use just a drop or two. Put a few drops on each point wherever metal moves against metal, for instance, at the center of the brake calipers. Then let the lube sink in.

Once you have applied the lubricant to the derailleurs, shift the gears a few times, working the derailleurs back and forth. This allows the lubricant to work itself into the tiny cracks and spaces it must occupy to do its job. Work the brakes a few times as well.

LUBING THE CHAIN

Lubricating the chain should be done after the chain has been wiped clean of most road grime. Do this by spinning the pedals counterclockwise while gripping the chain with a clean rag. As you add the lubricant, be sure to get some in between each link. With an aerosol spray, just spray the chain while pedalling backwards (counterclockwise) until the chain is fully lubricated. Let the lubricant soak in for a few seconds before wiping the excess away. Chains will collect dirt much faster if they're loaded with too much lubrication.

dirt northwest
www.dirtnw.com

The Ultimate Online Guide to Mountain Biking in the Pacific Northwest.

Dirt Northwest is an Internet-based mountain bike magazine created by Northwest riders for Northwest riders. The Web site is absolutely free and there is nothing to join. Each packed issue includes:

Trail Listings — Tons of trails throughout Oregon, Washington, Idaho and British Columbia. Trails include maps, photos and detailed descriptions.

Adventures — Explore scenic, challenging and exotic rides of epic proportions from around the world and your own back yard.

Product Reviews — The Dirty Boys review all the latest gear, saving you time and money.

Classified Ads — Buy, sell, barter, trade. Whatever you have or need, this is the place to sell or get.

Chat Forums — Interact and share ideas with other riders in your area with your interests and background.

Advocacy — Keep your favorite trails open. Learn what trails are at risk and what you can do to help.

Much More — Visit Dirt Northwest today at www.dirtnw.com to see all that the Northwest has to offer.

Off The Trail

Beachway Press' Adventure Directory

If you're anything like us, one sport just won't do it. To give you an exhaustive idea of what's out there in the way of outdoor recreation, we at Beachway Press have created Off The Trail, your one-stop adventure-guide catalogue. Since your mountain bike can't take you everywhere you'll want to go (it's virtually worthless on water), check out one of these guide companies and experience, under the direction of a local pro, the many facets of the Washington outdoors. You could start with a climb up Mount Baker, then ski down. Mountain bike the Chuckanut Mountains, kayak the San Juans, dive on the north shore of Orcas Island, land a few cutthroat in Cascade Lake. Pop open a cold one and call it a day!

Bicyling

America's Adventure/Venture Europe. Golden, CO 1-800-222-3595 or (303) 526-0806. Guided road and mountain bike tours of the San Juans.

American Wilderness Experience. Boulder, CO 1-800-444-0099 or (303) 444-2622. Guided trips in Washington.

Away From Here Adventures. Seattle, WA (206) 323-1641. Offer biking, hiking, and safari trips around the world.

Backroads. Berkeley, CA. 1-800-462-2848 or (510) 527-1555. Guided road bike tours of the San Juans.

Bicycle Adventures. Olympia, WA 1-800-443-6060 or (360) 786-0989. International bicycle tours; concentration on Pacific Northwest.

Cascade Wilderness Outfitters. Carlton WA (509) 997-0155. Deluxe and standard summer pack trips, ride or hike.

Where Discovery is the Adventure. Gravel Travel is very proud to announce that "Bicycling Magazine" has selected our "KVR Tour" as one of the top 50 on our planet. "The number one tour in British Columbia"—March '98 issue. Gravel Travel offers all-inclusive, fully supported, inn-to-inn, four-and-six day wilderness mountain biking adventures in British Columbia for the novice to advanced rider.

Gravel Travel
9708 Williams St.
Chilliwack, BC Canada V2P-5G7
1-800-429-2533
Tel/Fax (604) 852-3353
www.graveltravel.com

Mountain Outfitters. North Bend, WA (206) 409-0459. Guided mountain bikes trips.

Reachout Expeditions. Anacortes, WA 1-800-697-3847 or (360) 293-3788. Guided road and mountain bike trips in Washington and Oregon Cascades and Olympics.

Terrene Tours. Seattle, WA (206) 325-5569. Seattle bike tours.

Tim Kneeland & Associates, Inc. Seattle, WA 1-800-443-0528 or (206) 329-6090. Road bike tours in Washington State and around the globe.

MOAB DREAMRIDES! WWW.DREAMRIDE.COM. Dreamrides specializes in very small groups and classic Moab terrain. Originally a mountain bike film service, Dreamrides utilizes knowledge gained from years of ground and aerial scouting for the film industry to offer over 60 routes in the Moab area alone. A range of year-round vacation packages can include hiking, skiing, rafting, and aerial tours as well. Our web site, the best in the biz, has trail listings, weather updates, articles, vacation packages in Utah and elsewhere, and lots of photos.

DREAMRIDES
1-888-MOABUTAH
Fax: (435) 259-8196
e-mail: dream@lasal.net

Tri-Island Trek. American Lung Association of Washington. Seattle, WA 1-800-732-9339 or (206) 441-5100. Three-day, 130-mile, fund-driving race from Seattle to Victoria, B.C., to support the American Lung Association.

Mountain Biking at Ski Resorts

49 Degrees North Alpine Ski Area. Chewelah, WA (509) 935-6649 or (509) 459-9208. Many trails are open for mountain biking.

Crystal Mountain Resort. 1-800-852-1444 or (360) 663-2265. Many trails are open for mountain biking; rentals.

Mount Baker Ski Area. (360) 734-6771. Many trails are open for mountain biking.
Mount Spokane Ski Area. Spokane, WA (509) 443-1397. Many trails are open for mountain biking.

Stevens Pass. Skykomish, WA (360) 973-2441. Many trails are open for mountain biking.

Sun Mountain. Winthrop, WA 1-800-572-0493 or (509) 996-2211. Many trails are open for mountain biking.

The Summit at Snoqualmie. Snoqualmie, WA (425) 434-7669. Many trails are open for mountain biking.

Winter Sports

Beaver Creek Ranch. Leavenworth, WA 1-800-858-2276. Guided sleigh and snowmobile rides; snowshoeing and cross-country skiing trips.

Happy Trails Horseback Riding Ranch. Easton, WA (509) 656-2634. Horsedrawn sleigh rides from December through March.

Leavenworth Outfitters. Leavenworth, WA 1-800-347-7934 or (509) 763-3733. Guided cross-country ski trips.

Malamute Express. (509) 997-6402. Twisp River area dogsled rides.

Mountain Outfitters. North Bend, WA (206) 409-0459. Guided ski, snowboard, sleigh ride, and snowshoe trips.

Mountain Springs Lodge. 1-800-858-2276 or (509) 763-2713. Snowmobile tours out of Plain.

Northern Cascades Heli-Skiing. 1-800-494-4354 or (509) 996-3272. Backcountry ski drops.

Paradise Visitor Center. (360) 569-2211. Guided snowshoe walks around Mt. Rainier.

Reachout Expeditions. Anacortes, WA 1-800-697-3847 or (360) 293-3788. Guided cross-country ski trips in the Washington and Oregon Cascades and Olympics.

Rendevous Outfitters. Winthrop, WA 1-800-422-3048 or (509) 996-3299. Cross-country ski packages.

Tahoma Outdoor Pursuits. Tacoma, WA (253) 474-8155. Guided snowshoe and cross-country ski trips in Western Washington.

Horseback Riding & Pack Trips

Beaver Creek Ranch. Leavenworth, WA 1-800-858-2276. Hour-long and overnight horseback rides; lodging.

Blue Mountain Adventure Company. Troy, OR 1-888-258-3686 or (541) 828-7833. Guided, one to 5-day wilderness pack trips in and around the Blue Mountains.

Cascade Corrals. Stehekin, WA (509) 682-4677. Guided horseback rides in the Stehekin Valley.

Cascade Wilderness Outfitters. Charlton, WA; Guided pack trips into the Pasayten and Sawtooth wilderness areas, and Okanogan and Wenatchee national forests.

Chewack River Ranch Riding Stables. Winthrop, WA (509) 996-2497. Overnight campouts with dinner and breakfast; working ranch.

Chinook Pass Guides. Naches, WA (509) 653-2633. Guided horseback riding trips into the William O. Douglas and Norse Peak wilderness areas.

Eagle Creek Ranch. 1-800-221-7433 or (509) 548-7798. Guided rides, pack trips, and drop camp packages.

Early Winter Outfitters. 1-800-737-8750 or (509) 996-2659. Guided horse pack trips into the Pasayten Wilderness.

Elk Horn Ranch Outfitters. Lake Quinault, WA (360) 288-2750. Guided horseback rides in the Upper Quinault Valley of the Olympic Peninsula.

Gray Wolf Outfitters. Poulsbo, WA (360) 692-6455. Deluxe pack trips, drop camps, and day rides into the Olympic Mountains.

Happy Trails Horseback Riding Ranch. Easton, WA (509) 656-2634. Guided trail rides in Easton.

High Country Outfitters. Issaquah, WA 1-888-235-0111 or (425) 392-0111. Guided trail rides and 3-5 day pack trips into the Cascades.

Highland Stage Company. Tonasket, WA (509) 486-4699. Horsedrawn wagon train, camping adventures in the Okanogan and Colville national forests.

Icicle Outfitters & Guides. Leavenworth, WA 1-800-479-3912 or (509) 763-3647. Guided rides into the Cascades; pack trips; drop camps, and hike and pack trips.

Indian Canyon Riding Stable. Spokane, WA (509) 624-4646. Guided rides through the Indian Canyon Park.

Lake Quinalt Outfitters. Port Angeles, WA 1-888-452-9635 or (360) 928-0125. Guided horse packing trips and trail rides in Olympic National Park; hunting trips in the winter.

North Cascades Outfitters. Twisp, WA (509) 997-1015. Guided hike and pack trips in the Pasayten Wilderness; day rides available.

North Cascades Safari. Winthrop, WA (509) 996-2350. Guided horse pack trips into the Pasayten and Sawtooth wilderness areas, Okanogan and Wenatchee national forests.

Rock 'n' Tomahawk Ranch. Ellensburg, WA (509) 962-2403. Guided, hourly to extended day rides in Ellensburg's Green Canyon area; wagon and sleign rides available.

Rocking Horse Recreation. Winthrop, WA (509) 996-2768. Guided day riding and overnight trips in the eastern North Cascades; instruction available.

Sawtooth Outfitters. Pateros, WA (509) 923-2548. Guided horseback riding and horsepack trips into the Northern Cascades.

Sea Horse Ranch. Hoquiam WA (360) 532-6791. Guided horse and pony rides on the beach at Ocean Shores or at the ranch.

Stehekin Valley Ranch. Stehekin, WA (509) 682-4677. Guided horseback rides and rafting trips; meals and lodging.

Tiger Mountain Outfitters. Issaquah WA (425) 392-5090. Three hour, guided rides in the Tiger Mountain State Forest; instruction available.

Llama Treking

Kit's Llamas. Olalla, WA (253) 857-5274. Guided day and extended trips into the Olympic Mountains.

Llama Wilderness Pack Trips. Olympia, WA (360) 491-5262. Guided day trips; longer hikes in the summer.

Pasayten Llama Packing. Winthrop, WA (509) 996-2326. Guided day and extended trips into the Pasayten and Lake Chelan-Sawtooth wilderness areas..

Mountaineering & Climbing

American Alpine Institute. Bellingham, WA (360) 671-1505. Guided rock-climbing, mountain climbing, and ice-climbing expeditions in the North Cascades.

Pacific Crest Outward Bound. Portland, OR 1-800-547-3312 or (503) 243-1993. Mountaineering, backpacking, and canoeing; instruction available.

Rainier Mountaineering, Inc. Tacoma, WA (253) 627-6242 in winter or (360) 569-2227 in summer. Guided trips up Mount Rainier; instruction available.

Reachout Expeditions. Anacortes, WA 1-800-697-3847 or (360) 293-3788. Guided mountaineering trips in Washington and Oregon Cascades and Olympics; instruction available.

Tahoma Outdoor Pursuits. Tacoma, WA (253) 474-8155. Guided rock climbing trips in Western Washington; instruction available.

Valhalla Adventures. Seattle, WA (206) 782-3767. Guided mountaineering and climbing trips into the Cascade, Olympic, and B.C. mountains.

Hiking & Backpacking

Adventure Trails Northwest. Seattle, WA (206) 671-5711. Custom hiking trips.

Back Country Wilderness Outfitters. Seaview, WA (360) 642-2576. Offers drop camps and guided hunts around Mt. St. Helens and in the Gifford Pinchot National Forest.

Backroads. Berkeley, CA. 1-800-462-2848 or (510) 527-1555. Guided hiking tours of the Methow Valley.

Cascade Corrals. Stehekin, WA (509) 682-4677. Horse-supported hiking trips.

Cascade Wilderness Outfitters. Carlton, WA (509) 997-0155. Deluxe and standard summer pack trips, ride or hike.

Eagle Creek Ranch. 1-800-221-7433 or (509) 548-7798. Guided rides, pack trips, and drop camp packages.

Icicle Outfitters & Guides. Leavenworth, WA 1-800-479-3912 or (509) 763-3647. Guided rides into the Cascades; pack trips; drop camps, and hike and pack trips.

Mountain Outfitters. North Bend, WA (206) 409-0459. Guided hiking trips.

North Cascades Outfitters. Twisp, WA (509) 997-1015. Hike and pack trips in the Pasayten Wilderness; day rides available.

Olympic Park Institute/Rosemary Inn. Port Angeles, WA 1-800-775-3720 or (360) 928-3720. Field science, backpacking, and lodge-based trips.

Pacific Crest Outward Bound. Portland, OR 1-800-547-3312 or (503) 243-1993. Mountaineering, backpacking, and canoeing; instruction available.

Reachout Expeditions. Anacortes, WA 1-800-697-3847 or (360) 293-3788. Guided hiking/backpacking trips in Washington and Oregon Cascades and Olympics.

Sawtooth Outfitters. Pateros, WA (509) 923-2548. Guided, 3-10 day pack trips in the Northern Cascades.

Whatcom Skagit Outfitters. Sedro-Woolley, WA (360) 595-1136. Guided day hikes, overnights, and extended trips on Chuckanut Mountain.

Windsurfing

Adventure Out. Hood River, OR (541) 387-4626. Windsurfing trips.

Hood River Windsurfing. Hood River, OR (541) 386-5787. Windsurfing instruction, beginner to advanced.

Rhonda Smith Windsurfing Center. Hood River, OR (541) 386-9463. Windsurfing instruction, beginner to advanced; windsurfing vacations.

Sail World Hood River. Hood River, OR (541) 386-9400. Windsurfing instruction, beginner to advanced.

Rafting

Allrivers Adventures (Wenatchee Whitewater & Co). Cashmere, WA 1-800-743-5628 or (509) 782-2254. One to 3-day, guided rafting trips in OR and WA; instruction.

Alpine Adventures. Leavenworth, WA 1-800-926-7238. Guided rafting trips down 7 Cascade rivers; mild to wild.

Blue Mountain Adventure Company. Troy, OR 1-888-258-3686 or (541) 828-7833. Guided, one to 6-day rafting trips in and around the Blue Mountains.

Blue Sky Outfitters. 1-800-228-7238. Guided rafting trips down the Klickitat, White Salmon, Methow, and Suiattle rivers.

Cascade Corrals. Stehekin, WA (509) 682-4677. Guided rafting trips in the Stehekin Valley.

Chinook Expeditions. Index, WA 1-800-241-3451. Guided rafting trips down the Queets River, Skagit River, and Skykomish River.

Downstream River Runners. Monroe, WA 1-800-234-4644 or (360) 805-9899. Guided, one to multi-day rafting trips on 12 rivers; mild to wild; instruction available.

Enchanted Water Tours. Leavenworth, WA 1-888-723-8987 or (509) 548-5031. Guided rafting trips.

Hells Canyon Office. Clarkston, WA (509) 758-0616. Call for a complete listing of commercial guides.

Leavenworth Outfitters. Leavenworth, WA 1-800-347-7934 or (509) 763-3733. Guided rafting trips on the Wenatchee River.

Northern Cascades River Expeditions. 1-800-634-8433. Guided rafting trips down the Methow, Klickitat, White Salmon, and Sauk rivers.

Northern Wilderness River Riders. Pateros, WA 1-800-448-7238. Guided rafting trips down the Methow, Klickitat, White Salmon, and Suiattle rivers; mild to wild.

Olympic Raft & Guide Service. Port Angeles, WA (360) 452-1443. Guided rafting trips.

Orion Expeditions. Seattle, WA 1-800-553-7466 or (206) 547-6715. Guided rafting trips down class II to V rivers throught the Cascades; eagle float trips; instruction.

Osprey Rafting Company. Twisp, WA 1-800-743-6269 or (509) 997-4116. Guided rafting trips down the Methow, Wenatchee, and Tieto rivers.

Professional River Outfitters of Washington. (206) 726-4046. Guided rafting trips.

Reachout Expeditions. Anacortes, WA 1-800-697-3847 or (360) 293-3788. Guided rafting trips in Washington and Oregon Cascades and Olympics.

Redline River Adventures. Darrington, WA 1-800-290-4500 or (360) 436-0284. Guided, 1 to 4-day rafting trips on 7 rivers; mild to wild; instruction available.

Renegade River Rafters. (509) 427-7238. Guided rafting trips.

River Raft Rentals, Inc. Ellensburg, WA (509) 964-2145. Guided float trips up the Yakima River.

River Recreation. North Bend, WA 1-800-464-5899. Guided rafting trips down the Methow, Klickitat, and White Salmon rivers.

River Riders, Inc. Pateros, WA 1-800-448-7238 or (206) 448-7238. Guided rafting trips on 7 rivers; wild to mild.

Stehekin Valley Ranch. Stehekin, WA (509) 682-4677. Guided rafting trips and horseback rides; meals and lodging.

Wave Trek. Index, WA 1-800-543-7971 or (360) 793-1705. Guided rafting trips on the Skykomish River; kayaking and climbing courses.

White Water Adventure. White Salmon, WA 1-800-366-2004. Guided rafting trips down the Klickitat and White Salmon rivers.

Wild & Scenic River Tours. Seattle, WA 1-800-413-6840 or (206) 323-1220. Guided, half to multi-day rafting trips; wild to mild.

Wildwater River Tours. Federal Way, WA 1-800-522-9453 or (253) 939-2151. Guided rafting trips on the Methow, Klickitat, White Salmon, and Suiattle rivers; mild to wild.

Sailing

"A Trophy" Charters. San Juan, WA (360) 378-2110. Chartered sailing trips out of Friday Harbor.

Beachcomber Charters. Deception Pass, WA (360) 675-7900. Skippered sailboat charters.

Deer Harbor Charters. (360) 376-5989 or 1-800-544-5758. Skippered sailboat charters on Orcas Island; rents skiffs.

Emerald City Charters. Departs from Pier 56 (206) 624-3931. Sailboat excursions into the Puget Sound.

Harmony Sailing Charters. (360) 468-3310. Skippered sailing charters.

Kelcema Sailing Institute. Edmonds, WA (425) 771-8899. Custom sailing adventures.

Kayaking & Canoeing

Allrivers Adventures (Wenatchee Whitewater & Co). Cashmere, WA 1-800-743-5628 or (509) 782-2254. Guided kayaking and tubing trips in OR and WA; instruction.

Elakah! Expeditions. Bellingham, WA (360) 734-7270. Guided sea-kayaking trips in the San Juans and far off destinations.

Kayak Port Townsend. Port Townsend, WA (360) 385-6240. Guided kayaking trips.

Leavenworth Outfitters. Leavenworth, WA 1-800-347-7934 or (509) 763-3733. Guided kayak and canoe trips; rentals.

Northern Lights Expeditions. Bellingham, WA 1-800-754-7402 or (360) 734-6334. Guided, 6-day sea kayaking trips in British Columbia; lodge-based; focus on whales and wildlife.

Northwest Outdoor Center. (206) 281-9694. Guided kayak expeditions around Lake Union, Lake Washington, and Elliott Bay.

Northwest Sea Ventures. Anacortes, WA (360) 293-3692. Guided sea-kayak tours of the San Juans.

Olympic Outdoor Center. Poulsbo, WA (360) 697-6095. Guided sea and white-water kayaking in Puget Sound.

Outdoor Odysseys. (206) 361-0717. Guided kayaking trips to the San Juans and parts of Puget Sound.

Pacific Water Sports. Sea-Tac Airport (206) 246-9385. Guided canoe and kayak trips; instruction..

San Juan Kayak Expeditions. Friday Harbor, WA (360) 378-4436. Guided kayak trips; rentals available.

Sea Quest Expeditions. San Juan Island, WA (360) 378-5767. Guided, day or longer kayaking trips; educational tours.

Shearwater Sea Kayak Tours. Eastsound, WA (360) 376-4699. Guided kayak tours and classes; overnight trips for groups.

Tahoma Outdoor Pursuits. Tacoma, WA (253) 474-8155. Guided canoe and kayak trips on Western Washington rivers; instruction available.

Whale Watching

"A Trophy" Charters. San Juan, WA (360) 378-2110. Chartered whale watching trips out of Friday Harbor.

Cachalot Charters. West Port, WA; 1-800-356-0323 or (360) 268-0323. Whale watching trips out of Grays Harbor.

Eclipse Charters. Orcas Island, WA 1-800-376-6566 or (360) 376-4663. Whale watching trips.

Northern Lights Expeditions. Bellingham, WA 1-800-754-7402 or (360) 734-6334. Guided, 6-day sea kayaking trips in British Columbia; lodge-based; whales and wildlife.

Orcas Island Eclipse Charters. Orcas, WA (360) 376-4663. Sceduled whale-watching trips from Orcas Island.

Boating

Lake Chelan & Northern Cascades Tours. (509) 682-8287. Boat trips up the Lake Chelan and floatplane trips into the Cascades.

Fishing

Allrivers Adventures (Wenatchee Whitewater & Co). Cashmere, WA 1-800-743-5628 or (509) 782-2254. Guided fishing trips in OR and WA.

"A Trophy" Charters. San Juan, WA; (360) 378-2110. Chartered fishing for salmon, rock cod, and halibut out of Friday Harbor.

Barrier Dam Guide Service. Salkum, WA; (360) 985-2495. Guided salmon and steelhead fishing trips.

Bill Davis Guide Service. Kirkland, WA; (425) 822-8505. Guided fishing trips for steelhead, salmon, trout and bass.

Blue Mountain Adventure Company. Troy, OR 1-888-258-3686 or (541) 828-7833. Guided, fly and drift boat fishing trips in and around the Blue Mountains.

Buffalo Works. San Juan, WA; (360) 378-4612. Guided fishing trips.

C.C. Anderson Guided Service. Federal Way, WA; (253) 839-3584. Guided fishing trips for steelhead and salmon on western Washington rivers.

Cachalot Charters. West Port, WA; 1-800-356-0323 or (360) 268-0323. Chartered fishing trips out of Grays Harbor; whale tours.

Clancy's Guided Sports Fishing. Chehalis, WA; 1-800-871-9549 or (360) 262-9549. Guided fishing trips in the Northwest's premier rivers

Don's Guide Service. Enumclaw, WA; (360) 829-9296. Guided fishing trips for salmon, steelhead, and sturgeon on most Washington waters.

Drifting Fly Guide Service. 1-888-204-5327 or (206) 609-5327. Guided spin, drift, and fly fishing trips for steelhead, salmon, trout, and sturgeon.

Fish-On! Guide Services. Stanwood, WA; (360) 652-2359. Guided fishing trips for steelhead, salmon, and sturgeon on most Washington rivers.

Hell's Anglers. Silver Creek, WA; (360) 985-2449. Guided salmon and steelhead fishing in western Washington; Tillamook Bay, OR; and Alaska's Kenai.

Herb Jacobsen's Fishing Guided Service. Forks, WA (360) 374-5135. Guided trips for steelhead, trout, and salmon on the Olympic Peninsula.

Highland Stage Company. Tonasket, WA; 509-486-4699. Guided fishing trips from May to October.

Horizon West Guides. Vancouver, WA; (360) 887-3676. Guided fishing trips in southwest Washington and southeast Alaska.

Icicle Outfitters & Guides. Leavenworth, WA; 1-800-479-3912 or (509) 763-3647. Guided fishing trips.

Leroy's Guide Service. Chehalis, WA; (360) 748-1316. Guided fishing trips for salmon, steelhead, and sturgeon on western Washington rivers.

Mid-Columbia Guide Service. Entiat, WA; (509) 784-1782. Guided fishing trips for king salmon, walleye, Mackinaw, steelhead, and sturgeon.

Mike's Guide Service. Toledo, WA; (360) 864-6665. Guided fishing for salmon and steelhead.

Northwest Guide Service. Skamania, WA; (509) 427-4625. Guided fishing trips on the Columbia River; some lake fishing.

Olsen's Guide Service. Everett, WA; (425) 348-8053. Guided fishing trips for salmon and steelhead on the Skykomish, Snohomis, Satsop, Wynoochee, and Humptulips rivers.

Pacific Salmon Charters. Ilwaco, WA; (360) 642-3466. Year-round fishing charters.

Raleigh's Guide Service. Toledo, WA; (360) 864-6009. Guided fishing trips; specialize in salmon and steelhead on the Cowlitz River and other western Washington rivers.

Rich's Fishing Guide Service. Brush Prairie, WA; (360) 687-6149. Guided fishing trips for salmon and steelhead on the Cowlitz, Skagit, Snake, and Rogue rivers.

River Otter Guide Service. Lake Stevens, WA; (206) 399-7145. Guided fishing trips for salmon, trout, and steelhead.

Ron's Guide Service. Monroe, WA; 360-794-5540. Guided fishing trips on premier Washington rivers for salmon, sturgeon, and steelhead.

Rush's Fishing Guide Service. Chelan, WA; (509) 682-2802. Guided fishing excursions on Lake Chelan.

Ship's Guide Service. Mukilteo, WA; (425) 347-3434. Guided salmon and steelhead fishing trips from the Snohomish River to the Columbia River at Vernita.

The Drifting Fly Guide Service. Woodinville, WA 1-888-204-5327 or (425) 609-5327. Guided spin, drift, and fly fishing trips on Cascade and coastal rivers.

Washington Fishing Adventures. Marysville, WA (360) 653-5924. Guided bait and fly fishing for bass, salmon, steelhead, sturgeon, and walleye.

Diving

Emerald Seas Dive Center. Friday Harbor, WA; 1-800-342-1570 or (360) 378-2772. Guided dives in the San Juans; instruction and equipment available.

Kelcema Sailing Institute. Edmonds, WA; (425) 771-8899. Access to premier diving spots in Hood Canal.

Ads Up Aviation. (509) 682-8618. Charter flights in a 1941 open-cockpit bi-plane.

Aero West Aviation. Troutdale, OR (503) 661-4940. Charter flights over Mt. St. Helens, the Columbia Gorge, the coast, etc..

Chelan Paragliding. Chelan, WA; (509) 432-8900. Tandem or solo paragliding; instruction available.

Jim's Bipane Rides. Woodland, WA; 1-800-FLY-1929. Unique flightseeing trips in a 1929, open cockpit, TravelAir biplane; seats two passengers.

Lake Chelan & Northern Cascades Tours. (509) 682-8287. Boat trips up the Lake Chelan and floatplane trips into the Cascades.

Morning Glory Balloon. Winthrop, WA; (509) 997-1700. Balloon tours.

Nelson Air Services. Blaine Municipal Airport (360) 332-6346. Scenic flights and air charters.

Rite Bros. Aviation. Port Angeles, WA; (360) 452-6226. Charter flights over the Olympics.

Sound Flight Seaplane Charters. Renton, WA; 1-800-825-0722. Sea-plane tours to San Juans, Mt. Rainier, Mt. St. Helens, and salmon fishing trips.

Vagabound Balloons. La Conner, WA; 1-800-488-0269 or (360) 466-1906. Hot air balloon rides, April to September.

America's Adventure/Venture Europe. Golden, CO 1-800-222-3595 or (303) 526-0806. Guided, multi-adventure trips.

Hood River Trails. Hood River, OR 1-800-979-4453 or (541) 387-2000. Week-long, 6-sport, multi-adventure trips; custom trips also available.

Mount St. Helens Adventure Tours. Toutle, WA; (360) 274-6542. Van tours; overnight camping trips in the blast zone; hiking, fishing, and canoeing; meals included.

Progressive Travels, Inc. Seattle, WA; 1-800-245-2229 or (206) 285-1987. Guided, multi-adventure trips in Washington.

Reachout Expeditions. Anacortes, WA; 1-800-697-3847 or (360) 293-3788. Guided, multi-adventure trips in Washington and Oregon.

REI Adventures. Sumner, WA; 1-800-622-2236. Hiking, biking, walking, and kayaking trips worldwide.

Dear Reader: *It's the very nature of print media that the second the presses run off the last book, all the phone numbers change. If you notice a wrong number or that a business has disappeared or that a new one has put out its shingle, we'd love to know about it. And if you run a guide company or have a favorite one and we missed it; again, let us know. We plan on doing our part to keep this list up-to-date for future editions, but we could always use the help. You can write us, call us, e-mail us, or heck, just stop by if you're in the neighborhood.*

Beachway Press Publishing, Inc.
P.O. Box 5981
Glen Allen, Virginia 23058-5981
(804) 360-7581
offthetrail@beachway.com

Index

T

U

V

W

Y

Trails are not roads.

Roads go to malls and jobs and dental appointments.

Roads are for destinations.

Trails are for journeys.

Trails are for explorers and dreamers and wild hearts.

Trails are where nature beats a path past waterfalls

and volcanoes, through lush rain forests and

spectacular deserts, right into the middle of your soul.

Trails are for the important things like

pine cones and rivers and word of mouth. Trails can

make you wonder if you are going the right way.

Oregon has more trails than roads.

Oregon. Things look different here.

For more information about Oregon and its abundance of trails, call 1-800-547-7842. Or visit www.traveloregon.com.

See What Your Neighbors Are Up To.

When you can sit in a city café sipping lattés and be within an hour of an ocean and a glacier, you're not about to spend your days sipping lattés. No wonder the outdoors run deep in the blood of Oregonians. Let *Mountain Bike Oregon* give you an inside look into this land of a thousand faces, from its rugged, windswept beaches to its high, sage-brush deserts; from mile-high volcanoes to mile-deep canyons. Visit your local book, bike or outdoor retailer, or give us a call and see what's got your neighbors so busy.

To Order A Copy Call or Write:
1-888-BEACHWAY
9201 Beachway Lane, Springfield, Virginia 22153 www.beachway.com

Meet the Authors

Amy and Mark moved to the Northwest some time ago with the sole purpose of being near the mountains. Up from the plain plains of Texas, Washington's Cascade and Olympic mountains have opened up new worlds to them beyond what their southern brows could fathom. Now living and working in the Seattle area, Amy is a freelance writer and Mark, an independent business owner and musician. And while Amy has been writing for such magazines as *Mountain Bike Magazine*, *Bicycle Retailer*, *Snow Country*, *American Bicyclist*, and *Washington CEO*, Mark has been cycling through New Mexico, Canada, Texas, North Carolina, and as far away as Scandinavia and northern Europe. Amy and Mark explore Washington's outdoors together as much as they can and, like a true husband and wife team, debate regularly over who picks the next great adventure.

About The CD

This Washington Bike Trails CD contains USGS topographic map coverage for all trails mentioned in the *Mountain Bike America: Washington* guidebook. Also included is Maptech's TopoScout navigation software, for high-powered precision mapping. With TopoScout, you can measure exact distances, calculate trail elevation profiles, add your own symbols and comments, and print out customized maps! User-friendly and equipped with an extensive, point-and-click Help file, TopoScout is widely popular among all kinds of outdoors enthusiasts.

- On this Washington Bike Trails CD, one topo map (Hobart, WA), with complete coverage of the **Tiger Mountain Trail**, is immediately available for viewing and annotation with TopoScout's navigation tools. The remaining 39 trails, on 92 topographic maps, are locked.

- To obtain access to the entire contents of this CD, you will need a product key. Maptech will supply a key for use with this CD for a price of $34.50. To receive your key, call 1-800-627-7236, and have your Product ID (found in the previous message window) and your credit card ready. Maptech will issue you a product key specifically for use with this CD. As soon as you receive your key over the phone, you will be able to access all maps on this CD.

Maptech is the producer of the U.S. Terrain Series with TopoScout: USGS topographic maps on CD-ROM, for individual states in the USA. For the latest info on available map coverage and product releases, visit **www.maptech.com**, or call 1-800-627-7236.

MAPTECH®
Digital Mapping Technology